A SHORT HISTORY OF
SCOTLAND

A SHORT HISTORY OF SCOTLAND

BY

CHARLES SANFORD TERRY
LITT.D. CANTAB.

BURNETT-FLETCHER PROFESSOR OF HISTORY
IN THE UNIVERSITY OF ABERDEEN

CAMBRIDGE
AT THE UNIVERSITY PRESS
1921

CAMBRIDGE UNIVERSITY PRESS
Cambridge, New York, Melbourne, Madrid, Cape Town,
Singapore, São Paulo, Delhi, Mexico City

Cambridge University Press
The Edinburgh Building, Cambridge CB2 8RU, UK

Published in the United States of America by Cambridge University Press, New York

www.cambridge.org
Information on this title: www.cambridge.org/9781107681613

© Cambridge University Press 1921

First published 1921
First paperback edition 2013

A catalogue record for this publication is available from the British Library

ISBN 978-1-107-68161-3 Paperback

PREFACE

THESE pages are based upon my *History of Scotland* published in 1920. I am told, and my experience concurs, that there is need for a History of Scotland in smaller compass suited to the requirements of middle and upper forms in Schools, Training Colleges and similar institutions, for whom the larger Histories are both too detailed and too expensive. This volume will, I hope, meet their need.

C. SANFORD TERRY.

KING'S COLLEGE,
  OLD ABERDEEN,
    April, 1921.

CONTENTS

MAPS

(available for download from www.cambridge.org/9781107681613)

PEDIGREE TABLES

I. THE HOUSE OF ALPIN 844–1290

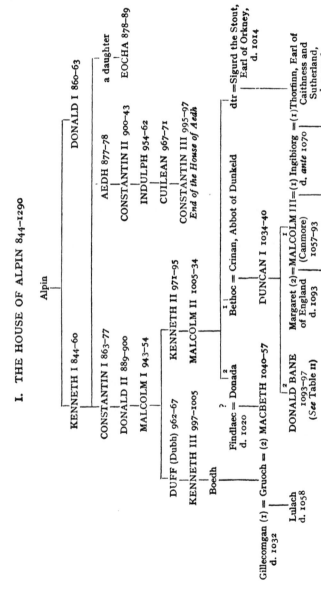

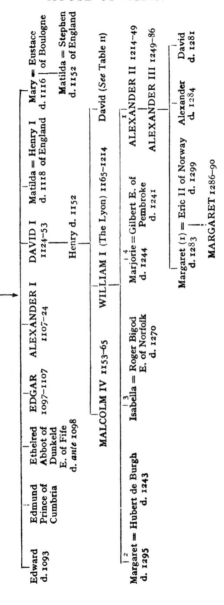

Edward d. 1093

Edmund Prince of Cumbria

Ethelred Abbot of Dunkeld E. of Fife d. *ante* 1098

EDGAR 1097–1107

ALEXANDER I 1107–24

DAVID I 1124–53

Matilda = Henry I d. 1118 of England

Mary = Eustace d. 1116 of Boulogne

Matilda = Stephen d. 1152 of England

Henry d. 1152

MALCOLM IV 1153–65

WILLIAM I (The Lyon) 1165–1214

David (*See* Table II)

Margaret = Hubert de Burgh d. 1295 [2], d. 1243

Isabella = Roger Bigod E. of Norfolk d. 1270 [3]

Marjorie = Gilbert E. of Pembroke d. 1244 [4], d. 1241

ALEXANDER II 1214–49

ALEXANDER III 1249–86

Margaret (1) = Eric II of Norway d. 1283, d. 1299

Alexander d. 1284

David d. 1281

MARGARET 1286–90

A →

II. THE CONTESTED SUCCESSION 1290–1371

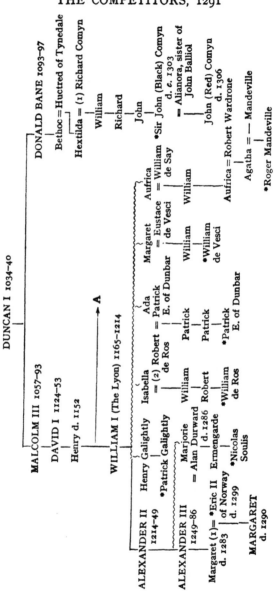

DUNCAN I 1034–40

DONALD BANE 1093–97

Bethoc = Huctred of Tynedale

Hextilda = (1) Richard Comyn

William

Richard

John

*Sir John (Black) Comyn
d. c. 1303
= Alianora, sister of
John Balliol

John (Red) Comyn
d. 1306

Aufrica = Robert Wardrone

Agatha = — Mandeville

*Roger Mandeville

MALCOLM III 1057–93

DAVID I 1124–53

Henry d. 1152

WILLIAM I (The Lyon) 1165–1214

Ada
= Patrick
E. of Dunbar

Margaret
= Eustace
de Vesci

Aufrica
= William
de Say

Patrick

Patrick

William

William

*Patrick
E. of Dunbar

*William
de Vesci

Isabella
= (2) Robert
de Ros

William

Robert

*William
de Ros

ALEXANDER II
1214–49

Henry Galightly

*Patrick Galightly

ALEXANDER III
1249–86

Marjorie
= Alan Durward
d. 1286

Ermengarde

*Nicolas
Soulis

Margaret (1) = *Eric II
d. 1283   of Norway
       d. 1299

MARGARET
d. 1290

An asterisk denotes a Competitor in 1291

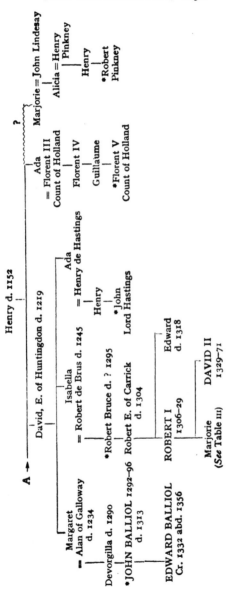

Henry d. 1152

A →

David, E. of Huntingdon d. 1219

Margaret
= Alan of Galloway
d. 1234

Devorgilla d. 1290

*JOHN BALLIOL 1292–96
d. 1313

EDWARD BALLIOL
Cr. 1332 abd. 1356

Isabella
= Robert de Brus d. 1245

*Robert Bruce d. ? 1295

Robert E. of Carrick
d. 1304

ROBERT I
1306–29

Marjorie
(See Table III)

Edward
d. 1318

DAVID II
1329–71

Ada
= Henry de Hastings

Henry

*John
Lord Hastings

Ada
= Florent III
Count of Holland

Florent IV

Guillaume

*Florent V
Count of Holland

Marjorie = John Lindesay

Alicia = Henry
Pinkney

Henry

*Robert
Pinkney

* An asterisk denotes a Competitor in 1291

III. THE HOUSE OF STEWART 1371–1807

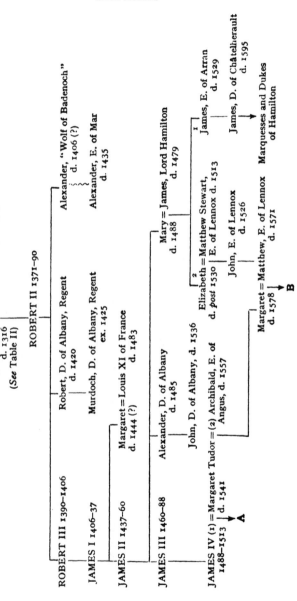

Marjorie Bruce = Walter Stewart, d. 1327
d. 1316
(*See* Table II)

ROBERT II 1371–90

Robert, D. of Albany, Regent
d. 1420

Alexander, "Wolf of Badenoch"
d. 1406 (?)

Alexander, E. of Mar
d. 1435

Murdoch, D. of Albany, Regent
ex. 1425

Margaret = Louis XI of France
d. 1444 (?)   d. 1483

Mary = James, Lord Hamilton
d. 1488   d. 1479

Alexander, D. of Albany
d. 1485

John, D. of Albany, d. 1536

Elizabeth = Matthew Stewart,   ¹ James, E. of Arran
² d. *post* 1530 | E. of Lennox d. 1513   d. 1529

John, E. of Lennox
d. 1526

James, D. of Châtelherault
d. 1595

ROBERT III 1390–1406

JAMES I 1406–37

JAMES II 1437–60

JAMES III 1460–88

JAMES IV (1) = Margaret Tudor = (2) Archibald, E. of
1488–1513 | d. 1541 | Angus, d. 1557

A

Margaret = Matthew, E. of Lennox
d. 1578   d. 1571

B

Marquesses and Dukes
of Hamilton

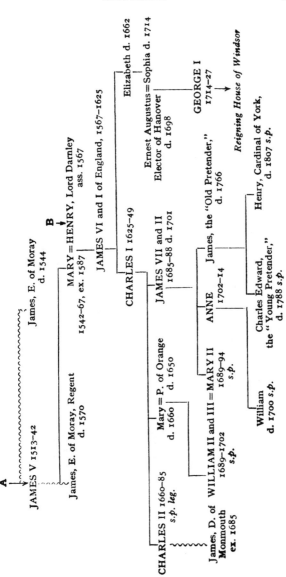

A

JAMES V 1513–42

James, E. of Moray
d. 1544

James, E. of Moray, Regent
d. 1570

MARY=HENRY, Lord Darnley
1542–67, ex. 1587   ass. 1567

B

JAMES VI and I of England, 1567–1625

Elizabeth d. 1662

Ernest Augustus=Sophia d. 1714
Elector of Hanover
d. 1698

GEORGE I
1714–27

Reigning House of Windsor

CHARLES I 1625–49

JAMES VII and II
1685–88 d. 1701

James, the "Old Pretender,"
d. 1766

Henry, Cardinal of York,
d. 1807 *s.p.*

Charles Edward,
the "Young Pretender,"
d. 1788 *s.p.*

CHARLES II 1660–85
s.p. leg.

James, D. of
Monmouth
ex. 1685

Mary = P. of Orange
d. 1660

WILLIAM II and III = MARY II
1689–1702   1689–94
s.p.   *s.p.*

William
d. 1700 *s.p.*

ANNE
1702–14

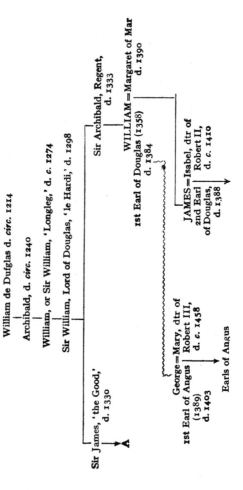

IV. DOUGLAS OF DOUGLAS

William de Dufglas d. *circ.* 1214

Archibald, d. *circ.* 1240

William, or Sir William, 'Longleg,' *d. c.* 1274

Sir William, Lord of Douglas, 'le Hardi,' d. 1298

Sir Archibald, Regent, d. 1333

WILLIAM = Margaret of Mar
d. 1390

1st Earl of Douglas (1358)
d. 1384

JAMES = Isabel, dtr of
2nd Earl Robert II,
of Douglas, d. c. 1410
d. 1388

Sir James, 'the Good,'
d. 1330

George = Mary, dtr of
1st Earl of Angus Robert III,
(1389) d. c. 1458
d. 1403

Earls of Angus

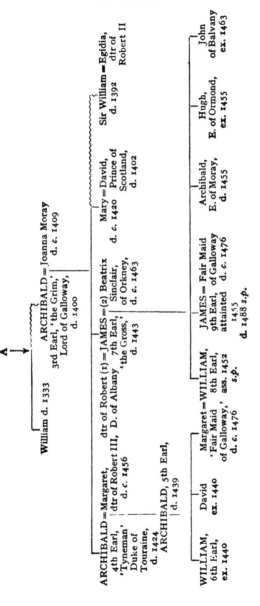

A
William d. 1333
ARCHIBALD = Joanna Moray
3rd Earl, 'the Grim,'
Lord of Galloway,
d. 1400
d. c. 1409
ARCHIBALD = Margaret,
4th Earl,
'Tyneman'
Duke of
Touraine,
d. 1424
dtr of Robert III,
d. c. 1456
ARCHIBALD, 5th Earl,
d. 1439
dtr of Robert (1) = JAMES = (2) Beatrix
D. of Albany
7th Earl,
'the Gross,'
d. 1443
Sinclair,
of Orkney,
d. c. 1463
Mary = David,
d. c. 1420
Prince of
Scotland,
d. 1402
Sir William = Egidia,
d. 1392
dtr of
Robert II
WILLIAM,
6th Earl,
ex. 1440
David
ex. 1440
Margaret = WILLIAM,
'Fair Maid
of Galloway,'
d. c. 1476
8th Earl,
ass. 1452
s.p.
JAMES = Fair Maid
9th Earl,
attainted
1455
d. 1488 s.p.
of Galloway
d. c. 1476
Archibald,
E. of Moray,
d. 1455
Hugh,
E. of Ormond,
ex. 1455
John
of Balvany
ex. 1463

CHAPTER I

THE FOUNDATIONS

WHO first inhabited Scotland? The patient antiquary, turning up the soil, brings to light elsewhere utensils, weapons, ornaments of the Stone Age, succeeded in turn by relics of the Bronze and Iron civilizations. They tell a story common to Europe in prehistoric times, of savage races hard put to it for defence against more savage beasts of prey; ignorant of agriculture, sheltering in natural caves, inadequately armed with rude arrow-heads of flint, bone harpoons, and roughly shaped stone hammers. Scotland yields few traces of these early populations. We conjecture their supersession by another race, better armed and more civilized, builders of houses, cultivators of the soil, clever hunters and fishers, not without rudiments of artistic culture, armed with polished axes of stone and quartz, cunning in boat craft and fishing shallow waters, who also had their day, passed across the stage, and vanished. With them closed an era. Primitive man makes his first raid upon the big secrets of nature. By fusing copper and tin he fashions bronze, a metal harder than either of its components. He forges swords, daggers, shields, spear-heads, sickles, even razors and trumpets. He adorns his women with beautiful decoration, bracelets, neck-rings, ear-rings, mirrors even, of gold. His tempered sword gives him victory over his predecessor, till in his turn he yields to a newcomer better armed than himself. For an Age of Iron supplanted the Age of Bronze. When Rome's ambition first revealed historic Britain, Caledonia housed a population of Goidels or Gaels, a people of Aryan origin, and Picts, a mysterious race, of whom we cannot say surely whether they were akin to the Gaelic pioneers or alien to

them. Centuries after Rome's legions abandoned these islands
the Pictish kingdom, by what processes exactly we cannot
tell, was merged into a wider monarchy which bore the name
Scotland, and the Pictish language was lost in the Scottish
speech to-day called Gaelic.

Meanwhile, Rome's long Empire rose and set for ever.
In her remote origins an insignificant fort upon the hills
overlooking Tiber, she embarked in B.C. 343 upon a course
of conquest which, in less than a century, made her mistress
of the Italian peninsula. With its acquisition she faced a
crisis in her development. In B.C. 264 she involved herself
in a life and death struggle with Carthage, a Phoenician
colony, which, stretching greedy hands across the Mediterranean, ruled Corsica, Sardinia, and a great part of Sicily as
well. To any maritime state it would have proved a foe of
metal. Rome was without experience of naval warfare and
lacked the resources to wage it. Yet, with confidence, she
launched her challenge, built ships to pursue it, and in the
span of four generations beat Carthage to her knees. Her
city was destroyed in B.C. 146 and lordship of the western
Mediterranean passed to the victor. Rome stood thus early
on the trail that beckoned to Britain and beyond. Less than
one hundred years later, Julius Caesar passed over the Straits
of Dover. In B.C. 55 and again in 54 he fought on British
soil. But the island's conquest was not achieved. All but
one hundred years passed before Caesar's collateral descen-
dant ordered a more persistent effort. In A.D. 43 the Emperor
Claudius campaigned in Essex. Thenceforward the tide of
invasion moved unrepelled northward. Yorkshire was added
to the Empire and Eburácum (York), its sometime capital,
was founded. In A.D. 79 Julius Agricola subdued Northumberland, the home of the Brigantes, and by A.D. 81 reached and
fortified the narrow isthmus of Clyde and Forth. Scotland
at length stood in the path of Rome's expanding rule.

It is not easy to picture Scotland as the Romans found it.
Almost the whole country was impenetrable jungle of oak

and pine, home of the elk, boar, and great red deer. Bogs, lakes, lagoons, and treacherous mosses covered great stretches of country. Sparse signs of agricultural activity appeared and the sites of *The Romans in Scotland* modern cities either lay waste or sheltered the rude hovels of a sturdy, stout limbed, tawny haired race, whom Tacitus describes in the first book written about Scotland. Their weapons were large iron claymores, inconveniently weighty for close fighting and lacking the sharp edge of the short Roman *gladius*, iron-headed spears, and battle-axes. Bronze-studded shields protected their bodies, which they clothed in hides or other material brightly coloured. A brave and warlike people, the Caledonians, as Rome called them collectively, consisted of many petty clans, whose divisions and poor equipment promised easy victory to the newcomers.

With the arrival of Agricola upon her borders Scotland's fortunes pass into the region of recorded fact. His activities inspired the pen of his son-in-law, Cornelius Tacitus, whose pages narrate Scotland's earliest historical experience. In the summer of A.D. 80 Agricola marched northward, 'ravaging the land,' says Tacitus, towards a tidal estuary called Tanaus, which may have been one of the two Tynes, or possibly was Tweed. Certainly Agricola advanced by the east coast and not through Cumberland. In the following year (81), he fortified the narrow neck of land between Forth and Clyde. Before challenging the clans beyond, Agricola turned to the west, doubtless to secure his flank. In 82 Ireland floated momentarily into his view, and Roman keels cruised the Kyles and waters of Kintyre. In 83 Agricola again pushed forward and at length entered

> Caledonia stern and wild,
> Land of brown heath and shaggy wood,
> Land of the mountain and the flood.

Agricola's line of march and the sites of his camps are hidden, but stiff fighting took place towards Tay before winter called him back to the fortified Forth-Clyde isthmus. In 84 his advance was resumed and Scotland's earliest hero, Calgácus, appears. Tacitus puts a spirited war-speech into his mouth, of which his taunt of the Romans has lived: 'they make a solitude and call it peace.' At Mons Graupius—a name whose misreading produced the modern word Grampian—the first recorded battle on Scottish soil was fought, a Roman victory dearly bought. Almost on the morrow of it Agricola was re-called. He had carried Rome's power effectually to the Forth and Clyde. Beyond it lay a people unsubdued.

With Agricola's departure, his policy of conquest, and the literary history of Roman Britain, so auspiciously begun, were abandoned. Rome substituted for Agricola's activity a frontier system which erected artificial defences wherever Nature's barriers were inadequate. In Britain the new policy was inaugurated by the Emperor Hadrian, who visited the island about A.D. 120. At his orders eighty Roman miles of solid masonry were drawn across Northumberland and Cumberland from Wallsend to Bowness. At a height of seventeen and from six to eight feet wide Hadrian's Wall marched undeviatingly over the bleak moorland, but proved no obstacle to its assailants. Constantly the Caledonians pierced its bare defences and raided Britain till, twenty years later (? A.D. 140), Antoninus Pius resumed Agricola's dis-carded policy and dispatched Lollius Urbicus to display Roman power beyond Hadrian's fortification. His activity is revealed in the Antonine Vallum built along the course of Agricola's earlier defences between Forth and Clyde. From Carriden on the Forth westward to Old Kilpatrick on the Clyde he raised a monument, the wonder of later genera-tions, who named it Grahame's, or Grime's, Dyke. On a foundation of stone twelve feet of turf sods were neatly laid, tapering somewhat from a width of fourteen feet at bottom. Parts stand to this day. To the north of the Vallum a deep ditch offered an obstacle to assailants. To the south of it a military road permitted rapid movement of its garrison to a menaced spot.

The northern Vallum proved as ineffective as Hadrian's Wall to defend the Romanized population. Fifty years later (*circa* 190) it was abandoned, wrecked and dismantled, it may be, by its retreating garrison. We hear of a new tribe, the Meatae, dwelling between the two Walls, a position of danger, which, perhaps, trained them to a high pitch of military daring. For the third time Rome stirred herself to vindicate her authority. In 208 the Emperor Severus led a great army into Caledonia. A man of sixty, racked with gout, the old campaigner was borne in a litter in the track of the legions. With Roman thoroughness he felled forests, drained marshes, and built roads along an unrecorded route. Roman camps at Ardoch in Perthshire, Raedykes, Normandykes on the Dee, and a large one at Auchterless, support the tradition that he marched to and saw the Moray Firth. No battle was fought. Wise in experience, the Caledonians preferred to harass their enemy's march through difficult country, and inflicted upon him heavy losses. Upon his return Severus repaired Hadrian's Wall, a labour which confessed the futility of his arduous campaign. In 211 the Meatae and Caledonians, Lowlanders and Highlanders, again rose in arms. Severus was organizing a new expedition against them when death removed him.

During the next half century the Roman Empire seemed on the verge of dissolution, and in the region between the British Walls its authority collapsed. Early in the fourth century (306) we hear for the first time of the mysterious Picts. Associated with them in fierce raids upon the Roman provincials were Scots from Ireland and Saxons from across the North Sea. In 368 Theodosius was dispatched by the Emperor Valentinian to rescue the unhappy province from their assaults. He repelled the audacious Picts, restored Imperial authority between the two Walls, and seemingly named the region Valentia in honour of his master. But ruin was only temporarily averted. Rome fell, in 410, to Alaric's victorious Goths. Already (? 407) the legionaries had been recalled from Britain, leaving the island to fight its battles unaided. Before the end of the century the Scots from Ireland settled in Argyll, and Englishmen sailed from over sea to the Kentish coast. From the two events North and South Britain took their separate courses and from the newcomers received their names.

For more than three hundred years the Romans had visited Caledonia and for intermittent periods occupied no inconsiderable part of it. But their departure was merely the exodus of a garrison. It is doubtful whether a single Scottish town can trace its ancestry to Roman foundation. Antiquities betokening Roman occupation have been found in many localities, and excavations at Newstead, near Melrose, reveal the existence of a considerable station. But Caledonia was never Romanized, never adopted the Roman dress, never spoke the Latin tongue, never lived as the Romans lived. Yet her contact with the masters of the ancient world must have united her divided clans. Their civilization was too impressive, their might too tremendous, to pass without stimulating development. Moreover, St Ninian (*circa* 397), Scotland's earliest evangelist, owed his Christianity to Rome, and imparted it to the Picts of Galloway under her protection.

Events in Scotland are veiled from us for a century and a half after Rome's evacuation. When the curtain rises again we observe a country whose geographical divisions had been remarkably simplified in the interval. The sixth century shows the territory of modern Scotland divided among four kingdoms, each ruled by its own monarch and confined within frontiers more or less respected. The largest

Pictland in area, that of the Picts, stretched from the Forth and Clyde to the Pentland Firth. Its people spoke a language allied to the Goidels', and though the conclusion is not established, have been dubbed Goidels themselves, akin to the Celts of Ireland and the Isle of Man. The Grampians cut them into two divisions: the South

Picts occupied the modern counties of Fife, Perth, Forfar, Kincardine: the North Picts the region beyond. Both divisions were subject to the same sovereign, whose seat was on the Ness. Sub-kings ruled the provinces, of which seven seems to have been the traditional number: the earldoms of Angus, Atholl, Fife, Lennox, Mar, Menteith, and Moray preserve their names. The kingdom was the first to disappear in the process of union which produced a single state. It survived till 844, when Kenneth MacAlpin linked it and Scottish Dalriada permanently.

The British, Welsh-speaking, Celts of Strathclyde formed the second kingdom. Like Lothian, it came into being during the advance of the English across   *Strathclyde* the island in the fifth and sixth centuries. Their ruthless pursuit drove back the Romanized Celts to the coast from Land's End to Solway Firth and forced a refugee population of Brythonic (Welsh-speaking) Celts into the region between Solway Firth and Clyde, separated from their kindred in Cumbria by a narrow arm of the sea and akin to the Scots of Ireland and Argyllshire. But the Britons were Welsh-speakers, the Scots used a Goidelic or Gaelic tongue, a fundamental distinction. Settled along the Clyde from the Derwent northward to Alclyde, afterwards called Dumbarton (Fortress of the Britons), the British Celts formed a kingdom which acquired the name Strathclyde. Two events contributed to detach it from English Cumbria, to which it was racially allied, and caused its inclusion in Scotland. Near the end of the sixth century (573) the Strathclyde Britons moved their capital from Carlisle to Alclyde. Forty years later (613), by his victory at Chester, Æthelfrith, king of English Bernicia, implacable enemy of the British, cut the Welsh-speaking Celts of the west in twain, and by the act decreed Strathclyde's attachment to the Scottish system. Within it, upon the modern counties of Wigtown and Kirkcudbright, a branch of the Pictish folk maintained itself stubbornly, provided a division to the host at the Battle of the Standard in

1138, and continued to speak Gaelic until the seventeenth century.

The third kingdom was English, the only one of the four not of Celtic, or presumably Celtic, origin. Its founder, Ida, in 547 became king of Bernicia between Forth and Tweed. His rule extended over Roxburgh, Berwick, Haddington and Lothian, and to one of his line Scotland's capital owes its name, Edwin's Burgh. Not until 1018 was this rich pastoral region detached from England to Scotland's permanent possession, an event of momentous import to her subsequent development.

Lothian

The fourth kingdom, Dalriada, was founded by the Scots, who took its name to their Scottish home from Ireland, whence they came. Late in the fifth or early in the sixth century a band of Irish emigrants, led by Fergus Mor and his brothers, settled in Argyllshire and founded the kingdom, which at its largest extent included Argyllshire and the islands of Islay and Jura. Fortune fared ill at first with the newcomers, who failed to withstand the power and enmity of the Picts until St Columba came from Ireland to their deliverance in 563.

Dalriada

Thus the Scottish nation is compounded of many racial elements once separate—Scoto-Irish, Picts, Goidelic Celts, Brythonic (Welsh) Celts, English, and, in the islands north and west, Danes and Norsemen, whose arrival was the event of a period we have not yet reached. In the main, persistent fighting hammered them into one people. But other processes were at work, and of especial efficacy was their profession of a common faith in Christ. The Scots were Christians since the days of Patrick, and for that reason, and as interlopers, were obnoxious to their Pictish neighbours. In 560 the Pictish King Brude inflicted on them a crushing defeat under which they were still staggering when Columba and twelve companions landed on Iona. He was of royal descent, high repute in counsel, learned, pious, and a busy founder of monastic societies in

St Columba

Ireland. Tradition alleges that he had been expelled from
Ireland in disgrace as a mischief maker. More probably he
came to rescue his kinsmen from their late disaster and to
convert their Pictish foe. Iona was the scene of his earliest
labours. He designed it to become a centre of monastic life
such as those he had planted widely in Ireland. Within a
high turf wall he reared a church built of wattle and clay.
Round it he raised the simple huts of the monks, some of
them novices in training, others performing the daily offices,
and others toiling on the land. For two years Columba
worked on Iona. In 565 he sought King Brude in his palace
on the Ness. The gates, close locked against him, flew open
at the sign of the Cross and admitted the Saint to the
astonished king. Brude declared himself a Christian, and
his people dutifully followed his choice. Their conversion
may fairly be held the governing fact in early Scottish
history. Aspirations were heightened, closer relations were
formed with Irish culture, and movements were put in train
which in time evolved a united kingdom and people.

Columba's success in restoring Dalriada yields in importance only to his conversion of the Picts. In a 'book of glass'
he is said to have singled out Aidan, who was not the
rightful heir, to sit on the Dalriadic throne. Aidan justified
his choice; for though he was decisively beaten by Æthelfrith of Bernicia at Dawstane, near Jedburgh, in 603, he
compacted his kingdom and restored to its monarch the authority the defeat of 560 had forfeited. He succeeded too, with
Columba's help, in breaking the bond which to this point made
Dalriada dependent on Ireland. In a synod held at Drumceatt
in 575 the Irish arch-king waived his superiority and recognized
Aidan as the first independent king of Scottish Scots.

The Britons of Strathclyde found an apostle in St Kenti
gern, better known as St Mungo. Of him we
have no account so trustworthy as that which   *St Mungo*
makes St Columba a historical figure. Mungo is said to have
been recalled from Wales by a Cumbrian king ten years

after Columba's settlement on Iona. Subsequently he worked in Aberdeenshire, where St Machar also was active. The prefix *Kil* in the place-names of Scotland often indicates localities where these early missionaries established their cells.

The conversion of Strathclyde, nominal though it seems
St Aidan to have been, left only Bernicia among the four kingdoms uninstructed in the Faith. The slow triumph of Christianity there is a narrative proper to the history of England. But it was from Iona that first tidings of the Gospel were borne thither. In 615, some twenty years after Columba's death, there entered Iona a pagan company of Bernician exiles driven before the sword of King Edwin of Yorkshire. Among them was the Bernician prince Oswald. He and his company submitted to be baptized and as a Christian Oswald grew to manhood. Twenty years later, Edwin having fallen in battle, Oswald returned to Bernicia in 634. His first act as king summoned from Iona missionaries to convert his people. In 635 the saintly Aidan settled at Lindisfarne, where for sixteen years he directed Christian enterprise throughout Northumbria.

Iona, however, was no longer the only Christian centre
Synod of   in Britain. In 597, a generation after Columba's
Whitby, 664 arrival from Ireland, St Augustine landed in Kent to strive in Rome's name for the salvation of the country her legions abandoned near two centuries before. Differences of rite and organization divided the Churches of Rome and Iona. The Scots kept the Feast of Easter on a different calculation. Their Church permitted rites which Rome denounced as barbarous. Their clergy were tonsured from ear to ear, not upon the summit of their heads. As a missionary agency, both in Britain and Europe, the Irish Church was more successful than Rome. On the other hand, neither its clergy nor its laity were skilled, as Rome's were, in the art of organization. Another weakness was its isolation. The Churches of Italy, France, and Germany were linked with Rome. To have surrendered to Iona the

spiritual direction of England and Scotland must have isolated both kingdoms from an organization and ideals which
could contribute to their development. Oswald's successor
Oswy prevented that disaster. At Whitby Synod, in 664,
he decreed the expulsion of the Scottish missionaries from
Northumbria and acknowledged Roman supremacy. 'I tell
you, you fight against the whole world' was the taunt that
won him to the Church of St Peter.

Rome's victory at Whitby is an event not less important
in Scotland's history than the coming of Columba one
hundred years earlier. The Roman Church had behind it
the imposing traditions of the Empire, represented the culture of the age, and in its territorial dioceses provided an
organization which the monastic institutions of Iona could
not afford. It is improbable that these reflexions weighed
with Oswy at Whitby. The unchallenged authority of St
Peter, holder of the keys of life and death, the poverty of
the Irish Church in apostolic tradition, and the power of a
see which ruled Christendom from the capital of Augustus,
were the considerations which expelled Aidan's Church from
Northumbria and later (710) moved Nectan, king of the
Picts, to conform to Roman discipline. Within ten years
thereafter Iona itself submitted to the rival order and, with
the apparent exception of Strathclyde, the whole of future
Scotland ranged itself under Rome's banner. The decision
opened a new world of ideas and endeavour. Yet, though it
exercised little influence upon the nation's development, the
Celtic Church was deeply cherished by the people. As late
as the eleventh century St Margaret sought to reform obstinate Celtic usages, and down to the fourteenth the Keledei
(Culdees), or Friends of God, perpetuated its traditions.

The supremacy of Northumbria, which ordered the retreat
of the Scottish Church from England, even
threatened to subjugate Scotland herself. King *England's
expulsion*, 686
Oswy's victory over heathen Penda of Mercia
at Winwaed, in 655, established him as the arch-king of

Britain. He is said to have subdued the Picts, and his power
extended along the east coast perhaps to Cromarty Firth.
For thirty years the Picts submitted, till, in 686, Ecgfrith,
Oswy's successor, leading a great host into Pictland, was
slain at Dunnichen (Nectansmere) in Forfarshire. The event
is memorable. It withdrew from Scotland a foreign power
capable of disturbing the nascent kingdom's growth. Pict
and Scot, Gael and Briton were left to work out the difficult
process of consolidation.

Following their victory at Nectansmere the Picts established a wide supremacy which embraced Dalriada
The Norse- and Strathclyde. Under King Angus MacFergus
men (731–61) they came near to anticipating the
achievement of Kenneth MacAlpin a century later. But his
successors lacked either his ability or his vigour. Bernicia
remained outside the limits of the future kingdom, and before the end of the eighth century (794) Norsemen from
Scandinavia made their first appearance in the Western
Isles, detaching from Scotland a part of her soil which was
not won back until the middle of the thirteenth century
(1266). In 802 they sacked Iona. The whole western coast,
as well as Caithness and Sutherland, surrendered to an increasing Scandinavian population which cut off the Scots
of Argyllshire (Dalriada) from their Irish kinsmen. Iona lost
its ecclesiastical primacy, and Constantin, king of the Picts
(d. 820), transferred the religious capital to Dunkeld.

The depredations of the pagan Norsemen were the imme-
Union of diate cause of the permanent union of Dalriada
Scots and and Pictland. In 844 Kenneth MacAlpin, king
Picts, 844 of Dalriada, united the two kingdoms in a partnership never broken thereafter. The circumstances of the
event are not clearly deciphered. By paternal descent
Kenneth was a Scot. On the maternal side he was a Pict,
and as by Pictish law the crown descended through the
mother, Kenneth had a good claim to both realms. Other
causes contributed to make permanent the union he achieved.

The two kingdoms had already been united. In Iona, and latterly in Dunkeld, they owned the same ecclesiastical capital. In blood probably and in language certainly they were akin, and the futile rivalries of three centuries may have suggested union as the better course, though Kenneth probably won the crown by taking advantage of a Norse invasion of Pictland or in collusion with it. That the union endured is the strongest proof that circumstances were ripe for its accomplishment. The event reduced the four kingdoms to three. In less than two centuries the three were compressed into one and, excepting the Norse regions, Scotland was geographically complete.

The accession of a Scottish monarch to the united kingdom was followed by a change in its name. By the beginning of the tenth century it was called Alban, after Albanacht, the mythical son of *Kingdom of Alban* Brude. Alban comprised a Highland region poor in soil, formed of hard and ancient rocks, and deluged by rains from the Atlantic. Below it lay the central Scottish plain, running from Dumbarton to Stonehaven in one direction, from Girvan to Dunbar in another, richer in soil and more open to commerce than the high lands which flank it north and south. Here the national life of Scotland was offered room to develop, and its acquisition was the chief ambition of Alban's rulers, a purpose which challenged the growing English monarchy, whose ambition gazed northward as that of Alban aimed southward. Hence at this stage the long rivalry of North and South, England and Scotland, begins. A king of Alban and his kinsman of Strathclyde succumbed to Æthelstan at Brunanburh in 937. Thirteen years earlier (924) the same king of Alban (Constantin II) entered into a relationship with Alfred the Great's son Edward upon which English lawyers of a later generation founded England's claim to Scotland's vassalage. His successor, Malcolm I, made a partnership with Edmund of England (945) to acquire Cumberland. Whether he accepted it as a dependency of the English crown is a controversial topic. Vassal or merely ally, Malcolm's intention to thrust Alban as far as he could into England is apparent. A generation later his son Kenneth II is declared to have received the Lothians from Edgar of England as vassal from suzerain. The event gains in importance from the fact that already, about 962, Dunedin or Edinburgh had passed into permanent possession of the Scots, with the region between the Pentlands and the Forth. From that vantage ground they coveted the rich corn-lands of Bernicia, the granary of the North. Some sixty

Battle of Car-ham, 1018 years later (1018) Malcolm II won them at Car-ham from King Cnut. The date is doubly memorable. In the same year the king of Strath-clyde died. For a century the British kingdom had been ruled by a branch of the Alban house of Alpin. In 1018 the line expired and Malcolm's grandson, Shakespeare's 'gentle Duncan,' took the throne. In 1034, when he succeeded his grandfather, the union of the four kingdoms was completed. The name Scotland has its modern significance from Malcolm's reign.

CHAPTER II

A FEUDAL KINGDOM

DUNCAN I's accession in 1034 brought together the four
kingdoms in a union never broken thereafter. But it
would be easy to exaggerate the thoroughness of their fusion.
He ruled discordant systems which exhibited neither sym-
metry of custom nor uniformity of race. The Isles and the
North gave him no obedience. England was soon to fall to
a Norman adventurer who, not content to be heir of the
English house of Cerdic, aimed at submitting Scotland to
the feudal obligations of a dependent fief. But the most
urgent problem that faced Duncan's successors was, to assimilate Celtic Scotland with the English leaven the cession
of Lothian introduced. For two hundred years scarcely a
king received the Crown who did not face the anger of his
Celtic subjects at his preference for English culture. Duncan
succumbed to his kinsman Macbeth, the Celtic champion, in
1040 in that quarrel, and in Moray, Macbeth's earldom, a
line of Celtic pretenders persisted till the reign of Alexander III, the first of Canmore's house whom the true Scots
took to their hearts. Hence, the two hundred and fifty years
between Duncan's accession and Alexander III's death in
1286 were a period of persistent racial rivalry. For ninety
years (1034–1124) Celt and Teuton, Scot and Englishman,
contended for the kingdom's mastery. With David I's accession in 1124 it passed conclusively under Anglo-Norman
direction, threw off its Celtic trappings, and entered the
society of European kingdoms equipped like them as a
feudal state.

Of these processes the reign of Malcolm Canmore (1057–93)
was the starting point. A lad of tender years when Macbeth

slew his father in 1040, Malcolm sheltered at the English
Malcolm Court of Edward the Confessor, grew to man-
Canmore, hood in England, spoke the English tongue,
1057-93 and by English help was restored to his crown
in 1057. Nine years later Norman William's advent to the
English throne (1066) closely affected his personal fortunes
and those of his kingdom. About 1068 the English Prince
Edgar and his sister Margaret, fleeing from the Conqueror,
besought Malcolm's hospitality. Soon—the date is not ascer-
tained—he married the maiden. By the match Edgar secured
an ally against his Norman supplanter. Malcolm received a
wife who promised to enlarge his kingdom with a dowry
of English lands. Margaret invested her marriage with the
responsibility of a mission, toiled to introduce the culture
of her English race, and upon her husband exercised influence
almost unbounded: of the six sons she bore him not one
received a Celtic name.

Malcolm's marriage necessarily embroiled him with Norman William. In 1070 he carried fire and sword into Yorkshire. Invasion provoked counter-invasion. In 1072 William
marched unresisted to the Tay and at Abernethy made
Malcolm his vassal, whether for his kingdom, or merely for
a gift of lands in England, is uncertain. Seven years later
(1079), enticed by William's absence in Normandy, Malcolm
again burnt and ravaged between Tyne and Tweed. Next
year (1080) William's son Robert entered Scotland, but
marched out again with nothing accomplished. For, as in
1072, Malcolm refused battle and Robert, staying his southward march, raised a new fortress (Newcastle) on the Tyne
to bolt the door into England against him. In 1091 Malcolm
again invaded England, and Rufus, the new king, hastened
from Normandy to meet the crisis. In 1092 he entered
Lothian, where Malcolm renewed the conditions of Abernethy. Next year Rufus fortified Carlisle to match Newcastle
as a sentry on the west. The event completed the Norman
conquest of English territory and disappointed Malcolm,

who hoped to make Cumberland his own. In anger he sought Rufus, lying sick at Gloucester. Rufus denied him audience and Malcolm made bold defiance. Before the year was out he crossed Tweed for the last time with an army at his back and met his death at Alnwick (1093). His eldest son Edward fell in the fight. Another, Edgar, galloping homeward with news of the double tragedy, found his mother upon her deathbed. She heard his tale and died.

Malcolm's reign increased Scotland's sparse population considerably, whether by English exiles fleeing before the Norman, or by English captives of Malcolm's wars. The bulk of this immigrant population was drawn to the Lothians, where it settled among men of its own race. Northward of the Forth other influences spread English settlements and English speech. A growing commerce built the towns upon the east coast, and English merchants introduced English culture along the seaboard.

Malcolm's English queen was the most unflagging agent of English culture. Margaret was a saintly, earnest woman, of strong character, who domi- *St Margaret* nated her husband and his court. Ignorant of Gaelic, she admonished her clergy upon the error of their ways, Malcolm acting as her interpreter. She read aloud to her unlettered husband, who bound her books in rare covers studded with jewels. In its appointments, dress, and tone, the court was moulded by her example. Especially upon the Church Margaret left her mark. On five points wherein Scotland stood apart from Latin Europe her persistency carried drastic reform. She caused observance of Lent to begin on Ash Wednesday and not, as heretofore, on the Monday thereafter. She bade all receive the Eucharist on Easter Day. She reformed the ritual of the Mass. She established stricter observance of Sunday as the Lord's Day. She suppressed irregular degrees of matrimony. Thus she completed the work Nectan began three centuries before, and brought the Scottish Church into harmony with Roman Christendom.

For four critical years Margaret's work was in jeopardy,
Donald and Celtic Scotland beyond the Forth threatened
Bane, to break loose from the English lands to which
1093-97 it was tied since 1018. Hardly had Margaret
yielded her last breath before Malcolm's brother, Donald
Bane, surrounded Edinburgh Castle, where his nephews
watched their mother's bier. Under cover of mist they
carried her body to her Church at Dunfermline and fled in
fear of their lives. As in 1040 under Macbeth so now under
Donald Bane hatred of the English rallied the Celtic Highlands. Donald fulfilled the hopes that set him on the throne
by driving the English from the positions to which Canmore
had advanced them. Informed of these happenings, William
Rufus spied an opening to reassert Malcolm's repudiated
homage. He held as hostage Duncan, Malcolm's son by his
first, Norse, wife, whom long residence in England made
virtually a Norman knight, and who gladly promised fealty
to secure an unexpected throne. In 1094 he overthrew
Donald Bane. Six months later Donald made an agreement
with Edmund, Margaret's eldest surviving son, proposing
to revert to the custom of an earlier time and hold Alban
apart from the British and English lands added in 1018.
Edmund agreed to the division, and the processes of union
in train since Carham seemed permanently checked till, in
1097, Margaret's son Edgar appeared, overthrew Edmund
and Donald Bane, and reigned for ten years over a united
kingdom. Donald Bane was the last king of Celtic birth.
After him no Gael by paternal and maternal descent sat
upon Scotland's throne.

Edgar (1097-1107) owed his throne to William Rufus and,
Edgar, there is reason to believe, acknowledged him
1097-1107 his suzerain. With Rufus' successor, Henry I,
also, his relations were intimate. He gave him
his sister Edith (Matilda) in marriage and gained a powerful
ally against his Celtic subjects. His sympathies were English.
Englishmen formed his court, and Edinburgh supplanted

Malcolm's Dunfermline as his capital. Secure in the friendship of his strong neighbour, Edgar's reign was little disturbed. The only troubler of his peace, Magnus Barefoot, King of Norway, subdued the Isle of Man in 1102 and received from Edgar ownership of those Western Isles between which and the mainland a helmed ship could pass. Not until 1266 were the islands recovered. Their loss Edgar accounted worth the Norsemen's friendship and his assured possession of the mainland.

In his measures for the devolution of the crown Edgar looked facts squarely in the face. Celtic Scotland was stubbornly opposed to English culture. The Lothians were as indisputably English. To treat both as separate systems promised to keep the peace between them. Hence Edgar, who had no son, proposed his brother Alexander for the throne as king, and their younger brother David as Count in Strathclyde and Lothian. The dual system set up neither an English nor a Celtic supremacy, and also evaded England's claims to feudal superiority. On Strathclyde and Lothian they were not lightly founded. But so long as David ruled there they could be admitted without diminishing the dignity of Alexander, the reigning sovereign.

For seventeen years (1107–24) Scotland was ruled from two centres. Edinburgh was Alexander's capital. David's charters do not guide us to the locality of his seat. He founded the Bishopric of Glasgow **Alexander I, 1107–24** and surrounded himself with men of Anglo-Norman birth, Lindsays, Bruces, Fitz-Alans, and others who played notable parts in Scotland's later history. Alexander, like his predecessor, was English at heart and did nothing to provoke England. Henry I, his brother-in-law, gave him his daughter Sibylla in marriage. He was a devout patron of the Church, recognizing, as did the other sovereigns of his family, the political value of its friendship. The bishoprics of Dunkeld and Moray were his foundations, and at Scone and elsewhere he settled monasteries of English monks. Since 1093 the

Bishopric of St Andrews, the only see north of Forth, lay vacant. One of Alexander's earliest acts appointed to it Turgot, his mother's English confessor and biographer. Turgot desired the Archbishop of York to consecrate him. But York claimed jurisdiction over Scotland as Metropolitan, and only with reservation of the rights of St Andrews did Alexander permit the consecration to take place (1109). As Turgot continued to assert York's supremacy, Alexander expelled him to Durham (where he died in 1115) and begged the Archbishop of Canterbury to send Eadmer, the friend and biographer of St Anselm. Eadmer came unconsecrated, took his pastoral staff from the altar instead of at the king's hand, and asserted Canterbury's supremacy as loudly as Turgot had alleged York's. He too was driven to England. Alexander then promoted Robert, Prior of his new foundation at Scone, who received consecration from the Archbishop of York, but without prejudice to the rights of St Andrews, where Culdee rule now ended.

Alexander died in 1124 and left no legitimate child. That fact, and the fortunate circumstance that his successor David was a statesman of rare ability, closed the division decreed by Edgar in 1107. Had it continued, Lothian and Strathclyde must have gravitated towards their English neighbour. It was the task of David as sole king to consolidate permanently the Celtic and English populations above and below the Forth.

The long reign of David I (1124–53) conclusively determined the form of Scotland's state and society. He was the last surviving son of Malcolm III and his English queen. A lad of nine in 1093, he grew to manhood in an English home. Close ties bound him to the Anglo-Norman Court. In 1100 his host, Henry I, married his sister Edith (Matilda). Alexander, David's brother and predecessor, wedded Henry's daughter Sibylla. David's own marriage linked him closely to Norman England. He took to wife Matilda, granddaughter of Siward of North

umberland, Shakespeare's 'Old Siward,' daughter of Waltheof
of Huntingdon. With her he received the Earldom of
Huntingdon, life-interests in the Earldom of Northampton,
many manors in several English counties, and a claim upon
the Earldom of Northumberland, which he made the object
of his reign to establish, so aptly did it assist the ambitious
policy of his reign. He failed to see that his feudal obligations to England as Earl of Huntingdon must compromise
his status as King of Scotland and afford his English relative
an opening to raise the question of homage.

As an English baron David pledged himself in 1127 to
acknowledge his niece Matilda as successor to Henry I upon
the English throne. When, eight years later (1135), Henry
died and Stephen seized the crown, David took the field
against Matilda's supplanter. Neither he nor Stephen dared
put the issue to an encounter, and therefore the two kings
made a treaty at Durham (1136) which reveals David's
selfish concentration upon his own purposes. Of Matilda's
rights no word was said. Stephen conceded that David's
son Henry should, as Stephen's vassal, hold the Earldom of
Huntingdon with the castles of Doncaster and Carlisle, so
recently built to hold the King of Scots in check. Stephen
also gave a contingent promise to recognize young Henry's
claim to the Earldom of Northumberland. In 1137 opportunity encouraged David to advance it. Stephen, however,
absent in Normandy, would not listen to the demand, and
David's motley host poured down upon the Border counties,
early in 1138, sending out marauding detachments into
Yorkshire and Lancashire. 'It is a war of men against beasts'
wrote a contemporary Englishman bitterly of David's Scots.
Near the village of Northallerton the English *Battle of the*
engaged him in the Battle of the Standard on *Standard,*
Cowton Moor. In David's ranks were Celtic 1138
levies from beyond Forth and out of Galloway, English from
Lothian, and 'Frenchmen,' they are called, nobles of Anglo-
Norman birth, the new aristocracy David had attracted to

Scotland. The battle was stoutly waged. But his enemy's superior equipment and his army's indiscipline turned the day against David, though Stephen's difficulties prevented him from following up the victory. In 1139 David a second time made with him an agreement at Durham which gave little heed to his niece's interests. The coveted Earldom of Northumberland at length was secured to Prince Henry, Stephen retaining Newcastle and Bamborough. Thus the Scottish frontier was carried southward to the Tees as already by the treaty of 1136 it was advanced to Carlisle and the Eden.

In 1141 the hitherto luckless Matilda made Stephen prisoner at Lincoln. David prudently joined his niece, and rode with her into London. But Matilda's cause collapsed as suddenly as it had revived and David barely extricated himself from her defeat at Winchester a few months later. Though Matilda maintained the contest for seven years, David held aloof from it until 1149, when her son, afterwards Henry II, sought him and received knighthood at his hands at Carlisle, promising, should the crown become his, to confirm David and his heirs in the lands between Tyne and Tees. Upon that compact David took the field for the last time, but returned homeward without striking a blow. For the rest of his reign the Eden and the Tees constituted his southern frontier. His policy, though successful, lacked chivalry and even honesty; he supported both English rivals and was true to neither. Had his only son Prince Henry survived him David's self-seeking might have won a permanently advanced frontier. But the prince died in 1152. His father followed him in less than a year (1153), and Scotland passed to the rule of a child. Never again did she hold over England the advantage David won for her.

More permanent than his territorial gains was the political *Feudalism* and social transformation of Scotland accomplished during David's thirty years of power. He made her a feudal kingdom. Feudalism flourished throughout Western Europe between the fall of the Roman Empire and the emergence of strong monarchies in England, France, Spain and elsewhere on the eve of the Reformation. It was the practical device of a period in which the king found it difficult to exert his authority directly over his people. Its essential feature was the employment of landed property as the basis of contracts in the public interest, land being the only national fund with which the king could bargain with his subjects. A modern landlord receives rent in money. The feudal sovereign demanded rent in service. Those who held his land were his vassals. They were bound to aid him against his enemies, attend his court, counsel him on matters of state, contribute to his exchequer on special occasions and for particular purposes. As these obligations rested upon the great nobles who were the tenants of the king, so these tenants-in-chief, as they were called, imposed similar conditions upon their own tenants. In this manner the whole nation was organized to fulfil the supreme national duty of military service.

It was David's purpose to surround the King of Scotland with a landed aristocracy charged with the feudal duty to himself which he, as Earl of Huntingdon, owed to the King of England. His early charters, before his accession, show him attended by friends of his English exile; the names Lindsay, Bruce, Fitz-Alan, are among them. To them and other Anglo-Norman lords David made princely gifts of land. Robert de Bruce, ancestor of Robert I, received nearly a quarter of a million acres in Annandale: the midmost regions of Ayrshire (Kyle), with Renfrewshire, were gifted to Walter Fitz-Alan, ancestor of the Stewart kings. Such grants, generously repeated in other districts to other re- cipients, introduced into Scotland colonies of Anglo-Norman landowners who built their castles, settled amid their new tenants, and spread English ideas, customs, and speech over their estates. In time the whole character of Scottish rural society was changed. The original inhabitants and

their descendants paid their masters the flattery of imita-
tion and, when the use of surnames became general, adopted
their names. But every part of the kingdom was not transformed in this manner. Neither Pictish Galloway nor the
Celtic Highlands succumbed to English culture, or at most
were superficially affected by it. Not until the eighteenth
century, after the abortive rising of 1745, was the process
begun in David's reign completed among the Highland clans.

David's generosity was not lavished only upon his English
The Church friends. He was, a later king complained, a
'sair sanct for the Crown.' An earlier Scotsman
wrote of him:

> He illumynd in his dayis
> His landys wyth kyrkys and with abbayis.

Holyrood, Kelso, Melrose, among others, owe their foundation to his munificence. Of the four existing episcopal
dioceses he was already founder of one (Glasgow). As king
he added five more—Dunblane, Brechin, Aberdeen, Ross,
Caithness. By the end of his reign, Scotland was carved into
nine dioceses, not counting Galloway, which was under
York's jurisdiction. Each diocese, ruled by its bishop and
his cathedral chapter, was divided into parishes served by
a priest, for whose support teinds (tithes of the land's produce) were exacted. Monasteries had been founded or were
in process of foundation in almost every part of the kingdom.
Thus David founded the vast wealth and influence of the
mediaeval Scottish Church. In the Celtic north and west
abbeys and towns were rare, and their absence, along with
the inaccessibility of mountainous country, held the region
behind the progressive south.

Along with these developments in the social structure of
Royal Council the nation proceeded a transformation of the
apparatus of government. Already in the reign
of Alexander I a Constable, Justiciary, and
Chancellor—feudal dignitaries all of them—made their ap-

pearance, the nucleus of a Royal Council which superseded
the Celtic Council of Mormaers (seven), if indeed that body
ever existed. David added to the feudal hierarchy a Chamberlain, Steward, and Marshal. All of these high offices imi-
tated English use, and were bestowed within the Norman
aristocracy: the hereditary Stewardship of the Household
and Constableship of the kingdom became hereditary in the
families of Fitz-Alan and de Moreville respectively. Like
his English brother, the Scottish king granted charters and
exercised the administrative functions of his office with the
advice and consent of bishops, earls, and barons, his tenants-
in-chief. No body resembling Parliament was yet in existence.

Anglo-Norman law necessarily accompanied an Anglo-
Norman aristocracy. A system of jury trial was   *Law*
probably introduced before David's reign and
tended completely to supersede ordeal and earlier forms of
legal procedure. Later, by the time of Alexander II, the
king was wont to delegate his judicial functions to Justiciaries,
one for Lothian, one for Galloway, and two for the regions
north of the Forth, taking cognizance particularly of the
'pleas of the crown,' *i.e.* murder, rape, arson, and robbery.
Thus, to other Anglicizing influences already in operation
an ordered legal system was added. Not only in Lothian,
but in the Lowlands from the Forth to the Moray Firth,
Anglo-Norman law won general currency.

The growth of commerce added to the influences which
cut off the Lowlands from the older Scotland   *Commerce*
behind the Highland line. Before David's reign,
federations of towns existed, as elsewhere, for the protection
of urban interests. A fourteenth century writer testifies to
the prosperity of the eastern Scottish ports through the
foreign merchandise which David's ordered rule attracted.
Flemish and English traders trafficked with Scotland and
settled in numbers upon the east coast. David's grandson,
William the Lyon, was quick to encourage commercial
enterprise, and the association of four southern burghs—

Berwick, Roxburgh, Stirling, Edinburgh—developed into the powerful Convention of Royal Burghs which still exists. Already in David's reign they elected their magistrates, monopolized the commerce of their area, and were not hampered by imposts. Though the creation of Scotland's urban life cannot be attributed to David, his encouragement of the towns makes his reign an epoch in their history.

Thus David's reign accomplished the consolidation of a kingdom so lately torn by the savage rivalry of two races. The Scotland of history was irrevocably made and moulded, equipped with the apparatus of a feudal state, meet to stand with the other kingdoms of Western Europe, and clogged no longer by the backward traditions of its Celtic past.

CHAPTER III

CONSOLIDATION

SUCCESSFULLY as David I had impressed himself upon the jarring elements of his kingdom, much remained to accomplish. Between his death in 1153 and that of his great-great-grandson Alexander III in 1286, an interval of one hundred and thirty-three years, four reigns intervened. Of the four kings only the last was not confronted by Celtic revolts in Moray or Galloway. The Western Isles still held allegiance to Norway. As to England, the seeds sown by David threatened an evil harvest. Two of the four kings were sons-in-law of the English monarch and their eagerness to acquire the Northumbrian earldom and Eden frontier afforded England opportunity to assert her unwelcome suzerainty. Under the menace Scotland turned her gaze towards France. As early as 1170 the 'auld alliance' was hinted, and both Alexander II and III took wives from France.

David I was succeeded by his grandson Malcolm IV, a lad of twelve, nicknamed 'The Maiden.' Once before, in 1034, a grandson succeeded his pre- **Malcolm IV, 1153-65** decessor on the throne, and now, as then, the Celts of Moray rose in revolt to uphold the Celtic system of Tanistry which assured an adult to the throne. Their leader was Donald, son of Malcolm Macbeth, great-grandson of King Macbeth's step-son Lulach, the Pretender of an earlier reign. In himself Donald was not formidable. But he had a powerful auxiliary in his kinsman Somerled, King of the Isles. For three years the struggle continued and disturbed Galloway, till Somerled turned after other booty and Donald was confined as a prisoner in Roxburgh Castle. Somerled remained at large and troublesome till 1164 when he was slain at Renfrew. In the interval Galloway again revolted, and was reduced with effort (1160). Fergus, its Celtic lord, took the cowl in David's foundation, Holyrood. On his own soil the Maiden showed himself the master.

Very different is the English aspect of the reign. Hardly had he triumphed over Macbeth in 1156 before Malcolm crossed the frontier to meet his cousin Henry II, who recently (1154) had succeeded to the crown for which his mother and Stephen so long contended. The sovereigns met at Chester, where Henry demanded surrender of Northumberland and Carlisle, conceding to Malcolm only the Earldom of Huntingdon. Lacking the power to retain his grandfather's spoils, Malcolm did homage at Chester for the earldom, as his grandfather before him, 'saving all his dignities,' that is, asserting the independence of his kingdom. Two years later (1158) he again attended at Carlisle, where Henry refused him knighthood, possibly because Malcolm had not borne arms in his service. He accompanied Henry to war in Toulouse and at Tours was dubbed knight. Scotland murmured against the absent king, the first to fight an English quarrel oversea, and on his return in 1160 a fruitless attempt was made to kidnap him at Perth. In 1163, Henry summoned him to England to do homage for Huntingdon to his son young Henry. Two years later (1165) he died prematurely in his twenty-fifth year after a reign whose permanent reduction of turbulent Galloway gives it importance.

For the second time in succession the crown passed from **William the** the king's direct issue. Malcolm, dying sonless, **Lyon,** was succeeded by his brother William, the **1165–1214** passionate purpose of whose reign was to recover from England what Malcolm had surrendered and their grandfather had won. With an eye to Henry II's favour, within a few months of his accession, William followed him to France, but failed to obtain from Henry more than the Earldom of Huntingdon which Malcolm had held. He did homage for it and parted on unfriendly terms. In 1168, associating himself with Henry's many enemies, William made overtures to Louis VII of France. No breach with England followed, and at Easter 1170, William, with his brother David, attended Henry at Windsor, did homage to Prince Henry, and received knighthood. Three years later, hankering after the status of kingship, young Henry conspired with Louis VII and offered Northumberland to William for his alliance. William rose to the bait and led an army over Tweed. In the summer of 1174, while he idly besieged Alnwick Castle, he was ambushed by a band of Yorkshire barons, who carried him off ignominiously, his legs hobbled under his horse's belly, to Henry II at Northampton. Thence he was hurried to Falaise, where he lay for six months before humiliating terms released him.

The Treaty of Falaise (1174) removed all doubt as to Scotland's feudal dependence on England. William acknowledged himself Henry's liege- *Treaty of* man expressly for Scotland and Galloway. *Falaise, 1174* Edinburgh and four castles in the Lothians were delivered to English garrisons: the king's brother David and twenty-one Scottish barons were surrendered as hostages. Upon these crushing terms William obtained his freedom and at York (1175) did homage to Henry and his heir. For the next fifteen years, till the death of Henry II, Scotland was a vassal fief over which Henry exercised his suzerainty.

The Treaty of Falaise also compromised the independence of the Scottish Church. In 1176 William and his bishops were summoned to Northampton to determine the conditions of their ecclesiastical dependence. But as the Archbishops of York and Canterbury both claimed supremacy over the Scottish Church, and the Scottish bishops as positively denied the authority of either, the Council separated without coming to a decision. Meanwhile, William involved himself in a quarrel with the Papacy similar in origin to the familiar contention between John and Innocent III. In

1179, upon a vacancy in the see of St Andrews, the cathedral body elected John Scot. William preferred his confessor Hugh and had him consecrated in his destined diocese. The Cathedral Chapter protested to the Pope, who supported and consecrated Master John. William thereupon impounded the revenues of the see. The Pope retaliated with a sentence of excommunication against the king, of interdict against the kingdom, and appointed the Archbishop of York to enforce the decree. William, holding his ground till 1181, when the Pope died, hastened to make peace with the new pontiff, who removed excommunication and interdict, settled Confessor Hugh at St Andrews and consoled John Scot with Dunkeld. In 1189, Pope Clement III took the Scottish Church and its nine bishoprics under the immediate protection of the Holy See, whose 'peculiar daughter' he declared that Church to be. At the price of submission to Papal authority it repudiated English allegiance.

The death of Henry II in 1189 broke the humiliating Treaty of 1174. Richard, Henry's successor, bent on winning Jerusalem from the Saracen, had two reasons to purchase Scotland's goodwill: he needed money, and also desired to protect his kingdom from an enemy neighbour in his absence. At a heavy price (Treaty of Canterbury, 1189) he restored the rights surrendered at Falaise: castles in English occupation were evacuated, and William received acquittance of all obligations which Henry had extorted from him in consequence of his captivity; saving only that he 'completely and fully perform to us [Richard] whatever his brother of right performed, or ought of right to have performed, to our predecessors.' The clause is vague; the obligations of Malcolm were and are undecided. But William was explicitly absolved from Henry II's exaction of homage.

The reign of Richard's brother John severely strained the relations of the two kingdoms. Clearly John intended to reinvolve Scotland in feudal dependence on England, and more than once threatened war. William, on his side, pursued the hope of acquiring Northumberland and on John's refusal (1199) to restore it was only deterred from taking arms, it is said, by divine warning vouchsafed in Canmore's church at Dunfermline. Other causes aggravated a situation already critical. English bishops, fleeing from their excommunicated king, sought William's hospitality, and moved John to threaten invasion. More provocative still was William's demolition of John's new castle at Tweedmouth. Thus challenged John led an army northward and William prepared to withstand him. But at Norham (1209) peace was quickly arranged. John abandoned the castle: William promised 15,000 marks for its damaged structure, and undertook to send his daughters Margaret and Isabella to be given in marriage by the English king, whose daughter ultimately married William's heir, while William's two daughters were matched with English commoners, Margaret with Hubert de Burgh, Henry III's powerful minister, and Isabella with Roger Bigod, Earl of Norfolk.

It was inevitable that a reign whose English ambitions were so active should provoke Scotland's Celtic areas. William's capture at Alnwick (1174) *Celtic revolt* stirred them to revolt. Galloway, lately subdued by Malcolm, flared up at the news and was not reduced until 1185. Ross also gave trouble: in 1181 Donald Bane (or MacWilliam), declaring himself a great-grandson of Malcolm Canmore by his first wife Ingibiorg, rose in revolt, laid waste and burnt the countryside and slew his prisoners. He mastered Ross and Moray until his death, in 1187, gave Scotland peace. In 1211 his son Guthred invaded Ross from Ireland. William, an old man, his son a stripling, appealed to John, whose English troops eventually (1212) defeated and hanged the pretender.

After a long illness William died, aged 74, in 1214, without having achieved the purpose of his reign. *Royal Burghs* But the revolution launched by Canmore moved steadily forward. The earliest charters to towns—Perth,

Inverness, Ayr, Aberdeen—were of William's granting,
though the burghs were not yet a recognized part of the
constitution. No organized Council or Parliament had as
yet developed: the king was attended by a retinue of barons
and churchmen on whose advice he acted. At periods he
held a Council of his vassals. Traces also exist of a code of
laws. Sheriffs had jurisdiction over 'pleas of the crown,' and
baronial courts, both secular and ecclesiastical, existed
widely for the repression of crime and inquest of feudal
services. Some of the burghs perhaps had limited jurisdiction within their bounds. The Lyon's Scotland already
boasted the apparatus of a feudal polity.

William, who

> Past off this warld till his lang hame,
> To the joy of Paradys,

was succeeded by his son Alexander II, a prince in his
seventeenth year. His reign and that of his son
The Golden Alexander III together spanned nearly three-
Age, 1214–86 quarters of a century, Scotland's Golden Age.
It saw the complete subordination of the kingdom to a
feudal organization. It achieved, excepting the Orkneys,
Scotland's expansion to her ultimate geographical frontiers,
the final disappearance of the Celtic pretenders, and the
reconciliation of the elements they represented ·to the
monarchy of a feudal State. In it the Scottish Church
assured its independence of England and in 1225 obtained
the Pope's license to hold provincial councils, thereby
gaining a national organization of its own. Moreover, throughout the seventy-two years no serious conflict menaced Scotland's relations with England, though Alexander II cherished
his father's hopes of Northumberland, and the English
sovereigns John and Henry III pursued an insidious policy
which threatened the independence of their Scottish neighbour.

Alexander II at once resumed his father's obstinate am-

bition. Across the border John was locked in strife with his
people: the situation was tempting, and a pro- **Alexander**
mise of Northumberland from the barons drew **II, 1214–49**
Alexander over Tweed. John found strength to
retaliate, burned Berwick, and boasted he'd 'hunt the red
cub [Alexander] from his lairs.' A second time Alexander
entered England, this time in collusion with Louis the
Dauphin of France. Again he backed a losing cause. Louis'
defeat at Lincoln Fair (1217) left Alexander no course but
to make terms with John's successor Henry III and his ally
the Pope, who had laid Scotland under the Church's ban.
At Berwick (1217) Henry received his homage for the
Huntingdon earldom, and gave Alexander his sister Joan
in 1221. A proposal that Henry himself should marry
Alexander's sister Isabella was resented by the English,
the elder being already wife of an English commoner.

Until the fall of his brother-in-law Hubert de Burgh in
1232 the relations of Alexander and Henry remained on a
pleasant footing. But so soon as Hubert's influence was withdrawn, Henry revived the policy of his grandfather and,
supported by the Pope, whom John's submission made
England's suzerain, reopened the claim to allegiance surrendered in 1189. In 1235, Pope Gregory IX summoned
Alexander to renew his father's homage, and on his refusal
dispatched a Legate to bring him to reason. The king fended
off the intruder: 'They be savage and uncivilized men who
inhabit my land,' he warned the visitor, 'and thirst for
human gore.' Meanwhile he prudently made terms with
Henry. A royal meeting at Newcastle was followed in 1237
by another at York at which the long controversy over
Northumberland at length was settled. Alexander resigned
his hereditary claim to the three northern counties, and received instead territory in Tynedale, with the stipulation
that no castle should be built upon it.

Thus an old sore seemingly was healed. But within a
twelvemonth the death of Alexander's queen (1238) threat-

ened a fresh quarrel. Joan died childless, and Alexander was
still young. He took his second wife from the French house
of de Coucy (1239), a union which Henry viewed jealously,
and the two kingdoms approached the brink of war. In 1242
one of Alexander's barons, cavilling at his forfeiture for an
alleged act of violence, fled to Henry and called for aid.
Military preparations were made by both sovereigns, Henry
alleging that Alexander, in collusion with France, was com-
forting his enemies and building castles with sinister purpose. But Henry's baronage gave no support; having a
quarrel with him, as with his father before him, they were
little disposed to weaken a Scottish ally. Hence, in 1244, a
new treaty was drawn at Newcastle; the provisions made
at York in 1237 were confirmed, and both sovereigns promised to abstain from alliances menacing the other. For the
rest of his reign Alexander and Henry were cordial neighbours.

Within his own kingdom Alexander showed his father's
vigour. Hardly was he seated on the throne before Donald
MacWilliam, son of his father's enemy, appeared in Moray
and was crushed in a swift campaign. Kenneth, last of the
Moray pretenders, shared his fate. In 1222, with the prestige
of his English alliance behind him, Alexander accomplished
the large exploit of his reign and reduced Argyll, which so
far evaded subjection to the Scottish crown. A sheriffdom
planted there brought the province to its proper allegiance.
In the following year an act of savagery called Alexander
to Caithness, whose people, resenting their bishop's im-
portunate demands upon their purses, spitted and roasted
him before his kitchen fire. Alexander avenged the bishop,
and a revolt in Moray alone broke the peace of the next ten
years. In 1234 Alexander made two campaigns in Galloway.
In that year the male line of the Lords of Galloway ended,
leaving three daughters co-heiresses, all of them married to
Anglo-Normans, one of whom, John de Balliol, was father
of the future king. Hating their ladies' husbands as foreigners,

the Galwegians petitioned the king to forfeit the lordship
and assume it himself. As policy and justice forbade Alexander to do so, the Galwegians set up a natural brother of
the heiresses, and broke into revolt which two arduous campaigns suppressed. Thereafter, for fifteen years peace reigned
till Alexander broke it and met his death. The Scottish kings
had ever regarded the treaty which divorced the Western
Isles from Scotland as a compact to be broken when opportunity allowed. Following his reduction of Argyll, therefore,
Alexander demanded of Norway restoration of the Islands
and offered purchase. Being refused he prepared to win them
by force, set sail on the adventure in 1249, and on the voyage
fell ill and died.

Alexander III, last king of Canmore's line, came to his
throne at the early age of eight. Crowned at
Scone upon the Stone of Destiny, acclaimed by **Alexander III, 1249–86**
a Celtic bard as rightful heir of 'Fergus, first
King of Scots in Albany,' and first of his house whom no
Highland pretender challenged, Alexander found a more
dangerous rival near the throne. Married as a boy of eleven
to Henry III's daughter Margaret (1251) it was not till 1262
that the birth of his child—mother of the Maid of Norway—
assured direct continuance of his house; while his own
tardy birth—he was not born till 1241, after his father had
been a quarter of a century upon the throne—had admitted his kinsman Robert Bruce, lord of Annandale, grandson of his great-uncle David, Earl of Huntingdon, as heir
to the crown upon the express nomination of Alexander II
in 1238. The birth of Alexander therefore snatched from
Bruce the prospect of a throne. But the king's infancy and
his own seniority as eldest male of the royal house kept his
ambition alive. Among the nobles a party gave him support.
Its leader was Alan Durward, Justiciary of the kingdom,
husband of a natural daughter of the late king. Opposed to
him was a party headed by Walter Comyn, Earl of Menteith, head of a powerful feudal connection holding lands

in Badenoch, Galloway and Buchan, and boasting royal descent which marked him Bruce's rival. The relation of these parties to the crown and to Henry III of England provides the history of the reign.

Factious strife at once involved the boy-king. Durward's party desired to postpone his coronation till Alexander had been knighted, a proposal inspired by the wish to secure Henry III's support. Comyn protested and prevailed. At Scone Alexander was forthwith crowned and two years later (1251) received from Henry III knighthood and his daughter Margaret to wife. The union encouraged Henry to press for homage from Scotland, a foreseen demand to which Alexander had been schooled to reply. He was, he said, a child uncounselled and without experience: his father was dead and his mother in her native France. 'Be to me father and mother,' he pleaded, 'and strengthen my weakness with protection and counsel.' Henry accepted the responsibility and fulfilled it.

In 1255, in collusion with Henry, Durward expelled the Comyns, and seized the youthful king and queen. Henry hurried to Scotland and at Kelso, acting as 'Principal Counsellor to the illustrious king of Scotland,' set up a Council of Regency to act pending Alexander's majority. It consisted of Durward and his faction, but its English complexion offended national sentiment hardly less than the humiliation of 1174. The Church opposed it: the Queen-Mother Marie returned from France to add her weight against it. In 1257, consequently, the Comyns carried a counter-revolution, seized the king, and (1259) made alliance with the Welsh, then at war with England. Henry took steps to restore Durward. But as Scotland so clearly opposed an English regency, he set up a new Council drawn from both factions. In 1261, under minute safeguards imposed by the Scots, Alexander and his queen visited Windsor. There, early in 1262, Margaret, afterwards Queen of Norway, was born. Alexander's tutelage was at an end.

Of Alexander's long reign one event is chiefly notable. Immediately after his daughter's birth, and upon attaining his majority, he repeated his father's embassy to Haco of Norway, demand-   *Battle of Largs*, 1263
ing the Western Isles and proposing purchase. Haco refused and next year (1263) sailed with a mighty fleet to Scotland to assert his rights. Off Arran a heavy gale smote his galleys and drove them, drifting wrecks, upon the mainland near Largs, where the storm-beaten crews, sturdily opposed, were denied a landing. Others fled to Ormidale. Mustering his shattered Armada, Haco sailed homeward and in Orkney died. The event permitted Alexander to follow up his victory and subdue the Western Isles. Three years later (1266), the Hebrides, including the Isle of Man, were ceded to the Scottish crown for 4000 marks and the payment of 100 marks annual rent in perpetuity. The marriage of the infant Margaret and Eric of Norway (1281) clinched the bargain.

The rest of Alexander's reign was peaceable. In 1278 he visited his brother-in-law Edward I and did homage 'saving his kingdom,' the Scottish record runs, though the English version asserts Edward's reservation of his rights as suzerain to such a time as he should choose to discuss them. The events that followed brought that moment inexorably nearer. In 1281 Alexander's younger son David, a boy of eight, died, the beginning of Scotland's woe. By 1284 Alexander's remaining children were removed by death—his elder son Alexander in his twentieth year, and his first-born Margaret, lately (1281) wed to Eric of Norway. Only an infant Maid of Norway, daughter of Eric and Margaret, stood between Canmore's direct line and extinction. Early in 1284 Alexander gathered his vassals to Scone to consider the succession. Failing issue to the king the Council, of whose 38 lay members at least 22 were Anglo-Normans, settled the crown upon the infant Maid of Norway. But the contingency of her succession was hardly contemplated. Alexander, a hale man of forty-four, married Joleta de Dreux in 1285. She was like to give him children. In fact she bore him none. A year later (1286), on a boisterous March day of gusts and snow, Alexander rode from Edinburgh to join his queen at Kinghorn across the Forth. A ferryman rowed him over to Inverkeithing. Dusk had fallen and the burgesses vainly bade him rest the night. With two guides the king picked his way along the coast. On a high cliff near the town where his French queen awaited him his horse stumbled and threw its rider. At the cliff's foot they picked him up, stark dead.

CHAPTER IV

THE WAR OF INDEPENDENCE

ALEXANDER III's death involved Scotland in a crisis unique in the experience of European monarchies and brought the looming problem of her relations with England to a solution. Though her nobles were pledged to the absent Margaret they observed the situation with dismay. So far only males had reigned in Scotland. But the new sovereign was an infant female, resident in a country lately hostile, and heiress to a foreign throne. In her absence, a month after the Kinghorn tragedy, the Council constituted a Regency of six Guardians, consisting of William Fraser, Bishop of St Andrews, with the Earls of Fife and Buchan (Alexander Comyn), for the districts north of the Scots Water (the Forth); the Bishop of Glasgow with the High Steward (James Stewart) and Lord of Badenoch (John Comyn) for the region south of it. Robert Bruce, excluded from the Regency, threatened trouble and, in the autumn, with his partisans formed a 'band' in his interests, 'saving their fealty to the King of England and the person who shall obtain the kingdom of Scotland, being of the blood of Alexander III and according to the ancient customs of the realm.' Now, as fifty years before, Bruce asserted his claims as eldest male of the royal house. The kingdom stood on the brink of civil war, and the Maid's succession in jeopardy.

The crisis called other interests to activity. In an English marriage Eric of Norway saw the surest security for his daughter's succession. *Edward I and the crisis* Edward I favoured a marriage between the Maid and his heir: it promised to give Scotland quiet and to solve the relationship of the two kingdoms in a peaceful manner. Therefore, upon receiving Eric's appeal, Edward invited an international conference to Salisbury (1289), where the two episcopal Regents, a testimony to the Church's influence, with the claimant Bruce and John Comyn met English and Norwegian plenipotentiaries. Application already had been made to the Pope to legalize the marriage of the cousins-german.

In November 1289 the Papal dispensation was announced *Treaty of* as on its way to Scotland, and in the following *Birgham,* March (1290) the Guardians summoned a Council 1290 to Birgham, which with deliberation debated the marriage of the queen and approved it, subject to safeguards which bear witness to its patriotic care. The Treaty of Alliance, approved on July 18, 1290, stipulated that union, if it resulted from the match, should be between two independent and freely contracting nations. Scotland's laws, liberties, rights and customs were declared inviolate in perpetuity, saving the rights of the King of England which belonged or ought to belong to him, an ominously vague qualification. The power of the English Parliament to legislate for Scottish affairs was expressly denied; a separate Great Seal was to remain invariably in the hands of a Scotsman; and the summons of Scotsmen to appear before English tribunals was forbidden. Failing lawful issue to Margaret, Scotland's crown was to revert 'wholly, freely, absolutely, and without any subjection' to the heir at law, with a reservation of English 'rights.'

A last calamity to Canmore's fated house shattered the scheme. In September 1290 the Maid sailed *Death of the* from Bergen on board a Norwegian vessel, her *Maid,* 1290 father having rejected an English ship sent for her conveyance injudiciously freighted with sweetmeats. Early in October 'a sorrowful rumour' of her death was bruited in Scotland. She expired on the voyage and her dead body was borne to the Orkneys. Accusations of foul play were made. She was alleged to have been murdered before she left Norway, a foolish tale. Norway believed her to have been kidnapped by interests that opposed her rule in Scotland, and twenty years later a Lübeck woman died at the stake for impersonating her.

The death of Margaret broke the conditions which, in terms of the Birgham Treaty, licensed Edward I to intervene. But he was now approached by the Scottish factions. The Bishop of St Andrews, acting with John Comyn as interim Governor, urged Edward to show himself on the Marches of the kingdom to aid the selection of a King of Scotland 'who will follow your counsel.' John Balliol was named for Edward's approval, and on the principal of primogeniture was rightly named. Before the end of the year (1290) Edward was also approached by Bruce, whom the Maid's death released to reassert his rights under Alexander's nomination of him in 1238. A body styling themselves 'The Seven Earls,' claiming a constitutional right to elect their sovereign, based on the traditions of Celtic Alban, named Bruce to Edward as heir of Alexander II.

Having received overtures from the rival factions, Edward ordered (March 1291) exhaustive search in monastic and other archives for documents elucidating the past relations of England and *Norham Council*, 1291 Scotland. A good deal of worthless material was placed at his disposal, credible to an age unschooled in the historic instinct. Edward then invited the vassals of the Scottish crown to meet him at Norham on Tweed on May 10, 1291, and summoned his own northern barons to attend him there three weeks later (June 3). On the opening day of the conference (May 10) Edward demanded of the Scots recognition of his status as Lord Paramount, exhibited the evidence—the Canterbury Treaty was not disclosed!—relied on to prove acts of homage to his predecessors by Scottish kings, and asserted his resolution to establish his undoubted prerogative. The Scottish magnates were granted three weeks to frame an answer. On June 2, when the conference reassembled at Upsettlington, near Norham, Edward's demand was conceded. Of the nine claimants so far in the lists, all, including Bruce, put their seals to a binding document: 'Forasmuch as the King of England hath evidently showed that the sovereign lordship of Scotland and right to determine our several pretensions belong to him, we, of our own free choice and without compulsion, have therefore agreed to receive his award as our Lord Paramount and bind ourselves to submit to his judgment.' Edward at once required and received custody of the castles throughout the realm and exacted an oath of fealty from the Guardians, to whose number he added the Bishop of Caithness, an Englishman, as Chancellor.

The process which awarded the crown of Scotland to John

The Claimants

Balliol did not terminate until November 1292. The claimants were thirteen in number, of whom only one, Patrick Galightly, was a Scot by paternal descent. Omitting Eric of Norway, who asserted a right derived from his dead wife, the competitors fall into four categories. Six were descendants of illegitimate children of Alexander II and William the Lyon. Three were legitimate descendants (Balliol, Bruce, and John Hastings) of David, Earl of Huntingdon. Two were great-grandsons of David's sisters. One, John Comyn of Badenoch, Balliol's brother-in-law, descended from Malcolm III's brother, Donald Bane. All rested their claims principally upon their relationship, near or remote, to the royal house and were quickly reduced to the three deriving from David of Huntingdon. Balliol, Bruce, and Hastings were descended from his daughters, Balliol from the eldest, Bruce from the younger, Hastings from the youngest. Bruce was a degree nearer to the common ancestor. Whether that advantage outweighed Balliol's descent from the eldest daughter Edward's judgment had to determine. No other claimant could compete with these two in descent, possessions, or influence. Hastings, whose claim could not be preferred to theirs, conveniently contended that the kingdom was partible, and he heir to one-third of it.

The procedure by which Edward determined the most famous suit of the Middle Ages was carefully *The* Centum- planned. In the practice of England, France, virale and Scotland herself, the king administered Judicium justice through 'auditors,' before whom causes were unfolded and whose finding declared his judgment. The originality of the Court constituted by Edward to determine the Scottish succession is in the fact that the number of 'auditors,' namely 105 (including the Lord Paramount), corresponded with the membership of the ancient Roman court of *Centumviri*, which had as its peculiar function the hearing of causes involving rights of property and hereditary succession, matters closely cognate to the subject Edward as Lord Paramount was charged to determine.

On June 3, 1291, Edward issued from Norham an order for the nomination of 'auditors.' On June 5, Bruce and others named forty, Balliol, Comyn and others a similar number, and Edward himself twenty-four, a total of 105, including the king. Two months later (August 3, 1291) the 'auditors' sat at Berwick to receive statements from the claimants and adjourned until June 2, 1292. On reassembling the issue was found to lie between Bruce and Balliol, and, after further adjournment, Edward put a question to distinguish the merits of the two which drew a unanimous answer, that Balliol, though of remoter degree than Bruce, was to be preferred as descending from the first-born daughter of Huntingdon. But it had been urged by some of the interests concerned that the prize could be divided. Further questions to the 80 Scottish 'auditors' drew an answer that the kingdom was not partible. On November 17, 1292, in full Parliament in the hall of Berwick Castle, Edward therefore awarded the kingdom whole and undivided to John Balliol, who swore fealty to his suzerain and on the last day of the month was crowned at Scone.

Edward's decision was in accordance with the modern
rule of primogeniture and helped to establish it.
But it gave Scotland an indifferent king and,
in Edward, a suzerain resolved to exact the last
**John
Balliol,
1292–96**
ounce of obligation Balliol's vassalage entitled him to demand. The new king, a man of forty-three at his accession,
represented a family of Anglo-Norman descent domiciled in
Galloway since the reign of David I. His character was
feeble: 'Toom Tabard' his subjects dubbed him derisively:
'a simple creature' an English contemporary described him.
He permitted cancellation of the Treaty of Birgham and
its safeguarding of Scottish autonomy. He had not been a
month upon the throne before he was vexatiously summoned
to London by his liege. In the following year he was condemned in damages upon a matter affecting the Earldom
of Fife. In 1294 he was called to London to provide Edward
with aid in his impending campaign in Gascony. Whatever
the limits of his own complacence, Balliol was aware that
his people would not fight an English quarrel in France.
Therefore, Edward's hands being already full with warfare
there and in Wales, Balliol in 1295 concluded a defensive
alliance with France which for the next three hundred years
powerfully influenced Scotland's fortunes. In October he
denounced his homage and threw down the gage to his
superior.

The first blows in the War of Independence were struck
in the spring of 1296. Scottish raids upon Northumberland
and Cumberland were visited upon the people of Berwick
with savage brutality by Edward. A month later Balliol
fought his last battle at Dunbar, and in July (1296) made
his submission at Stracathro, near Brechin, closing his
uneasy reign. It was not in Edward's mind to set up another
king. Advancing to Elgin, he exacted homage as he went.
The Scottish nobles submitted to him: before
he left Scotland the Ragman Roll recorded
two thousand earls, barons, ecclesiastics, freeholders, and
Ragman Roll

others, the Bruces among them, who pledged him their fealty. Leaving English garrisons to maintain his authority and a triumvirate of Englishmen to execute it—John de Warenne, Earl of Surrey, as Governor; Hugh de Cressingham as Treasurer; and William Ormesby as Justiciar—Edward turned his back on a country apparently subdued. He took with him the Stone of Destiny from Scone and three boxes of Scottish archives. So far as could be judged, every avenue to the expression of a national voice in Scotland was closed.

But in the moment of Scotland's humiliation the voice of the 'community' found utterance. While the nobility were cowed or bound by oaths, a *William Wallace* second Calgacus emerged in the winter of 1296–7. Of William Wallace little is known before his short public career. He is believed to have been the younger son of Sir Malcolm Wallace (le Waleys) of Ellerslie near Paisley, and, like Bruce after him, beginning his public career as a fugitive from justice, soon revealed himself a master of men. In May 1297 he was the leader of a guerilla band. By the summer he was the champion of a cause whom even the time-serving Bruce, old Bruce's grandson, afterwards king, ventured to follow, though Wallace was working for Balliol, for whose restoration Bruce had little desire. Dissension therefore did its work, and in July 1297, at Irvine, where Wallace's force lay expecting attack, Bruce and others made peace with Edward. Two months later, however, Wallace's victory at Stirling Bridge placed Scotland at his feet. Warenne rode precipitate to Berwick: Cressingham was slain: English rule toppled to the dust and the castles of Roxburgh and Berwick alone maintained it. Wallace and his colleague Andrew of Moray administered the kingdom as 'Generals of the Army of King John.'

History records few instances of so meteoric a rise from insignificance to power, and the achievement reveals the depth and resolution of patriotic stirring to which Wallace's

obscure personality had given a voice. But his triumph
was short lived. In the summer of 1298 Edward led a formidable army across the frontier and at Falkirk overthrew
his brief supremacy. The disaster was fatal to Wallace's influence over his jealous followers, and in 1299 he crossed to
France to enlist King Philip's aid and the Pope's sympathy.
Meanwhile, the hero s failure rang the knell of Balliol's hopes
and invited Bruce to assert his claim. But Comyn, Balliol's
nephew, had to be reckoned with. At a meeting of the two
men in the summer of 1299 dirks were drawn and Comyn
had his rival by the throat. But, before they parted, Bruce,
Comyn and the Bishop (William Lamberton) of St Andrews
agreed to fill the absent Wallace's post as Guardian, and
the surrender of Stirling Castle gave good augury for their
government.

Only Edward's difficulties enabled the Guardians to
maintain a show of independence for a few years. No help
came from France, whose sovereign seized and imprisoned
Wallace, and whose sister's marriage with Edward seduced
him from the Scottish cause. Pope Boniface VIII summoned (1300) Edward to desist from attacking a kingdom
whose allegiance, he declared, was due to the Holy See.
But his injunction was not regarded. Ineffectual campaigns
in 1300, 1301, 1302, however, failed to bring Scotland to
her knees and Bruce trimmed his course with characteristic
versatility. At length, in the summer of 1303, at peace with
his barons and France, Edward in person set out to achieve
the task and marched almost unopposed to the north of
Scotland. Bruce and Comyn hastened to renew their broken
oaths and Bruce assisted with engines of war against Stirling
Castle, whose fall in July 1304 made Edward master of the
kingdom. Wallace's capture and execution in 1305 completed his triumph.

The way was clear to a settlement. At a Parliament held
at Westminster in September 1305, three weeks after
Wallace's execution, Edward issued an 'Ordinance for the

establishment of the land of Scotland.' The outcome of
joint deliberations between Edward's coun-   *Edward's*
cillors and ten Scottish delegates, the scheme   *Settlement,*
established Edward's direct lordship over Scot-   1305
land but confirmed to the kingdom its administrative and
legal systems. Edward's nephew, John of Brittany, was
named Lieutenant and Warden. The 'custom of the Scots
and the Welsh,' that is, the laws of the Highlanders and
Strathclyde Celts, were abolished, and the codes of Scottish
monarchs from David's reign were ordered to be corrected on
details 'plainly against God and reason.' Scotland's constitutional Council was retained and Edward seemingly contemplated Scottish representation in the Parliament of
England. The Ordinance otherwise professed a conciliatory
spirit wanting in his relations with Balliol. Bygones were to
remain bygones, and liberal and efficient government was
relied on to bring two systems lately hostile into harmony.
But Edward reckoned without the spirit Wallace had
stirred. Efficient administration was a poor exchange for
independence. Within six months the Constitution of 1305
was abandoned and Scotland, under a new leader, received
the crowning mercy of Bannockburn.

His father's death in 1304 made Bruce Lord of Annandale
and Earl of Carrick, a man of thirty years, whose   **Robert**
career to that point exhibits duplicity unusual   **Bruce,**
even in an age not squeamish. After Wallace's   **1306–29**
defeat at Falkirk Bruce took his place, with Red Comyn
and Bishop Lamberton of St Andrews, as Guardians of Scotland's cause. But directly Edward displayed activity Bruce
hastened to join his stronger power. In 1302 he became
Edward's Sheriff for Lanarkshire and Governor of Ayr
Castle, had his suzerain's summons to attend his campaign
in 1303, and after Comyn's surrender in 1304 received Edward's thanks for diligence against the patriot party. His
father's death brought him a fourth time to swear fealty
to Edward for his English estates, and he aided his suzerain's

capture of Stirling Castle. In 1305 he was present at one or both Parliaments at Westminster summoned to accomplish the settlement of Scotland, swore a fifth oath of allegiance, and early in 1306 left London ostensibly to assist the newly constituted Scottish executive, actually to work his own purposes. Already in the summer of 1304 he was in secret league with Lamberton for mutual assistance 'against all comers,' and thereby gained the Church's powerful aid to set him on the throne to which his father's death made him heir. Having seduced Lamberton Bruce needed to assure himself of Comyn, who had a rival claim to advance; he too was of Huntingdon's blood. The rivals met in the cloister of the Church of the Grey Friars at Dumfries. Bruce revealed his ambition, offered a bribe, and invited Comyn's countenance. Comyn objected his oath to Edward. High words were bandied and blows were struck. Comyn, wounded, sought sanctuary within the church, while Bruce, joining his companions, told the news, 'I doubt I've slain Red Comyn.' 'I'll mak siccar,' said one of them, and did so.

However unpremeditated the deed, the sequel had been planned. The new Constitution, to which Bruce was sworn, had spurred his purpose; more forcibly than Balliol's abdication it declared Scotland's thraldom to a foreign rule and promised him national support. His 'band' with Lamberton reveals him already in 1304 contemplating action. Comyn's murder, planned or not, was a detail in a considered design. From the scene of his crime Bruce rode to Glasgow to gain from the bishop absolution for his blood guilt. Thence he passed to Scone with Good Sir James Douglas, his leal man for over twenty years. Six weeks after Comyn's death he was crowned there. The Stone of Destiny was at Westminster: the crown had gone with Balliol into exile: a simple band of gold replaced it for the ceremony. Duncan, Earl of Fife, who claimed hereditary privilege to encircle the sovereign's head, was Edward's man. His sister, though married to the Earl of Buchan and kin to murdered Comyn, took his place. Bruce was duly crowned. But of all whom the day's ceremony made his lieges only two earls, three bishops, and one abbot were present.

Bruce now faced the superior he had deceived and dared. While Edward, vowing to avenge Comyn, stripped Bruce of his English honours, sentence of excommunication was passed upon him in the Pope's name from St Paul's Cathedral. In June 1306 the Earl of Pembroke surprised and scattered his slender force at Methven, near Perth, and drove the king to the hills. His brother Nigel, taken at Kildrummy in Aberdeenshire, was executed at Berwick. His queen, daughter, and sisters were confined closely. The valiant Countess of Buchan also paid penalty for her devotion. Near twenty knights taken at Methven shared Nigel Bruce's fate; age and his infirmities alone prevented Edward from taking the field in person against 'King 'Hobbe,' so he dubbed King Robert.

By September Bruce was pushing through the heather westward to the Islands. In February (1307) he was in Arran, facing his earldom and his birthplace, Turnberry Castle. In March, on a chance blaze of heather interpreted as a signal, he landed at Turnberry, attacked the garrison, and flung himself into the fastnesses of Loch Trool. There he held his own valiantly till Scotland began to stir. Early in May he encountered and confounded his encircling enemies at Loudon Hill. The news called Edward, 'Hammer of the Scots,' to the last effort of his life. On July 3 he mounted horse at Lanercost for the Border. On July 6 he was at Burgh-on-Sands, but moved no farther. On July 7, as they raised him in bed to take his morning meal, he fell back dead with Scotland full in view.

Edward's death is the turning-point of Bruce's reign. The new king's worthless character was known, and by the end of August 1307 he was out of Scotland. Bruce had his opportunity. His first task was to subdue the Comyn faction in the north. In

Bannock-burn, 1314

1308 he made such havoc upon their lands that 'the herschip [harrying] of Buchan' was a wonder for fifty years. Success gained adherents: the whole of the north had passed under Bruce's power when, in 1310, the clergy announced at Dundee their acceptance of him as lawful king. He challenged the remaining English garrisons and even crossed the frontier into Durham (1311). In 1312 the barking of a dog alone saved Berwick. In 1313 Bruce in person headed the assault on Perth. Dumfries was won a few weeks later, and Linlithgow fell in the autumn at the assault of a peasant, who played on the garrison (busy at the corn harvest) the ruse of the Trojan horse. Early in 1314 Roxburgh and Edinburgh were taken and by the spring of the year the English flag flew only above Stirling beyond the Forth. From Lent to Midsummer 1313, Edward Bruce, the king's surviving brother, closely girt the fortress and stipulated surrender if the garrison was not relieved from England before Midsummer Day 1314. Spiritless Edward II was spurred to effort. On the eve of Midsummer Day 1314, he came in sight of the beleaguered fortress and on the morrow, at Bannockburn, staked his fortune and lost. Had Scotland been defeated the history of Britain must have run another course. As it was, Scotland vindicated her independence, survived to develop her distinctive national life, and was ready to enter as an equal the United Kingdom of a later time.

Bannockburn gave Bruce the heart of his people as no king before him possessed it. But a faction remained irreconcilable. Alienated by a blood feud founded on Comyn's murder and his treatment of that house, a party among the nobles resented Bruce's elevation over them and staked their hopes on English intervention. Bruce struck them with ill-judged severity. Four months after Bannockburn his Council passed sentence of forfeiture on all who denied his authority. Subsequent charters of the reign prove the immense amount of

The Disinherited

landed property which consequently changed hands, particularly in the north and north-east where the Comyns had
prevailed. The 'Disinherited' carried their woes to England
and on Bruce's son fell the consequences of his father's unwisdom.

Scotland's independence was won at Bannockburn. But
England stubbornly refused to acknowledge *The Chapter*
Bruce's sovereignty. To compel it was the pur- *of Mytton,*
pose of his remaining years. Sir James Douglas' **1319**
name became a terror on the Marches, where English mothers
rocked their cradles to the crooning song:

> Hush ye, hush ye, little pet ye,
> Hush ye, hush ye, do not fret ye,
> The Black Douglas shall not get ye.

Berwick was recaptured in 1318 after being in English hands
for twenty years. Next year an English attempt to recover
the town was countered at Mytton-on-Swale in Yorkshire,
where, led by their Archbishop, so many clerks were slain
that the mellay passed in England as the 'White Battle,'
and in Scotland as the 'Chapter of Mytton.' To the same
end Bruce concerned himself with Ireland, where an invitation from the Ulster O'Neills to assist them against English
oppression attracted him. In 1315 Edward Bruce landed in
Ireland, was crowned, and for three years fought an uphill
battle till he fell at Dundalk in 1318.

Bruce's Irish policy failed, but hinted the consequences
to England of Scotland's implacable enmity. Hence Edward II sought the intervention of Pope John XXII, whose
summons to Bruce to appear at Avignon was answered by
a famous letter from Arbroath (1320) in which his Council
declared their resolution never to bow down to England.
Its tone impressed the Pope, who now directed Edward to
seek a lasting peace. Edward preferred a last appeal to force.
In 1322 he swept the Lothians and burnt Dryburgh Abbey
to the ground. Bruce followed his retreat and at Biland

inflicted so sharp a defeat that Edward sued for peace, admitted Bruce's kingly dignity, and accepted a truce (1323) to endure for thirteen years. Within a twelve-month the Pope also recognised Bruce's royal status, while the birth of the king's son David (1324) promised to establish his dynasty. But England's persisting claim to suzerainty and her insistence upon the restoration of Berwick prevented a closer approach to peace. Hence in 1327 Edward III broke the truce, but, faring no better than his father in 1322, was forced to offer peace instead.

The Treaty of Northampton (1328) put the seal upon
Treaty of Bruce's life-work and brought the War of Inde-
Northampton, pendence to an end. As categorically as the
1328 earlier Treaty of Canterbury it surrendered
English claims to suzerainty. Documents, including the Ragman Roll, claiming to establish Scotland's political servitude were to be given up. The Stone of Destiny was retained, in deference, it is said, to English opinion. With some exceptions Bruce's drastic forfeitures were to stand; hence the 'Disinherited' sore festered to discharge its venom at a later time. The marriage of Prince David (aged four) and Princess Joanna of England (aged six) proposed to clinch the new friendship. It took place two months after the Treaty. Bruce was not present. He had not reached his fifty-sixth year. But the rigour of his reign left him 'right sore aged and feeble, so greatly charged with the great sickenes' [leprosy], that 'ther was no remedy with hym.' He died on June 7, 1329, a man of rare force, sagacity and decision, qualities the lack of which sorely vexed his Stewart successors.

Chiefly memorable in another aspect, Bruce's reign is
notable also as a landmark in Scotland's con-
Parliament, stitutional history. In 1326 he convened at
1326 Cambuskenneth a Council which properly may
bear the name Parliament. The burgesses apparently were summoned for the first time, and though they are not found regularly in subsequent Parliaments until 1455, their ap-

pearance in 1326 connotes Scotland's tentative progress along
a path of constitutional development which England had
already pursued with greater thoroughness.

Sir Thomas Randolph, who assumed the regency for
Bruce's son, faced a menacing situation. By
the Treaty of Northampton he stood bound to   **David II,
1329–71**
reinstate barons whom Bruce had deprived of
their Scottish estates. At the head of the 'Disinherited' was
Edward Balliol, eldest son of King John, whom Edward III
permitted to return to England from France in 1330, the hope
of many whose opposition to Bruce had sacrificed their Scottish properties. In August 1332 Balliol and his disinherited
band, small in numbers but well equipped, landed in Fife and
advanced towards Perth. 'We are sons of the magnates of
the land,' they announced, 'and are come hither with the
Lord Edward of Balliol, rightful heir of this realm, to demand
the lands which are ours by right.' Randolph was newly
dead and his successor, Bruce's kinsman Donald, Earl of
Mar, showed small ability. Despising caution, he attacked
and met death and defeat at Dupplin Moor. Unopposed
Balliol occupied Perth and in September was crowned as
'Edward I' at Scone. On English Edward he depended
and a treaty at Roxburgh in November acknowledged his vassaldom. But Balliol's kingship   *Edward
Balliol*
had a sudden end. On a dark December night
the brother of Black Douglas and the son of Randolph
sought out the Winter King at Annan, surprised his
household, and made him flee precipitately

> On a barme hors wyth leggis bare

while

> all that cumpany
> Dyscumfyt ware all halyly.

Next year Balliol was again on Scottish soil with an
English force behind him and England's king in his company. The foolhardiness of Mar at Dupplin was repeated

at Halidon Hill (1333). The boy king David and his queen
were shipped to France, while his supplanter again acknowledged Edward III Lord Paramount, and ceded Berwick for
ever (1334). For the moment, the country between Tweed
and Forth also was abandoned. But its possession was in-
secure. By rifling Scotland of her fairest provinces Edward
III intensified the hatred of a people whom his house had
failed to subdue. His puppet king was a shadow, like his
father, scorned by his people, distrusted by his kingmaker,
and vexed by the factious spleen of the Disinherited, whose
greedy demands it was not easy to satisfy. At no time was
Balliol really sovereign, though in 1336 Edward paraded
the country to Inverness as conqueror. But it was his last
stroke in Scotland. In October 1337 he published his claim
to the crown of France, an act which diverted his activities
elsewhere and proved decisive for Scotland's recovery. The
tide turned. The patriots rallied under Robert Stewart, the
future king. Bruce's cautious tactics were resumed, the
English-held castles were recovered. Perth fell in 1339.
Edinburgh and Stirling followed, and by 1341 it was
deemed safe for David and his queen to return from France.
Scotland again had a king of her own choice.

David returned, a stripling of eighteen, young, stout,
Battle of   and jolly, who loved the splendid pageantry of
Neville's   an age which glitters in Froissart's pages, and
Cross, 1346   held of little account his people or his throne
save so far as they could contribute to his pleasure. For five
years the strife of parties continued, till in 1346 David was
ill-guided to attempt in England a diversion in the interests
of France, where Edward III was threatening Calais. At
Neville's Cross, near Durham, led by the clergy of the
north, an English host faced him. Deriding an army of
'miserable monks and pig-drivers,' David gave battle, was
defeated and carried into captivity. For eleven years he remained in England, nor was greatly regretted in Scotland,
where his nephew Robert Stewart passably filled his place.

The years of David's captivity were memorable for two events. In 1350 the Black Death laid its grim hand upon Scotland, raged for a full year, and carried off a third of the people. Four years later the French alliance caused another calamity. Anxious to prevent an agreement between Scotland and England, a considerable French force was dispatched to encourage Scotland to attack France's enemy. In 1355 Berwick was captured. Next year Edward retook it, and pushed on to Edinburgh over a trail of black ruin: the 'Burnt Candlemas' men called the event. The aged and childless Edward Balliol surrendered his empty title for a generous pension. His house troubled Scotland no more.

The Burnt Candlemas, 1356

In October 1357 David gained his liberty, but upon onerous terms. One hundred thousand marks were demanded in ten annual payments, and David's personal extravagance swelled the kingdom's burden. In 1363 his nephew Robert Stewart and others banded in protest against the king's heedlessness. David had no love for his heir and put down the movement with decision. So intolerable remained the financial situation that David, upon a visit to London in 1363, offered acknowledgement of Edward or his son Prince Lionel as heir to Scotland's throne provided the ransom was remitted. The unworthy proposal was rejected peremptorily by David's Parliament (1364). At length in 1369, Edward's position in France demanding an understanding with Scotland, the annual, and so far infrequently paid, instalments were reduced to 4000 marks and a truce of fourteen years was arranged. David survived the treaty for two years. He died in 1371 leaving his kingdom in debt to England for half the ransom his release had cost. His reign in no aspect was worthy and is significant chiefly as showing the kingdom's tenacity to the traditions of Bruce and Wallace. England's claim to superiority was not formally abandoned. But to press it ceased to be an absorbing and persistent purpose.

Like his father's reign, David's supplies a landmark in *Committee of* the kingdom's constitutional development. Cir-*the Articles,* cumstances afforded Parliament opportunities, ₁₃₆₇ of which it took advantage, to assert its powers at the expense of the royal prerogative. A development of far reaching consequence took place in 1367, when so large a number of burgesses presented themselves at Scone that it was resolved to delegate their authority to a Committee of twelve drawn from the six most prominent burghs: the others returned home to attend to the harvest. This was the origin of the 'Committee of the Articles,' so large a detail in the mechanism of the Scottish Parliament almost throughout its existence.

Significant of Scotland's expanding culture is the fact that *Barbour and* in David's reign her first authentic authors *Wyntoun* lived. John Barbour, Archdeacon of Aberdeen, wrote *The Brus*, an epic of David's heroic father. Andrew of Wyntoun, Canon Regular of St Andrews and Prior of St Serf's, compiled his *Original Chronicle*, a vernacular metrical history from the Creation to the accession of James I. Both were contemporaries of English Chaucer, but their remoteness from his more modern spirit measures the relative backwardness of their country and proves its energies absorbed in the sterner tasks troubled times imposed. The War of Independence, indeed, was a testing experience calculated to strengthen rather than refine the national character.

CHAPTER V

THE EARLY STEWARTS

ROBERT II, first of a line of kings who reigned for more than three hundred years, came of a house whose founders were of Breton stock, sometime of Dol in Brittany, emigrants thence to Wales, and thence to Scotland under the patronage of David I. Walter, **Robert II, 1371–90** first of the Scottish line, received great estates in Kyle and Renfrewshire, made his principal residence at Renfrew, founded Paisley Abbey, and died in 1177. Robert II, first of the royal Stewarts, was sixth in descent from him. From the first to the third Walter, Robert's father, who mated with Robert Bruce's daughter, every generation held the office of High Steward, and the title became the family name.

The period of the early Stewarts—Robert II, his son Robert III, the Albany Regency, and James I (1371–1437)—is a record of turbulence, rebellions, bitter blood feuds, burnings and slayings, border raids and invasions. As in England, in France, in Germany, the monarchy fought feudal anarchy, and, lacking great possessions, the Stewarts, at the outset, were hard put to it to hold their own. Happily the contest was not protracted: Flodden, in 1513, closed the struggle's secular stage, permitting the Crown, as elsewhere in Western Europe, to found a new Monarchy upon the ruins of feudal arrogance.

The accession of the Stewarts at once evoked protest from a family which chiefly menaced their rule. William, first Earl of Douglas, is stated *Douglas of Douglas* to have claimed the throne in virtue of his alleged descent from the Comyns and Balliols, though he did not carry his protest against Robert II's accession into action. His eldest son, James, received the king's daughter Isabel in marriage, and Douglas himself became Warden of the East Marches, a position of importance in view of England's enmity: there the Douglases built up a reputation for valour and patriotic vigilance which soon overshadowed the Crown:

> So many, so good, as of the Douglases have been,
> Of one surname in Scotland never yet were seen.

When the Stewarts began to reign, their rival, as superior of Annandale and Galloway, was master of South Scotland, a region whose proximity to England imposed on him the brunt of patriotic resistance. He was Warden of the East Marches and Justiciar below the Forth. Saving his allegiance his position in ancient Strathclyde and Lothian was royal: six children of the first and third Earls of Douglas married sons or daughters of the royal house.

James, the second Earl, holds a prominent place in Scotland's story as hero of the heroic event of Robert II's reign. The king was fifty-five when he came to the throne, an old man already, 'worthi, wise, and leil,' tall, handsome, stately, tender-hearted, not endowed with qualities to contest the brave deeds of his great vassal. The fourteen years' truce of 1369 with England still had years to run. And, though half of David II's ransom was unpaid, the troubled accession of Richard II (1377) removed the probability of invasion. But Border disturbances were constant. Avenging the death of a retainer, the young Earl of March fell upon the English garrison at Roxburgh in 1377, gave the town to fire and put its population to the sword. The Percies retaliated in the 'Warden's Raid,' Berwick was recovered and recaptured, till in 1380 John of Ghent, Richard's uncle, came to impose peace upon the Marches. Douglas met him and arranged a truce to last till 1384, when that of 1369 expired. The date was eagerly awaited on the Scottish side, and Douglas had

scarcely buried his father (1384) before he was over the
Border with a band of adventurous French in his company.
Next year (1385) a larger body of French, escorted to Scotland by John de Vienne, Admiral of France, joined Douglas
in a more formidable raid. But, faithful to the Bruce tradition, Douglas was not minded to risk battles, and Richard,
retaliating, burned Edinburgh, Perth, and Dundee.

The state of England in 1388 encouraged reprisals. At
a meeting in Aberdeen, Douglas and the king's
son, the Earl of Fife, made plans to avenge the *Otterburn,*
desolation wrought by Richard in 1385. The *1388*
king was not privy to the design: he was near seventy years
old: his eldest son, a lame man, was hardly more vigorous.
In the summer of 1388 a strong force rode over the Border.
The main body, under Fife, passed round the head of Solway
and ravaged Cumberland. A smaller force, under Douglas,
crossed Tweed and carried destruction to the walls of Newcastle, where Harry Hotspur, driven before superior numbers,
had taken shelter.

> To the Newe Castell when they cam,
> The Skottes they cryde on hyght,
> Syr Harye Percy, and thow byste within,
> Com to the fylde, and fyght.
>
> Sir Harry Percy cam to the walles
> The Skottyshe oste for to se;
> 'And thow haste brente Northomberland,
> Ful sore it rewyth me.
>
> Yf thou hast haryed all Bambarowe shyre
> Thow hast done me grete envye;
> For the trespasse thow hast me done
> The one of us schall dye.'
>
> Where schall I byde the? sayd the Dowglas,
> Or where wylte thow come to me?
> 'At Otterborne in the hygh way,
> Ther maist thow well logeed be.'

Following the retreating Scots, Hotspur came on them in
a grassy plain at Otterburn near midnight. Till daylight

the fight raged. Douglas was struck down, mortally wounded. His men rallied, till Hotspur, his brother, and other knights were led captive to Edinburgh. Of little moment in itself, the Battle of Otterburn set the house of Douglas upon a pinnacle for national applause and lit the sunset of the first Stewart reign. Almost upon its second anniversary Robert II laid down his undistinguished sceptre.

Robert III inherited his father's character and, like him, came past middle age to the throne. Of im-
Robert III, 1390–1406 posing stature, though lamed by the kick of a horse, with long snow-white beard, the new king had the affection of his people but feebly ruled the land. He had received the name John, whose tragic associations in English, French and Scottish history prompted the substitution of Robert at his coronation, a name of good augury unfulfilled. His brother, Earl of Fife, who acted as Lieutenant in the last months of their father's reign, continued in that capacity until 1399, when his nephew, the king's son David, displaced him. The rivalry of the two men disturbed the reign and developed to a tragedy.

Almost the last act of Fife before his fall procured the title Duke for himself and Prince David. The dignity was strange to Scotland: a desire to meet the English on equal terms perhaps suggested it. David took his title from the town of Rothesay. Fife received the designation Duke of Albany, sometime name of the kingdom north of Forth. It was proposed to elevate the house of Douglas to the same rank. But when the heralds called him 'Sir Duke, Sir Duke,' the third Earl, Grim Archibald, quacked back at them, 'Sir drake, Sir drake,' contemning the honour.

Charming in person, Rothesay was dissolute, irresponsible, and soon gave Albany opportunity for revenge. His first act drove into the English camp one who had done yeoman service against the English. Rothesay was betrothed to the daughter of the Earl of March. He now rejected her and in her stead married Mary Douglas, daughter of Grim

Archibald. March, incensed, betook him to England, where
Richard II's recent murder had given the throne to Henry IV,
whom March's offer of service moved to revive the claim to
suzerainty, the more readily because the Scottish Court was
harbouring a pretender whom the credulous asserted to be
Richard II himself. In 1400, and for the last time in person,
an English king led an army into Scotland. Douglas and
Rothesay shut themselves in Edinburgh Castle. Henry appeared before it, but his depleted commissariat soon required
him to withdraw from a fruitless adventure. In the same
year the deaths of Rothesay's mother and Grim Archibald,
his father-in-law, removed restraint upon his actions. With
a few attendants he rode to St Andrews to seize the Castle
of the vacant see. By the king's orders, or with his permission, the young prince was arrested by Albany and
Rothesay's brother-in-law, Archibald 'the Tyneman,' the
new Earl of Douglas. He was conveyed to Falkland Tower,
where, in 1402, he died. How far Albany is justly suspect
as his destroyer cannot be resolved.

Meanwhile March was active on the Border and Douglas,
the king's son-in-law, was already in the saddle.
In company with Albany he was defeated at   *Homildon*
Nesbit Muir in the Merse (June 1402). Three   *Hill*, 1402
months later, at Homildon Hill, near Wooler, Douglas was
severely wounded, lost an eye and was made prisoner.
Albany's son, Murdoch Stewart, shared his fate. Otterburn
was avenged. Douglas and his fellow prisoners were hurried
to London. Murdoch Stewart was handed over to the royal
grace. The Percies refused to yield Douglas till their mone-
tary claims on the Crown were discharged. So, in anger,
Henry ordered out his levies and Hotspur answered with rebellion. Douglas and other Scots were enticed into the plot
and early in July 1403 Anglo-Scottish forces started from
Northumberland to confront the king. A fortnight later they
were overthrown at Shrewsbury. Hotspur was killed, and
Douglas fell at length into Henry's custody.

Douglas did not regain his liberty fully till 1408 and for the last years of Robert's reign Albany ruled unopposed. They were years of gathering gloom for the old king, whom in 1406 a crowning tragedy bowed to his grave. Fearful lest the fate of Rothesay should meet his surviving son James, a boy of twelve, Robert sent the lad to France for safety and education. Off Flamborough Head the ship was brought-to by privateers who sent the prince to Henry, a valuable prize. The news killed his father. On April 4, 1406, he died.

Albany, almost a septuagenarian, but of vigour unabated, **The Albany** was appointed Regent and till his death, four-**Regency,** teen years later, ruled the absent James' king-**1406–24** dom. Three events give these years distinction, and two of them are eloquent of Scotland's cultural progress.

In Scotland as elsewhere the fourteenth and fifteenth *Lollardy* centuries were an age of torpor in the Church. David I's ill-judged generosity had corrupted it and the cause of true religion suffered most at the hands of clergy whose office charged them to advance it. The worldly Papacy itself was the gravest scandal, against which Wykliffe in England and John Hus in Bohemia raised loud voices. Their views were echoed in Scotland where, in 1407, James Resby, an English priest of Wykliffe's school, was burnt for alleged heresy. A quarter of a century later (1433) Paul Crawar, a Bohemian physician, met Resby's fate, asserting ideas which simmered till the Reformation.

Of equal significance was the founding of St Andrews University. To this point Scottish students, *The* *Universities* denied opportunities at home, sought instruction outside the kingdom. In the rare intervals of peace Oxford and Cambridge attracted them to their halls, one of which owed its foundation to a Balliol. But from the beginning of the fourteenth century that avenue to learning was closed. Opportunely the Franco-Scottish League attracted Scottish students in great numbers to Paris and Orleans. In 1326 a Scots College was founded at Paris which, restricted at first to students from Moray, threw open its gates to all Scotland. The enthusiasm of these pilgrims of learning suggested a home University, while the need for an educated clergy, able to confound heretics, influenced the Church to provide one. In 1413 a series of Bulls was obtained from Pope Benedict XIII, constituting a *Studium Generale* or University at St Andrews, where instruction should be given in theology, canon and civil law, medicine, and the liberal arts. Forty years later (1456) a second College, St Salvator's, was established at St Andrews. Glasgow had already founded a University (1451) and Aberdeen possessed one before the end of the century (1494). As at St Andrews, the Church was the founder of both.

The third event reveals the rough ground wherein these new developments had precarious root. For a century and a half the Western Isles had been *Harlaw*, 1411 severed from Norway. But their allegiance to the Scottish crown was perfunctory, and until the eve of Flodden the Lords of the Isles constantly threatened the stability of the realm. John of the Isles followed a tortuous course between Bruce and Balliol and was brought tardily to obedience. Donald, his son, flung down the gage at Harlaw. Alexander, his successor, challenging James I, was twice imprisoned as a rebel. John, last Lord of the Isles, suffered sentence of attainder. The record of their house ranks them with the Douglas, types of the disorderly baronial license of their day.

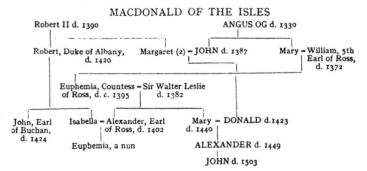

MACDONALD OF THE ISLES

Donald of the Isles' quarrel was on a point of property. By the death (1402) of the Earl of Ross, the earldom devolved on his heiress Euphemia, whose mother was Albany's daughter. Euphemia, becoming a nun, was influenced to resign her dignity to her uncle John, Earl of Buchan, Albany's son. The transaction was arbitrary and prejudiced the rights of Euphemia's legal heir, her aunt Mary, wife of Donald of the Isles. Donald asserted her interests and claimed the earldom. Upon Albany's refusal, Donald, like the renegade Earl of March, offered Henry IV his worthless allegiance and amity, counting, vainly it proved, on English assistance.

> Then haistylie he did command
> That all his weir-men should convene,
> Ilk ane well harnisit frae hand,
> To meit and heir quhat he did mein;
> He waxit wrath and vowit tein,
> Sweirand he wald surpryse the North,
> Subdew the Brugh of Aberdeen,
> Mearns, Angus, and all Fyfe to Forth.
>
> Then he a proclamation maid
> All men to meet at Inverness,
> Throw Murray land to maik a Raid,
> Frae Arthursyre unto Spey-ness.
> And further mair, he sent express
> To schaw his collours and ensenzie
> To all and sindry, mair and less,
> Throchout the boundis of Boyn and Engie.

Marching southward, lured by promise of the plunder of Aberdeen, Donald's caterans were brought to a halt at Harlaw, a few miles from that city, where Albany's nephew, lately settled at Kildrummy as Earl of Mar, with a small force of Lowland gentry and burgesses stemmed the avalanche (1411).

Albany died in 1420, ruler in fact though not in name for fifty years. His policy was based on an understanding with Douglas, the Crown's most powerful vassal. Otherwise he lacked the means, even if he had the will, to restrain the turbulence which surged around him and to which the royal house contributed. The death of Rothesay places him under suspicion. His indifference to his nephew James' long exile increases it. The charges are not proven. But Albany stands condemned as one whose weakness encouraged the feudal anarchy that cost James I his life.

Murdoch Stewart, released from English captivity, took his father's place and held feeble rule for four years. In the course of them Henry V's death (1422) opened an avenue to James' freedom. Murdoch, who probably did not inherit his father's ambition, and also the English Court favoured the king's release: a heavy ransom was not unwelcome to a needy treasury; and it was judged that James would be too closely employed at home to prove troublesome abroad. Scotland agreed to pay £40,000 for his 'costage' in England. Perpetual peace was covenanted between the two realms and the recall of the Scottish men-at-arms in France was stipulated. The terms were concluded in the autumn of 1423. But James lingered in England to celebrate his marriage with Joan Beaufort, Henry VI's kinswoman. In April 1424 the young sovereigns crossed the Border and took up their heavy task. 'Let God but grant me life,' said James, 'and there shall not be a spot in my kingdom where the key doth not keep the castle, and the furze-bush keep the cow, though I myself live the life of a dog in bringing it to pass.'

Succeeding two sovereigns of enfeebled health and indifferent ability, James I came to the throne at the age of thirty in splendid physical and mental vigour. Long captivity had not excluded exercise in every manly accomplishment. He was a good horseman, excelled at games, was tireless in martial discipline. Moreover he displayed gifts which give him honourable place in Scotland's roll of letters. During his imprisonment in England, or perhaps in later years, he wrote, in the school of Chaucer, *The Kingis Quair* [Book], telling in it the story

James I,
1424–37

of his love for the 'milk-white dove,' Lady Joan Beaufort, whom he made his queen.

James began his reign with his purpose bent unrelaxingly on taming the feudal baronage, whose order bears an ill name in Scottish history. The War of Independence, and particularly the reign of David II, gave their class vast power. Lavish grants of land provided resources with which to oppose alike the Crown, the wealthy and privileged Church, and democracy represented by the towns. Accident enlarged the opportunity these resources conferred. Neither Robert II nor Robert III displayed qualities justifying the unexpected succession of their house to the throne; and after the death of Robert III a singular fatality dogged their line. From the accession of James I to that of Charles I in 1625—a period of two hundred and one years—every sovereign entered upon his reign as a minor. James I's widow was the first of a succession of Queen Mothers left to guard a juvenile king. The nobility took their advantage from the circumstance. Their addiction to private vendettas, subordination of patriotic to class interests, and the contempt for royal authority which their resources permitted them to indulge, collectively constituted a menace to national welfare which the monarchy could not brook. James held it his mission to subjugate these disorderly elements, and if he was little scrupulous in the discipline he employed, the disease called for drastic surgery.

James did not delay to fulfil his elected mission. Little more than a month after his return from exile he arrested Murdoch Stewart's eldest son, Walter, on grounds that are obscure, though the destruction of Albany's line was already in James' mind. Five days later (May 26, 1424) he met his first Parliament at Perth. It showed extraordinary subservience to James' anti-feudal policy, gave the king power to summon his vassals to produce charters and justify possession of their properties, forbade private vendettas, so disturbing of the public peace, and inhibited noblemen from travelling attended by bodies of armed retainers. Such tireless activity made the king's lieges uneasy, and from his second Parliament, held at Perth in March 1425, many held aloof. While Parliament was in session Murdoch and his younger son Alexander were seized, with Murdoch's wife. If their fate was ever in doubt Murdoch's son James More decided it. Descending on Dumbarton he gave the town to flames and slew the garrison, including the castellan. When Parliament reassembled in May after brief adjournment, in presence of the king and before an assize of his peers, Walter Stewart was tried, condemned and executed in one day on the Heading Hill at Stirling. Murdoch, his son Alexander, and his father-in-law followed the same road.

In the spring of 1427, carrying his authority to a remoter locality, James called a Parliament to Inverness and summoned to it Alexander, Lord of the Isles, son of Donald of Harlaw, who, with royal sanction, had taken the Earldom of Ross, the bone of contention in 1411, and affected semi-royal airs of independence. Alexander and some forty Highland chiefs were seized and imprisoned, while the most formidable were tried summarily and executed. Alexander was spared. But in 1429 he was up in arms and Inverness smoked in ruins. As he marched southward by Lochaber to reach the Lowlands, the king met and dispersed his force. Abandoned by his Celts, Alexander made submission at Holyrood and, presenting a naked sword, offered his body to the sovereign's mercy. He obtained enlargement after brief imprisonment, and his quarrel with the Stewart passed to his descendants.

Such strenuous acts of royalty could not fail to win enemies. But the tragedy which ended James' life was contrived within the royal house by descendants of Robert II's marriage with his second wife, Euphemia Ross, of whom James' half-uncle, Walter, Earl of Atholl, Robert II's son, was head and representative. Being childless, James' almost complete elimination of the house of Albany necessarily encouraged Atholl, whose hopes were dashed in 1430, when the king's son James was born after six years of matrimony. Atholl, the disappointed heir, was a septuagenarian whom James had treated with consideration. The active contrivers of the tragedy that ensued were Sir Robert Graham, whom James had imprisoned and released early in his reign, and Atholl's grandson, Sir Robert Stewart, whom James had taken into his household, probably with an eye to his succession to the throne should James himself leave no heir.

James cannot have been unaware of these hopes and disappointments. But his conduct shows him strangely incautious. It was the custom of the Court to quarter itself upon the wealthy religious houses, and for the winter of 1436–37 James planned to receive the hospitality of the Black Friars outside the walls of Perth. Till February 1437 all was well. But the conspirators were maturing their plans, and Graham, in the Atholl highlands hard by, raised a force of caterans ready to come out at a word. On the night of the tragedy (February 20, 1437) Sir Robert Stewart, on duty as the king's private Chamberlain, made ready for Graham's approach: the moat was bridged with planks, the locks of the doors were spoiled. Within, the king, before retiring, held conversation with the queen and her ladies. At a sudden sound of hoarse tumult James sought to bar the door, found the great bolt withdrawn, and, raising a flag, dropped to a vault below the flooring which formerly communicated with the courtyard outside. Here the king was trapped. Graham with others burst into a room empty of all but women, searched, and rushed out to seek his quarry. Either at a sound from below, or on the prompting of a traitor, Graham returned, tore open the flooring and spied the king unarmed. James maintained an unequal fight, and fell, stabbed with sixteen wounds.

James' reign holds an important position in the constitutional development of the kingdom. The Scottish Parliament never exercised the authority which marked its English counterpart, nor was it James'

Parliament

purpose to confer it. His utmost wish was to establish his royal power on a foundation of popular consent; the reform associated with his name was inspired by the will to strengthen in Parliament a section of the community which so far had been of little consequence there. In principle the royal burghs took their place as members in Bruce's Parliament of 1326. The county lairds below baronial rank who held of the crown possessed from an early period the right to attend. In fact they did so perfunctorily or not at all. James purposed to correct their indifference and by placing the county lairds alongside the burgesses to give the Crown support against the feudal baronage. To that end, in March 1428, he released them from obligation to attend Parliament in person, provided that from each sheriffdom came two or more of their order—Clackmannan and Kinross were limited to one—competent to speak on their behalf. The Act remained inoperative, and more than a century passed before county representation was rescued from chaos.

James was more successful in other innovations. He set up the Court of Session by an Act (1426) which directed the Chancellor and other persons to sit thrice annually to undertake judicial work so *Court of Session* far grappled with in an unsatisfactory manner by temporary Parliamentary Committees. His busy activity secured a rich harvest of legislation from the frequent Parliaments of his reign. The arms and armour of all classes liable to attend military musters were prescribed: *Legislation* wapenschaws were recommended: an obligation (little heeded) was laid on all men above twelve years to 'have usage of archery,' to which end archery practice-grounds were to be provided: the competing game of football was proscribed under penalties. Other Acts regulated the sowing of peas and beans, laid penalties on those who failed to dislodge destructive rooks 'biggand in treis,' ordained a close time and honest tackle for the taking of salmon, insisted upon vigorous hunting of wolves, threatened poachers of orchards and slayers of red deer, regulated the price of victual and the costume of all classes, enjoined precautions against the outbreak of fires, ordered an inquisition of idle men, regulated weights and measures, established a standard for the coinage, provided for the maintenance of hospitals, and required ale and wine houses to be closed on the stroke of nine.

James was zealous against heresy. Parliament in 1425 passed a law against heretics under which Paul Crawar, a Bohemian, was burnt eight years later. In the spirit of Wykliffe James admonished the Church to employ in the interests of religion the wealth with which his predecessors had endowed it. He founded a Carthusian monastery at Perth—the only house of that rule in Scotland—to set an example. Towards the Papacy he maintained an attitude of independence, and to the Council of Basel, which asserted the liberties of Christendom against Papal usurpation, he sent representatives (1431).

Heresy

His irksome exile in England, the romance of his marriage, his poetic vein, his tragic end, have coloured James' portrait. Probably he was rapacious, hasty and imprudent, intent upon augmenting his high prerogative. But his innovations give him an abiding place in the constitutional development of his kingdom, while his legislation proclaims his despotism paternal.

CHAPTER VI

THE FALL OF THE DOUGLAS

JAMES II, James Fiery Face men came to call him, was not seven years old when his father died. His English mother, with implacable spirit, hunted her husband's assassins to their doom and, with her children, returned to Edinburgh. Scone not being safe ground, Holyrood for the first time witnessed a corona- tion. There James was crowned in March 1437, and his reign, so charged with tragic incident, began.

James II, 1437-60

Memorable for an act of royal decision at a supreme crisis, James' rule opened hopelessly enough. While the queen, a foreigner, received the custody of her son, the Lieutenancy of the Realm was confided to Archibald, fifth Earl of Douglas, grandson of Robert III. Throughout the reign of James I the earl had played an inconspicuous part and his death in 1439 denied him opportunity to disturb the young king's minority. Those whose ambition chiefly menaced the realm were men of minor rank. Sir William Crichton had been in favour with James I, who knighted him, admitted him to the Privy Council, and made him Keeper of Edinburgh Castle. The queen was encouraged to place herself under his care after her husband's murder by his record of faithful service. But his ambition was not proof against the opportunity custody of the king's person afforded. The queen soon suspected his intention to exploit the lad in the interest of his ambition, and outwitted him. Alleging her wish to visit the shrine of Our Lady at Whitekirk, in East Lothian, she transferred herself and her son, concealed in bales of luggage, to Stirling Castle, commanded by Sir Alexander Livingstone of Callendar, who, like Crichton, had served James I faithfully.

Though a meeting of Estates at Stirling in March 1439
authorized Livingstone to arrest Crichton, he failed to capture Edinburgh Castle and, on the queen's behalf, resolved
to win Crichton by obtaining for him the Chancellorship,
while he himself held the royal family in his custody. The
bargain was struck and was not disturbed by the death
(June 1439) of the Earl of Douglas, in succession to whom
no Lieutenant of the Realm was appointed. But at this
point the queen confused the situation by taking a second
husband, Sir James Stewart, the 'Black Knight of Lorn.'
Holding her act a breach of trust as the king's guardian, or
fearing its effect upon his own position, Livingstone confined her in Stirling Castle, arrested her husband, and a few
weeks later received from the queen surrender of her son
until his majority. On her renunciation Joan Beaufort slips
out of Scotland's story, though the sons of her second marriage played parts in it. Jealous of Livingstone's sole ward-
ship of the king, Crichton now kidnapped the young sovereign,
carried him back to Edinburgh Castle, and struck a new
bargain with Livingstone in an audacious blow at the house
of Douglas.

William, sixth Earl of Douglas, a boy of fifteen in 1440,
had succeeded his father in 1439. Whether they
anticipated impediment to their influence over
the king, or realised the menace which Douglas'
family power offered to the crown, Crichton and his partner
resolved upon the earl's death. In November 1440 they used
James' presence in Edinburgh Castle to decoy him and his
younger brother David thither. Sir Walter Scott tells the
story of the black bull's head served at dinner which told
the youths their sudden fate. From the table they were
hurried to a mock trial and thence to the scaffold:

*The Black
Dinner*, 1440

> Edinburgh Castle, towne and toure,
>   God grant thou sink for sinne!
> And that even for the black dinoir
>   Erl Douglas gat therein.

Both lads were without issue. The vast Douglas heritage consequently broke up. The entailed estates and earldom passed to the dead earl's grand-uncle, James the Gross. The duchy of Touraine in France, which the fourth earl received in 1424, reverted to the crown of France. The Lordship of Annandale escheated to James II. Galloway fell to the dead earl's sister, Margaret, the Fair Maid of Galloway. Thus the house of Douglas was spoiled, but not destroyed.

William, eighth Earl of Douglas, a youth of eighteen, inherited a rifled patrimony in 1443, and set himself to restore his house's position and avenge its humiliation. Soon after his father James the Gross' death he appeared at Court, obtained the favour of Livingstone, and probably of his ward the king, now thirteen years of age, who appointed him Lieutenant of the Realm. In 1444 Papal dispensation permitted him to marry his cousin, the Fair Maid of Galloway, who, still a child, brought him as her dowry Galloway and other lands torn from the earldom by the tragedy of 1440. At about the same period William made a 'band' with the Earl of Crawford, the most formidable noble north of the Forth, who represented the interests and wrongs of the fallen house of March, whose alliance Douglas sought for the humiliation or overthrow of the house of Stewart. His sinister purpose was suspected by Bishop James Kennedy of St Andrews, the king's cousin, who prepared to meet it by winning Crichton, whom Douglas and Livingstone had ousted from the Chancellorship in Kennedy's favour. Instigated by Douglas, Crawford thereupon harried Kennedy's diocese (1445), while Douglas himself made alliance with John of the Isles, Earl of Ross.

The threatened conflict between the Crown and its most potent vassal was delayed until 1450, when *The Fall of* Douglas' departure on a stately mission to *the Douglas,* Rome to celebrate the Papal Jubilee, with em- *1452* bassies from other countries, provided a seemingly auspicious opportunity to pursue the court's vendetta. James, who lacked the literary accomplishments of his father and sisters, was endowed with qualities which the crisis demanded. The air of camps was agreeable to him, and he was inured to a life which stimulated vigour of mind and body. His first blow fell actually before Douglas' departure. At the first Parliament of his majority James denounced the earl's ally Livingstone on a charge of treason. Livingstone escaped: his sons went forthwith to the block. Douglas raised no finger to protect them and accepted a portion of their forfeited properties. After the Earl's departure James more clearly exposed his enmity. Disorder upon Douglas' territory was alleged to justify an assertion of royal authority there. Several Douglas strongholds were captured and oaths of fealty to the sovereign were exacted. By April 1451 the earl was back in Scotland and, in spite of what had happened in his absence, he and his sovereign seemed on friendly terms, so that 'all good Scots were right blythe of that accordance.' The King kept Christmas at Stirling, and when the festival was over summoned Douglas as his guest. The earl presented himself in February 1452, bearing a safe-conduct under the king's seal. His retinue found quarters in the town: Douglas was housed in the Castle with the king. On the morrow, at James' invitation, the earl supped with him. Afterwards, withdrawing to an inner room, king and guest conversed. The topic of the Crawford-Ross 'bands' was broached. James demanded their dissolution and perhaps pleaded their inconsistence with the kingdom's well-being. Douglas answered, 'he might not, nor would not.' At the word the king, unsheathing his dagger, threw himself on his guest: 'False traitor, since you will not, this shall,' and dirked him in the neck. Attendants pressed in and stabbed the dying man: one with a pole-axe struck out his brains. His body was flung from the window to the court below and had hasty burial.

Nearly a month after the crime the dead earl's brother and successor, at the head of a powerful retinue, ap-

peared at Stirling, made open defiance (March 1452), denouncing James as a perjured covenant-breaker, and with
ignominy paraded the violated safe-conduct through miry
streets, tied to the tail of a sorry horse. The moment
was arrived to settle conclusively whether the house of
Stewart or that of Douglas was master of Scotland. Crawford
raised his banner in the north. Douglas made treasonable
overtures to England, renounced his allegiance to the
King of Scots, and offered homage. Early in June 1452
Parliament gathered at Edinburgh to face the crisis,
Douglas showing his contempt for its deliberations by ex-
hibiting a letter of defiance. The Estates exonerated James
as having done justice upon a proved traitor. Crawford was
attainted, and a powerful army was summoned. Lavish
grants of forfeited property drew to the king a formidable
following, of whose number the most distinguished was
Douglas' kinsman the Earl of Angus, of whom it was said
that 'Red Douglas put down the Black.' Awed by these
formidable preparations, before the end of August 1452
Douglas and his brothers made unconditional surrender,
dissolved the 'bands' prejudicing their loyalty to the crown,
and abandoned plans of vengeance upon the dead earl's
slayer. Crawford yielded to the king's lieutenant in the north
and made his submission, bareheaded and barefooted, at the
king's feet.

As a mark of reconciliation Douglas was permitted to
marry his brother's widow, the Fair Maid of Galloway, and
so regained that province (February 1453). Immediately
thereafter James appointed him a commissioner to England
to negotiate a truce. His disloyal relations with that court
are probable and the menacing demeanour of Macdonald of
Ross may be connected with his intrigues. Whatever the
immediative motive that actuated him, James resolved to
complete the ruin of his vassal. In March 1455, joined by
Highland and West Country levies, he took the field, while
Angus led the van. Douglasdale, Avondale, and other

Douglas lands were wasted: Douglas himself fled across the Border. At Arkinholm (Langholm) his brothers were defeated in May: only the youngest of the three escaped and joined the earl in England. Deserted by their leaders, the last stand of the Douglases was made at Threave Castle, the strongest in Galloway, built by Grim Archibald on an island in the Dee. Mons Meg, the king's 'great bombard,' dragged heavily to the spot, reduced the fortress and crowned James' triumph. In June Parliament attainted the earl and his surviving brother. A second Parliament annexed great tracts of his property to the Crown, declared his Wardenship of the March no longer hereditary, and forbade communication with or assistance to him. He remained in England for full thirty years, implacable enemy of his lawful sovereign.

That a single subject should have defied his sovereign so long was due in great measure to the relative poverty of the Crown. The attainder of Douglas conveniently forfeited to the sovereign a vast tract of property, and Parliament took the opportunity (August 1455) to attach inalienably to the Crown certain lordships and estates which the public safety required not to pass into the hands of subjects. Most important of them were Ettrick Forest and the Lordship of Galloway, taken from the Douglas; the Castle of Edinburgh, with the royal domains in Lothian; Stirling Castle, with the neighbouring Crown lands; Dumbarton Castle; the Earldom of Fife, with Falkland Palace; the Earldom of Strathearn; the Lordship of Brechin; the Castles and Lordships of Inverness and Urquhart; and Red Castle, with the lordships in Ross pertaining to it. James I had laid hands freely on his vassals' properties. James II far exceeded his father's appropriations, and by their means removed the Crown from the menace which the comparative poverty of the Stewarts had invited.

James ruled for five years after suppressing the Douglas. Their interest is chiefly in his relations with England, his policy being guided by his relationship to the house of

Lancaster and the treasonable intrigues of exiled Douglas with the house of York. On York's reconciliation with Henry VI in March 1458, a strong force entered Annandale in the earl's interests, a danger intensified by York's victory at Northampton in July 1460 and the subsequent agreement which established him as heir to Henry's crown. James saw in the confusion of English politics an opportunity to recover Roxburgh Castle, the last spoil, excepting Berwick, of Edward III's Scottish conquests. The defence was obstinate, though Scotland was equipped with the new artillery which already was transforming the art of war and the political systems of Europe. While watching, 'mair curious than became the majestie of ane king,' one of these hooped monsters, the piece burst, a fragment broke James' thigh-bone and killed him on the spot (August 3, 1460). Roxburgh fell, but at this heavy price.

James died in his thirtieth year and had been king for twenty-four. His dirking of Douglas is matched by Bruce's murder of Red Comyn. Both crimes promoted the interests of the kingdom at large. Scotland's future depended upon the supremacy of the monarchy, for nothing else could tame feudal turbulence or create an ordered state out of jarring elements.

The first five years of the new reign afforded no warning of troubles to come. James III, a lad of ten years, with his Flemish mother, Mary of Gueldres, **James III,** hastened to the army at the news of his **1460–88** father's sudden death, rallied its discouragement, and was rewarded by the fall of Roxburgh. He was hastily crowned in Kelso Abbey and, in February 1461, met his first Parliament at Edinburgh. Their close association with the late king marked out Bishop Kennedy or the Earl of Angus for the Regentship. But the Queen-Mother, a woman of character, received the king's charge, while the Castles of Edinburgh, Stirling, and other strengths were entrusted to her partisans. Until the end of 1463 she ruled wisely in

her son's name: had she survived, the history of his reign
would have followed another course.

Upon Scotland's horizon at the moment of James' acces-
Anglo-   sion the most urgent question was her relations
Scottish   with England, where, in March 1461, the Yorkist
Relations   rebellion triumphed on the accession of Edward IV. Opposed by such another rival in his own kingdom,
and himself related to the Beauforts, James II's interest
had inclined to the Lancastrian Henry VI. Kennedy and
Angus shared his view of Scotland's fitting policy, seeing in
the more vigorous rule of a Yorkist king, and his encouragement of the exiled Earl of Douglas, menace to the kingdom's
security. Moreover, the Yorkists' victory synchronised significantly with a renewal of English claims to superiority.
Hence, Scottish diplomacy inclined to Lancaster, nor was
discouraged by the disasters which befell the Red Rose in
1460. In January 1461 Margaret of Anjou, Henry VI's determined queen, visited Scotland to seek alliance, but found
Mary of Gueldres won to the Yorkist cause through the intervention of her uncle, the Duke of Burgundy, though Kennedy, true to the traditions of his late sovereign, continued
to urge an understanding with Lancaster. Scottish counsels
consequently were divided.

In April 1461 Margaret was again in Scotland, Henry VI
with her, fugitives from the Lancastrian rout at Towton.
She offered a princely gift for assistance. With intervals
Berwick had been in England's hands since 1296. In April
1461 it was restored to Scotland and invited recompense to its
donors. Edward IV thereupon stirred up forces which could
be counted on to serve his interests. Douglas was dispatched on a mission to John of the Isles, whom James II
had reduced to his lawful fealty, but whom the country's
preoccupations tempted to mischievous activity. The result
of Douglas' embassy was an astonishing treaty signed at
Westminster in February 1462. It covenanted that John of
the Isles should become vassal of Edward IV and his heirs,

his ally in his wars in Scotland or Ireland; if successful he should hold the entire country north of the Scots Water (Firth of Forth) by homage and fealty to England; Douglas, in like manner, if he gave proper aid, should be reinstated in Scotland as Edward's vassal. Meanwhile the Lord Paramount promised liberal pensions 'for fees and wages.'

While thus sowing trouble for the Scottish government Edward was also in communication with Mary of Gueldres, who led a Yorkist party among the younger nobles, though Kennedy's influence prevented the assembling of a Parliament summoned to support her policy. Edward was thrown back upon Douglas and John of the Isles; need for instant action arising through the return of Henry's indefatigable Margaret in the summer of 1462 and her successes in Northumberland. Angus led a Scottish force to her assistance, but with little good fortune. John of the Isles came out and Douglas harried the Marches in preparation, it was supposed, for Edward's army of invasion. But before the end of the year Margaret and her son were again in flight, and Kennedy, who had been entertaining Henry at St Andrews, was fain to turn him adrift. France was equally impressed by the futility of further assistance, and in 1463 made truce with England, the first for fourteen years. Its conclusion disposed Kennedy to make terms with the victorious Yorkists. In 1463 he secured a truce, to last till October 1464, which was soon prolonged by agreement for fifteen years.

Bishop Kennedy, 'wondrous godlie and wyse, weil leirned in devine syences,' died in 1465. The Queen *The Boyds* Mother was already deceased, leaving James, in his fourteenth year, his own master. Within a twelvemonth he was prisoner of an upstart family whose fall was as sudden as its rise. The chief actors in a rapid drama were Robert Lord Boyd and his brother Sir Alexander Boyd. Their family, though not of high distinction, had an honourable record of national service. Sir Alexander was the king's instructor in knightly exercises and held Crichton's former

post as Governor of Edinburgh Castle. The office tempted
him to repeat Crichton's career. Accomplices being found in
the dead bishop's brother, Gilbert Lord Kennedy, Robert
Lord Fleming, and others, in February 1466 the customary
'band' proposed the king's detention by Boyd and Kennedy, who pledged themselves to secure for Fleming 'any
large thing' conveniently falling to the patronage of the
Crown. In July 1466 the conspirators played their stroke.
On pretext of escorting him to a hunting party, James was
carried to Edinburgh Castle. Three months later (October)
the Estates appointed Lord Boyd sole Governor of the
Realm, keeper of the king and his two brothers, and cus-
todian of the royal fortresses. Soon he was constituted Lord
Chamberlain for life. That he was acting in collusion with
the Yorkist dynasty in England is probable. But his chief
object was to enrich his family. His son Thomas was
singled out for special distinction, received the title Earl
of Arran, and in the same year (1467) married James'
sister Mary.

Boyd's rule promoted an event of first-rate service to
Orkneys and the Scottish realm. Even before the death of
Shetlands an- James II, Christian I, King of Denmark, Nor-
nexed, 1472 way and Sweden, complained of Scotland's
failure to pay the 'annual' for the Western Isles. An
appeal to the French king's mediation received his suggestion of a marriage between Christian's daughter and the
King of Scots, and in 1468 an embassy dispatched to Denmark and headed by the Earl of Arran secured an agreement
extremely valuable to Scotland. James' proposal for Margaret
of Norway was accepted. Of her jointure, 10,000 florins were
to accompany her to Scotland. For the balance (50,000 florins)
the Orkney Isles were pledged, and full discharge was given
for arrears and future payment of the 'annual' for the
Western Isles. But the princess brought only 2000 of the
promised 10,000 florins. Her father therefore pledged the
Shetlands too. Neither Orkneys nor Shetlands were ever

redeemed and in 1472 both were annexed to the Scottish crown.

Escorting the child bride from Norway, Arran returned to Scotland in 1469, and the royal marriage took place forthwith at Holyrood. But the star of the Boyds had set. The chief cause of their fall was the nobles' jealousy of Arran's presumptuous alliance with royalty. His father and uncle, impeached of treason, were sentenced to forfeiture. Arran himself led a roving life upon the Continent until his death. His wife, compelled by James to desert his fallen fortunes, gave her hand to the first Lord Hamilton, to whom she took the Arran title. From the union sprang the powerful houses of Lennox and Hamilton.

Meanwhile, within the royal house dissension was growing to a head and burst in 1479. James III, now in his twenty-eighth year, was upon uneasy terms *Albany* with his brothers, Alexander, Duke of Albany, and John, Earl of Mar, whose tastes and temperament despised his unkingly occupations, which gained him the contempt of his lords. His low-born favourites, rightly holding their master's preference the object of his brothers' anger, insinuated suspicion of them in his mind and hinted sorcery and enchantment as weapons they would not scruple to employ. But, inert by nature, James was capable of sudden effort. In 1479 Albany, who held the Earldom of March, was lodged in Edinburgh Castle on a charge of disloyalty amply supported by his subsequent conduct. Mar, at about the same time, was thrown into Craigmillar Castle, where he died suddenly, murdered, said some.

Intent upon his own ambition, Albany fled to France, where Louis XI showed no disposition to adopt his quarrel. But in another quarter his estrangement from his brother was found opportune. At peace with France (1475), the Yorkist Edward IV was not averse from giving his dynasty the foundation which vindication of England's claim to superiority over Scotland would afford. Albany was an instrument providentially provided. Anti-

cipating his enmity and collusion with Edward, war was
loosed upon the Border, Bamborough was fired by Archibald
Bell-the-Cat, Earl of Angus, in the spring of 1480, and the
remonstrance of the Pope, who urged Christian princes to
turn their arms rather against the Turk, lately lodged in
Europe, alone stayed James from leading a great host into
England.

Again, therefore, England and Scotland were on the
precipice of war through Edward's revival of
the old Plantagenet ambition. Albany was summoned from France, and in June 1482 made a
treaty at Fotheringay with Edward which exposed his ambition and disloyalty. It bound him within six months of
his restoration in Scotland to do homage to Edward, surrender Berwick, Lochmaben, Eskdale, and Annandale, and
marry Edward's daughter Cecilia, a girl of thirteen. A week
later he joined Edward's brother Gloucester (Richard III),
and marched with a force of 10,000 to recover Berwick.
The crisis brought the barons' quarrel with the king to a
head. Accompanied by the whole band of unpopular
favourites to whose ill-counselling the estrangement of
Albany was attributed, James took the field. But at Lauder,
where the army encamped, Archibald 'Bell-the-Cat'—he promised to play the game of cat and mice with James' minions
—and others let the king understand that only on condition
he dismissed his favourites would they follow him farther.
James proudly refused. Incontinently the lords hanged his
favourites over Lauder Bridge, and incarcerated James in
Edinburgh Castle. Opposition to Gloucester and Albany
collapsed, and the dukes entered Edinburgh in triumph. The
Church now intervened between James and his brother. On
condition of owning allegiance Albany was restored to his
estates and offices. Gloucester withdrew, and upon his return
march mastered the Castle, as already he possessed the town
of Berwick, which passed finally from Scotland's possession
(1482).

*Lauder
Bridge*, 1482

Albany still stood pledged to Edward IV to fulfil the Fotheringay contract. In January 1483 his agents were at the English Court, where the compact was repeated. His brother's perfidy *Fall of Albany*, 1484 was known to James, who, in March 1483, prohibited Albany from coming within six miles of the Court. The duke thereupon acknowledged his treasonable relations with Edward, and undertook to break with his confederates, while Edward IV's death a few weeks later removed his main prop. In July Parliament visited his treasons upon his head, and attainted him in absence, he being already in flight across the Border. A year later (1484) he threw his last stake with exiled Douglas. Dispersed at Lochmaben, their small force scattered. Douglas ended his days as a monk. Albany, passing to the Continent, was killed in a tournament a year later (1485).

The accession of Henry VII to the throne of England in 1485 brought James' relations with his neighbour into smooth water. He had freed himself *Sauchie Burn*, 1488 from Arran, Douglas, and Albany, and the future beckoned with promise. But the fair prospect was delusive; within three years of his triumph James' death swelled the tale of Stewart tragedy. His favour of 'abandoned wretches,' men 'of the lowest description,' 'sycophants and cowards,' so his favourites are described, remained a grievance. His employment of ecclesiastics, the favour he showed them, was another. But the immediate cause of revolt was a quarrel with the Homes upon his intention to attach the Priory of Coldingham to the Chapel Royal, Stirling, his own foundation. The Homes, who had an interest in the Priory, formed a powerful confederacy among the nobles of the South, and both sides appealed for English assistance. But a decision was obtained without intervention from outside. With an army drawn from the North, James met the rebels at Blackness on the Forth in 1488. But instead of striking he chose to parley, and pro-

mised to submit himself to none but prelates, lords, and
others of wisdom for the guiding of his realm. The tragedy
was only delayed. Young James joined his father's enemies,
whose army had kept the field, alleging the king's intention
to cheat them with English aid. Early in June, on the
Sauchie Burn, near Bannockburn, the forces met. James,
carrying the sword of Bruce, was mounted on a grey charger
beyond his management, which carried him from the field.
At night-fall the king sheltered in a mill distant from the
battle-field. His enemies, drawn to the spot by his rider-
less horse, entered the room where the king lay and dispatched him in cold blood (June 11, 1488). Details of the
tragedy were never divulged; the king 'happinit to be slain,'
the curious were told.

So ended an unhappy reign. Kidnapped by the Boyds,
betrayed by Douglas, hurt by the disloyalty of a brother
and a son, James from first to last was the sport of circumstances which his unstable spirit could not control.

CHAPTER VII

THE FRENCH ALLIANCE

THE reign of James IV was coincident with a new period of human progress. In the recovered literatures of Greece and Rome men discovered a *The Renaissance* secular outlook unfamiliar to the sombre Middle Ages, and received a stimulus which spurred endeavour in every sphere of human activity. The vernacular Bible, a gift of the Renaissance, awoke a spiritual sense long dormant: judged by the standard of the recovered Book of God the formalism of the mediaeval Church was found unsatisfying. The very limits of the known world were extended by a new insatiable curiosity. Vasco da Gama and Columbus respectively linked Western Europe with India and a New World upon which, before the middle of the sixteenth century, the chief Powers staked out claims whose development vitally affected the course of human history. Enormously stimulating also were the scientific discoveries of the period. The employment of the compass and astrolabe facilitated maritime adventure and a wide expansion of geographical knowledge. The use of gunpowder revolutionized the art of war and hastened the break-up of mediaeval society. The invention of printing widened the appeal of literature and learning.

In James IV Scotland received a sovereign qualified to preside over such a period of transition. A foreigner described him in 1498, when James **James IV, 1488–1513** was twenty-five years old, as a man of noble stature, handsome, agreeable in address. He spoke Latin 'very well': French, German, Flemish, Italian, Spanish, and Gaelic were also known to him. He inherited his father's taste for music: at an early meeting with his bride, 'incontinent the king began before her to play on the clarichord and after on the lute, which pleased her very much.' In chemistry and the primitive physical science of his period he showed intelligent interest. His charter set up the first printing press in Scotland in 1507, and painters had his patronage. He was a mighty hunter, proficient in knightly exercises, an accomplished rider, impulsive in temperament, deficient in self-control; one who knew him remarked his 'young adventurousness' and 'simple wilfulness,' for which his kingdom paid heavy penalty. For the Church and the clergy he had high regard. Never before was Scotland so closely involved in the web of Western diplomacy, and at home the reign stands in happy contrast to the disorders of its predecessor and successor. To James' personality both circumstances must be attributed.

James' distinctive achievement was the reduction of the *The Islands* Islands to a state of order which they had not formerly known, and their absorption as an integral part of the kingdom. Since John of the Isles made submission to James III in 1476 and surrendered the Earldom of Ross, his Lordship had been an arena of disorder. In May 1493 Parliament passed sentence of forfeiture upon him: he died at Dundee ten years later (1503). But the work of pacification was incomplete. In 1497 and again in 1498 James visited the Islands, whose chiefs found a leader in Donald Dubh, John's grandson. In 1503 under their new champion the islanders descended upon Badenoch. Next year James summoned the whole military array of the kingdom, quelled the revolt, and incarcerated Donald Dubh in Edinburgh Castle. Two sheriffdoms were created to control the rebellious territory. Thereafter the Islands remained comparatively quiet. Their chiefs followed James' banner to Flodden and at length held themselves subjects and not rivals of the monarchy.

To the judicial administration of the kingdom James gave

personal care. Throughout his reign his pleasure progresses
were put to administrative uses, and constant
justice-ayres under his supervision protected the   *The Daily*
people from the nobles, kept the nobles in har-   *Council*
monious peace, and enriched the treasury. To the same end,
Parliament in 1504 ordained a 'Daily' Council to sit at
Edinburgh, or where the Court happened to be, to hear
summonses in civil matters, complaints, and causes, exercising powers conferred in previous reigns upon the Lords
Auditors of the Court of Session, whose authority only ran
during the sessions of Parliament. It became their custom
after 1504 to pass on unfinished causes to the Lords of
Council. Hence, upon the foundation of the College of Justice
in 1532, its Senators were styled Lords of Council and
Session. Until that date the Daily Council constituted the
supreme judicial Court of the kingdom.

His ambition to establish Scotland's naval power shows
James alive to the opportunity which the decay   *The Navy*
of Mediterranean sea-power opened to the mon-
archies of the West. An Act of 1493 ordained every burgh
to construct fishing boats of not less than twenty tons'
burthen. With Flanders commercial relations were particularly close. At Campvere, the seat of the Scottish
staple, a Conservator was specially charged to facilitate the
operations of Scottish merchants. These over-sea interests
directed James to the need for an adequate navy. The *Great
Michael*, the largest ship afloat, was the biggest of a national
fleet of nearly thirty vessels, large and small, and in Sir
Andrew Wood of Largo and Andrew Barton James possessed
sea-captains of ability.

With the Papacy James' relations were close throughout
his reign. Absolution for those involved in   *The Church*
James III's death, the erection (1492) of Glasgow
into an archbishopric to match St Andrews (erected in 1472),
and the title 'Protector of the Christian Religion,' were
successive marks of the Pontiff's favour. But the abuses of

the Scottish Church were scandalous. To the Arch-See of
St Andrews James appointed his brother, the Duke of Ross,
and, upon his death, his own bastard son, a minor. Another
of his natural sons received the Abbey of Dunfermline. The
Church possessed too large a proportion of a poor country's
wealth; its fat endowments afforded benefices for illegitimate
sons of the royal house or younger and portionless members
of the nobility, a scandal which already exercised thoughtful
minds. In 1494 the Archbishop of Glasgow sent up thirty
persons from the districts of Cunningham and Kyle on charges
of heresy. Many of their opinions were extravagant. But
the Reformation was already foreshadowed in them.

Abundant as are the signs that Scotland under James
The Yorkist Hoax 'issued from her northern gloom into the full
light of western civilisation,' nowhere are they
so evident as in the international arena. James'
contemporaries upon the English throne were the first two
sovereigns of the House of Tudor. Mystery enveloped the
fate of the two sons of Edward IV murdered in the Tower.
Hence Yorkist pretensions were exploitable by foreign
and unfriendly Powers. Their opportunity presented itself
in astonishing circumstances. In 1491 a Breton merchant-
man, entering Cork harbour, landed a handsome youth
named Peter (or Peterkin or Perkin) Warbeck (or Osbeck),
whose father, on his son's confession, was a native of Tournai.
Cork, where adherents of the White Rose were numerous,
hailed Perkin as the younger of Edward IV's murdered sons.
Declaring himself the prince, Perkin, as 'King Edward's son,'
opened communications with James IV. For the moment
James was not drawn into the imposture. But by the summer
of 1495 he concluded that Perkin was genuine or employable
to Scotland's advantage. In June he offered support, and
in November received the pretender as 'Prince Richard of
England,' giving him a pension of £1200 a year and the hand
of his kinswoman, Lady Catharine Gordon, daughter of the
Earl of Huntly.

In September 1496 James made his inglorious effort in
the pretender's behalf. No English response answered him.
Perkin himself was but two days on English soil, and James
returned to his capital after a fruitless raid. Each assailed
the other with reproaches. Perkin disliked the savage warfare of his Scottish auxiliaries. James answered with a
rankling retort: 'You call England your land and realm; yet
not one man will show himself to aid or assist you in the
war begun for your cause and in your name.' But he was
loath to abandon the 'young fond foundling,' and in 1497
Northumberland was again raided. Henry VII, confronted
by a Cornish rising, took no measures to retaliate, but opened
negotiations for Perkin's surrender. In July, 1497, the
pretender, with his wife, sailed from Ayr in a ship felicitously
named the *Cuckoo*. Her destination was Cornwall, where
three months later a surprising adventure ended in Perkin's
capture and confession. 'My masters of Ireland,' Henry is
reported to have said, 'ye will crown apes at last.' His interests, now that Scotland was no longer behind Perkin,
inclined Henry to peace with his neighbour, and the Spanish
sovereigns also were anxious to relieve England of Scotland's
enmity in hope of Henry's participation in their Continental
plans. Their mediation prevailed. At Ayton a seven years'
truce was signed in September and five months later
(February 1498) was prolonged for a year beyond the death
of the survivor of the two sovereigns.

The truce encouraged the idea of a match between James
and Henry VII's daughter, Margaret, which had   *The Tudor*
been mooted in 1495 but was broken by James'   *Marriage,*
support of the White Rose. Early in 1502 a   *1503*
marriage treaty was concluded. On the same day the two
countries pledged themselves to perpetual peace, the first
pacification, distinguished from a truce, since the Treaty
of Northampton (1328) nearly two centuries before. Eighteen
months later (1503) James was wedded to his fifteen years'
old bride at Holyrood, whose Palace he had just completed

for her reception. From the couple the spouses descended whose marriage united the kingdoms a century later. William Dunbar celebrated the event in a hymeneal poem, *The Thistle and the Rose*, interesting as the first reference in literature to Scotland's national emblem.

So long as Henry VII lived his sagacity maintained peace with Scotland. But upon the accession of *Flodden Field*, 1513 Henry VIII in 1509 English policy abandoned its cautious reserve. Jealousy of French prestige won in Italy inclined the new sovereign to join the Holy League against France. In November 1511 he did so, pledging himself to war upon her in the coming spring. In 1512 the storm burst, and France's plight appealed alike to James' interest and honour. In May he confirmed the Ancient League, in chivalrous answer to the Queen of France, who named him her champion and sent him a ring. Hence, when, in June 1513, Henry invaded France, James sent his challenge to him, and before August was out crossed the Border. Norham surrendered to him after a six days' siege. But already the Earl of Surrey was bringing relief. Twice James had evaded conclusions with the English captain, whose challenge to him, to test 'the righteousness of the matter' between them on an appointed date, he was not a man to shirk. He awaited Surrey on Flodden Edge, on the left bank of the Till. On September 9, on the afternoon of a waning day, Surrey mounted the ascent where James' standards flew. Before darkness fell, gashed and riddled with bills and arrows, the king lay dead upon the field, the flower of Scotland's nobility and manhood round him.

Flodden plunged Scotland into anarchy. The king was an infant, eighteen months old. His mother, a *James V*, 1513–42 woman of twenty-four, was a foreigner. The heir apparent was John of Albany[1], a man of thirty-two, son of the traitor Albany of James III's reign,

[1] Strictly, the heir was John of Albany's half-brother Alexander whose rights the Estates subordinated to John's in 1516.

a naturalized Frenchman, and knowing no other tongue. Next heir after Albany was the Earl of Arran, head of the house of Hamilton. Complicated already, the queen-mother's swift marriage to the sixth Earl of Angus, Bell-the-Cat's grandson, added a detail of confusion to the situation and revived the traitorous relations with England which were an inherited tendency in the Douglas blood. Behind these personalities operated the tireless diplomacy of England, resolved to spare no effort to humble France, and prepared to employ in Scotland every artifice to counter the menace of the Ancient League. Driven by English provocations into the arms of France, Scotland for years to come was an arena for the antagonism of her jealous neighbours.

James IV fell on September 9, 1513. Before the end of the month his infant son was crowned at Stirling and his widow was appointed Guardian and Regent. The Archbishop of Glasgow (James Beaton), the Earls of Arran, Angus (Bell-the-Cat), and Huntly were named her advisers. But her second marriage provoked civil dissension, and on the Borders after Flodden fighting was constant. Anxious eyes were turned to France, and many interests desired Albany's coming. In the early weeks of the reign messages were dispatched by well-wishers urging that course, and in March 1514 the Estates formally summoned him. A year later (May 1515), secretly plenished by France, Albany landed at Ayr after eluding English cruisers instructed to prevent his passage to Scotland. James IV's two infant children alone stood between him and the crown, and their guardianship, with the Regency of the kingdom, was accorded him three months after his arrival (July). He was welcomed with enthusiasm by a people who had not yet measured the impotence of France's friendship.

Possession of the infant sovereign was essential to Albany's undeclared mission in France's behalf. But English plots to abduct the queen and her children were active. Immediately upon his appointment as Regent Albany pro-

cured the appointment of four peers into whose hands
Margaret was required to surrender her children
at Stirling. They were refused admission, and
Angus and the English March Warden, Lord
Dacre, plotted to carry the queen and the princes to England,
though Angus' brother, Sir George Douglas of Pittendreich,
approaching the Castle with a body of horse, failed to extricate its occupants. So, in August 1515, when Albany
appeared in force, Margaret made unconditional surrender.
The princes were delivered up. Margaret with her husband
rode for the Border and gave birth to 'a fair young lady'
who became the mother of Darnley and grandmother of
James VI. To complete Albany's triumph Angus deserted
his wife before the end of the year, her infant Duke of Ross
died, and Arran's chief fortress, Hamilton Castle, passed
into the Regent's hands. But Albany was discovering the
difficulties of his position and complained of his neglect
by France, on whose support hung the interests he represented. Anxious to quicken France's activities, he obtained
permission to return thither, and meanwhile assured his
position in Scotland by securing an admission of his rights
as heir apparent. In June 1517 he sailed for France, undertook to return in six months, and was absent for more than
four years.

The years of Albany's absence were filled by the feuds of
Angus and Arran: a famous encounter was the scuffle known
as 'Cleanse the Causeway,' which took place at Edinburgh
in April 1520 and has its name from the completeness of
Angus' victory: Arran barely escaped with his life, and his
brother was slain by Angus himself. Albany's return alone
promised to quiet these tumults. In November 1521, he
was once more in Scotland, on a visit even shorter than the
first and less satisfactory. Arriving at a moment when France
and England were on the brink of open war, his return was
viewed from London as a stroke in France's policy. Henry
vainly sought his expulsion. The Douglas friends of England

Albany
Regent

charged him to have murdered the infant Duke of Ross and
with neglecting the king. Whispers that he contemplated a
match with the queen-mother were put abroad. He had in
fact taken steps to procure her divorce from Angus, but
'prayed he might break his neck' if marriage with her was
in his mind. The Estates, little heeding these charges, repudiated Henry's attempt to interfere, and when, in August
1522, an English army crossed the Straits to France, Albany
at the head of a large army threatened Carlisle and the de-
fenceless western frontier. But he reckoned without the
memory of Flodden: those even whom he chiefly trusted
refused to risk another catastrophe for the sake of France.
Perforce Albany accepted a month's truce, disbanded his
army, and returned to France, leaving Huntly, Argyll,
and Arran to act as a Council of Regency (October
1522).

Albany's departure encouraged Henry to tempt Scotland
from her French attachment. Early in 1523 he offered the
youthful king peace, with the hand of his daughter Mary.
The Estates would not listen and Surrey, son and successor
of the conqueror of Flodden, was let loose upon the Border.
Jedburgh was given to the flames on the day (September 25,
1523) Albany landed at Dumbarton with foreign auxiliaries
and artillery. A second time he summoned Scotland to arms.
But once more, as in 1522, his levies melted away on the
news of Surrey's approach. His Frenchmen were deported
to France with little cordiality, and Albany begged for
permission to accompany them, convinced that neither
his own interests nor those of France could be served
further in Scotland. In May 1524 he left Scotland, and
never returned.

Albany's departure at length surrendered Scotland to
Henry and the English party. Angus, who had retired to
France on Albany's return in 1522, now left that country
for England. To Scotland Henry sent money, and an English
guard of 200 men replaced the royal bodyguard. With their

aid James was brought to Edinburgh (July 1524) and proclaimed king regnant. But Henry required the association
of Angus with James' rule, a proposal obnoxious to Margaret, whose divorce from Angus was still unaccomplished,
though her mature affections already settled upon Henry
Stewart, a youth of twenty, whom she appointed Lord High
Treasurer. At this inconvenient juncture Angus returned to
Scotland and consequently threw Margaret upon the support of the French faction. Beaton, whom she had imprisoned, was released, and though Margaret repulsed Angus,
in November 1524, when he raided Edinburgh in hope
of abducting the king, English gold was irresistible. Angus
entered the Council of Regency.

English interests, of which Angus was the subsidized agent,
Fall of Angus,
1528
were now in the ascendant. A new Privy Council
was constituted of which he was master. But
he could not win the sovereign's affection.
James was a gloomy, passionate youth, whose strongest
emotions were affection for his mother and hatred of his
stepfather. 'Nane at that tyme durst stryve with ane
Douglas nor yet ane Douglas man, for gif they wald they
gat the war.' But James took courage and prevailed. In
April 1528 Margaret married her third husband, Henry
Stewart, later Lord Methven. In the king's name Angus
separated the spouses, and stung James to action. He complained of his 'thraldom' to Angus, and, alleging a plot to
abduct him to England, betook himself to his mother at
Stirling, ordered Angus to withdraw beyond Spey, and prohibited any of his name to come within six miles of his
person. In September 1528 the Estates passed sentence of
forfeiture upon the earl, and as Henry was not prepared to
act in his support, England and Scotland concluded a five
years' peace which sacrificed him. Angus made his way to
England as Henry's pensioned guest. There he lived till the
death of James V in 1542.

James was in his seventeenth year when the fall of Angus

made him his own master. Squat and broadly built, with
grey eyes shrewd and penetrating, he inherited his father's
complexion—he was called the 'Red Tod'—physique, and
love of sport. He was accomplished, a poet and musician,
a patron of letters and the arts. But his character was
undisciplined, though he won affectionate remembrance as
'the poor man's king.' Many stories record kindly acts of
the 'Goodman of Ballengeich'—so he called himself after
the hollow behind Stirling Castle—upon his adventures
incognito among his humbler subjects.

The hostility of Catholic Europe and the definitive sever-
ance of his Church from Rome made Scotland's support of
consequence to Henry VIII; if James was influenced to
follow in his footsteps the Franco-Scottish alliance could
not survive Scotland's breach with the Pope. On the other
hand, Scotland's friendship was rendered more precious to
France as an ally to chastise heretic England. While
Henry conferred the Garter on James, the sovereigns of
France and the Empire hastened to bestow on him the
Orders of St Michael and the Golden Fleece. James was not
blind to the need for reformation in his Scottish Church. At
the same time the memory of English hostility made it
venturesome to terminate the French Alliance. The Church
clamoured for its maintenance to buttress her against heresy
and threatened spoliation. In vain therefore Henry in 1535
dispatched one of his bishops to argue James into a
Protestant mood, suggesting an interview at York or elsewhere. James' Council dictated refusal. Nor would it enter-
tain his marriage with Henry's daughter, Mary. Instead,
James asked the hand of Marie de Bourbon, and in 1536
sailed to France to bring home his bride. The decision
definitively bound him to the Catholic and French
interest.

Presenting himself at St Quentin, where his bride was
staying, James found her humpbacked and deformed, and,
though received with cordiality by her parents, could not

bring himself to make a match. Proceeding to Paris, he was
The French Marriage captivated by the beauty of Francis I's daughter Madeleine, a passion which the princess reciprocated. At the New Year of 1537 they were married in Nôtre Dame and James brought home his bride. But within two months Madeleine died and James again sought a wife in France. During his visit he had admired Mary, daughter of Duke Claude of Guise, recently widowed. In the spring of 1538 David Beaton, the future Cardinal, was dispatched to obtain her hand. Comely and wealthy, she was also a woman of character and decision, possessed by the passionate hatred of Protestantism which was the characteristic of her house. In the summer of 1538 she arrived in Scotland, to play in its history a larger part than any who had worn the crown matrimonial since Canmore's English Margaret.

Twelve months after the queen's arrival, David Beaton
The Protestants was preferred to the See of St Andrews. Elevated to the Cardinalate by Paul III in 1538, a man of firm will, not scrupulous, a master of the age's tortuous diplomacy, he was well qualified to stand by Mary's side in the crisis that faced Scotland. Under these two dominating personalities James' reign approached its closing catastrophe. His second marriage and Beaton's ascendancy spurred him to action against the Protestants. Patrick Hamilton had been burnt for heresy in 1528. In 1534 three sufferers met the same fate. At the close of 1539 a bigger effort was made to eradicate their sect. At Glasgow and Edinburgh several were sent to the stake. Otherwise Henry's interests urged him to an understanding with James for the overthrow of Beaton, than whom, he was convinced, 'England hath no greater enemy.' In 1540 Sir Ralph Sadler was sent to Scotland charged to discredit Beaton, and to suggest the spoliation of Scottish monasteries as an agreeable source of revenue. In 1541 Henry proposed a meeting at York, and arrived there; James never came. There was a

burst of indignation from Henry, whose sister Margaret's
death a few weeks later (1541) snapped the last link binding
the two Courts. Scotland was threatened with invasion unless
she accepted inexorable terms—a perpetual alliance between
the two countries effectual against every quarter, and therefore operative against Scotland's friends, France and the
Papacy. The harsh conditions were rejected, and Henry revived the slumbering claim of suzerainty. Only war could
resolve the issue.

In October 1542 Norfolk, son of the victor of Flodden,
led a force across the Border, burnt Kelso
Abbey, and was out of Scotland in a week. *Solway Moss,*
James advanced to Fala Moor to give him *1542*
battle and, finding him withdrawn, would have marched
into England. But none would follow him. Some of his nobles
were eager to plunder an over-rich Church; all remembered
Flodden and were unwilling to risk disaster for France's
sake. As a counterstroke to Norfolk's deed, James therefore
resolved to raid the Debateable Land. In November a force
some 18,000 strong advanced, burning and ravaging, till
Sir Thomas Wharton cornered them between the Solway
Firth and the Esk. The day is disastrous in Scotland's
military history. Two earls, five barons, 500 lairds and
gentlemen, twenty pieces of ordnance and thirty standards
fell to the English. Thousands of horses were bogged and
lost. Only seven English lives were the price of the victory.
The news was carried to James, who rode to Falkland
Palace, where he sought his bed mortally wounded in spirit.
News of his child's birth was brought to cheer him. 'The king
inquired whether it was man or woman. The messenger said
it was a fair daughter. The king answered and said, Adieu,
farewell, it [the Stewart crown] came with a lass, it will pass
with a lass, and so turned his back unto his lords and his
face unto the wall.' A week later 'He gave a little smile and
laughter, and thereafter held up his hands to God and yielded
the spirit.'

With James V ended the period of 'The Jameses.' Underneath the turmoil which fills the page of history the country advanced in wealth, established itself in the fraternity of European states, and responded to the call of the Renaissance and Reformation. James' death did not at once weaken the tradition of Franco-Scottish friendship, but it left Scotland at the parting of the ways: France and Rome beckoned to one, England and a new age to the other. For a quarter of a century the issue was in suspense, till, galloping from Scotland in 1568 to the inhospitable shelter of an English roof, Mary Stewart resolved it. Protestantism and the English alliance triumphed, a transformation of their relationship essential to the already imminent union of the two countries.

CHAPTER VIII

THE REFORMATION

SOLWAY MOSS seemingly prostrated Scotland at England's feet. The sovereign was an infant a few days old, her one near relative a Frenchwoman. The Franco-Papal alliance had encountered humiliating disaster and could be supposed discredited. Henry stood to Scotland as Edward I in 1286: a child queen offered the means to unite the realms by marriage with a juvenile Prince Edward. At once upon the news of James' death Henry laid his plans. The Solway Moss prisoners, released on parole, were speeded to Scotland to do his business. 'They have not sticked to take upon them to set the crown of Scotland on our head,' Henry could assert. They were pledged to seize the infant queen, kidnap the Cardinal, and secure the chief fortresses of the kingdom. Should Mary die they undertook that Henry should be king. Early in 1543, he intimated to the Scottish Council his resolve to unite the two realms through the marriage of their queen and the Prince of Wales. Angus, who signed the discreditable bond with Henry, and his brother Sir George Douglas were restored to Scotland to further his purposes.

Mary Stewart, 1542–67

The next heir to the crown after the infant queen was the Earl of Arran, head of the house of Hamilton, a man lacking character, 'half an idiot,' in the opinion of a contemporary. His career proves him devoid of ability, but his position could not be ignored. Early in January 1543 he was named Regent and tutor of the young sovereign, and looked to Henry for support. Opposed to him were Beaton and the priests. On the Cardinal's determined shoulders rested the continuance of the French alliance and the old Church. At him in chief Henry's enmity was aimed.

Henry's emissaries returned to Scotland to find Arran
installed in power. Boasting Henry's support,
Arran Regent Angus and the other lords easily influenced the
weak Regent 'to have the Cardinal by the back.'
He was arrested and confined. Five weeks later the Estates
helped the plot upon its course. The English marriage was
discussed, ambassadors were appointed to treat. At the
same time, following the example of Henry, the Old and New
Testaments were ordered to be circulated in the vulgar
tongue. In July 1543 two documents were signed at Greenwich. The first was a treaty of peace, in which France was
included. The second sanctioned the Anglo-Scottish marriage:
Scotland's independence and autonomy were safe-guarded.

Beaton's arrest, the promise of a vernacular Bible, and
Henry's revival of pretensions to suzerainty gathered indignation to a head. The priests refused to say Mass, christen,
or bury so long as the Cardinal was in ward. Their hands
were strengthened by the return from France of two men
whose attachment to the old Church made them willing
partisans of the Cardinal—Arran's cousin Matthew, Earl of
Lennox (father of Lord Darnley) and John Hamilton, Arran's
natural brother, later Archbishop of St Andrews. Lennox
was next heir to the throne after Arran and stood before
him if his legitimacy was challenged. Hence, their arrival
moved Arran to propitiate the Catholic party. Beaton
recovered his liberty: his demand to share the custody of
the infant queen was conceded, and Arran, succumbing
to his stronger will, did public penance for his 'apostasy':
Beaton as Chancellor, the Queen-Mother, and a number of
Francophile bishops were added to the Council. The Estates
denounced the Greenwich treaties, renewed the French
alliance, and ordered the bishops to make inquisition into
heresies. It was clear to demonstration that on their own
resources his Scottish partisans were powerless to achieve
Henry's purposes. If Scotland was to be won it must be
by his own wooing, and a rude one he was preparing.

In May 1544, Edward Seymour, Earl of Hertford, uncle of the infant Mary's destined bridegroom, appeared in Scotland by sea with a powerful force to demonstrate the consequences of Beaton's *The English Wooing* ascendancy. He was charged to destroy Edinburgh, Holyrood, St Andrews, and fulfilled his task with excessive rigour. For five miles round Edinburgh the country was laid in ruins and of James IV's Palace Hertford raised 'a jolly fire.' 'Wo worth the Cardinal' the women cried who saw the blaze. Through the summer and autumn raids were constant, and an English force was severely handled at Ancrum Moor in February 1545. In the spring Henry offered friendship on condition that the Greenwich treaties were confirmed. He was repulsed, and auxiliaries from France arrived in May. In the following August a Franco-Scottish army took the old road into England but achieved little. Hertford again crossed the Border and retired, leaving a blackened country behind him and the Abbeys of Kelso, Melrose, Dryburgh and Jedburgh smoking ruins. Seven monasteries, sixteen castles, five market towns and two hundred and forty-three villages were demolished.

Meanwhile the Protestant leaven was working. Arran had approved the plunder of the wealthy Church and the rabbling of the religious at Dundee, Lindores, Arbroath and elsewhere. Beaton addressed himself to curb this aggressive spirit. Bishops were urged to hold searching inquisition. Heavy punishments were threatened, and by the summer of 1545 Beaton boasted with ill-founded confidence that 'heresy is dead.' Most notable of his victims was George Wishart, who had been exiled in 1538, and re- *George Wishart* turned to Scotland after James V's death in company with the released Scots on whom Henry relied to destroy Beaton. At the New Year of 1546 he came to Haddington to denounce the 'mummeries' whose observance marked the season. The occasion is memorable; John Knox steps upon the stage of history in the scanty audience who

greeted the preacher. At midnight after the meeting Wishart
was arrested. A few weeks later he was 'brynt to poulder'
as a heretic in front of the Cardinal's seat at St Andrews.
There is a legend that Beaton gazed exultingly on the scene
from a tower of his castle and that Wishart foretold the day
not distant when the Cardinal's body should hang lifeless
from its battlements.

Wishart's death invited retaliation. In May 1546, a few
Assassination weeks later, men were at work on Beaton's
of Beaton, castle when, early one morning, a dozen or
1546 more Protestant stalwarts, mingling with the
workmen as they passed in to their tasks, overpowered the
sentinels, closed the gates, and upon a staircase, or within
his own chamber—the accounts are conflicting—found Beaton and did him to death. Assembling at the rumour of
tumult, the townsfolk beheld the Cardinal's body suspended from the tower whence he had witnessed Wishart's
death. Both sides had now immolated a martyr to their
convictions and more passionately rallied for a stern conflict.

Beaton's death was a damaging blow to the Ancient
League and removed from Henry's path the most obstinate
obstruction to the alliance he sought. But Arran knew that
the country would not tolerate an understanding with
England, and continued to pursue the path the Cardinal
had chosen. The Catholic Earl of Huntly replaced Beaton
as Chancellor; the rejection of the English alliance was
unanimously confirmed by the Estates; and even the
Douglases denounced the marriage between their queen and
their paymaster's son. A veto was placed upon the rabbling
of religious houses, and the authors of the Cardinal's murder
were marked for punishment. They had seized their victim's
castle, proposing to use it for their protection against the
law and as a refuge for their partisans. Its accessibility to
English naval succours added a reason for the castle's re-
tention. To reduce it was Arran's chief purpose and succours
for that purpose reached him out of France. Late in July

1547 a breach was made in the walls and the garrison capitulated. Their lives were spared, but all were transported to France, where Knox and others for nearly two years toiled as slaves in the galleys. Beaton's murder was avenged, and a flicker of vitality lit up the expiring French alliance.

England, at length committed under Edward VI to a Reformation more thorough than his father had permitted, could not stand indifferent to the *Pinkie, 1547* situation in Scotland. French forces had seized St Andrews, frequented the streets of Edinburgh, and, it was suspected, proposed to carry the young queen to France's protection. Early in September 1547 Hertford, now Duke of Somerset and Lord Protector, with a force 16,000 strong entered Scotland, counting on Protestant co-operation. The fiery cross was sent round by the priests, but many of the 23,000 who faced Somerset at Pinkie were Irish archers brought up by Argyll. Confident in their numbers the Scots for the first time in half a century gave battle. On September 9 the two hosts faced each other. On the morrow—'Black Saturday'—abandoning commanding ground, the Scottish host crossed the Esk to threaten the English left. Ere nightfall the battlefield was a shambles; at least six thousand lay dead upon the field, and fifteen hundred were captives. Pinkie was the bloodiest and last of Scotland's disasters in her contest for national existence.

Somerset's victory induced a decision of far-reaching import. A few days after the battle he declared his master's determination to 'forward the godly *Mary sent to France, 1548* purpose of the marriage' by force if other measures could not prevail. The Queen-Mother, therefore, removed her charge to the Island of Inchmahome on the Lake of Menteith, half-way between Stirling and the Highlands. Already appeal had been made to France, where the new king Henry II and his Guise advisers were fixed to prevent Scotland from following England along the paths of heresy. Possession of the Scottish queen being essential to their design, a request was dispatched for her union with the Dauphin and her instant passage to France. In July 1548 'in ane voice' the Estates accepted a proposal which assured the queen's safety and promised to divert England's enmity to another target. Scotland's laws and liberties were jealously safeguarded and the French king undertook to pursue her quarrels as his own. At the end of the month the queen sailed to France. For thirteen years it was her home.

One thing was needed to complete the French victory. The queen was in France, shortly to be married *Mary of Guise, Regent* to the heir of that monarchy. Scotland was supported by a French garrison. But Arran remained Regent. His substitution by the Queen-Mother would link the two kingdoms' policy. In September 1550 Mary of Guise visited France to take counsel with her brothers. Could Arran's ambition be conciliated? Solaced by the duchy of Châtellerault, he gave reluctant assent to Mary's assumption of the Regency when her daughter reached the age of twelve in December 1554. Impatient to await that period, Mary in April 1554 assumed an authority which Knox declared 'as seemly a sight (if men had eyes) as to put a saddle upon the back of an unruly cow.' Her elevation gave France a status in Scotland which, except at the sword's point, England had not held since the reign of Henry III.

The short Regency of Mary of Guise witnessed the most drastic revolution in Scotland's experience. France's alliance was definitively rejected. Burying the animosities of centuries, Scotland turned to the friendship of England, and joined the forces of reform and progress. Mary Stewart, returning to her native land in 1561 after thirteen years' absence, found Beaton's Church in ruins, France no longer regarded, and herself the head of a Protestant establishment.

The Regent's task was to administer Scotland in the interests of France, attempting a purpose which England's armed might had abandoned. Sympathetic as Scotland had shown herself to French ideas and culture, the two races never mingled agreeably on Scottish soil. The French troops on whom the Regent relied provoked popular violence. The suspicion was well founded that the distant queen was not a firm champion of Scotland's rights and independence, and the 'crown matrimonial' worn by her husband suggested the rule of a foreign prince. What the Scottish community had so stubbornly withheld from England was, in fact, abandoned to France by Scotland's sovereign. The Reformation, under Knox's leadership, weakened the alliance at another angle. Hence, in a situation which involved sharp antagonism to the stubborn convictions of her daughter's subjects the Regent's ability availed little.

The Regent's earliest acts were ill-liked. She neglected the nobles, and, in spite of her people's suspicion of foreigners in their high places, set her countrymen in authority. As her principal adviser she chose the French agent whose diplomacy had smoothed the young queen's departure for France. Huntly was superseded by another Frenchman, to whom the Great Seal was entrusted. The chief fortresses of the kingdom, excepting Edinburgh, were in Frenchmen's hands. Hence, within a twelvemonth, Mary faced an angry opposition. Stubborn resistance was offered to her proposal to maintain a standing army, after the example of France, and to impose its burden upon the property owners of the kingdom. The Regent yielded, but encountered a further rebuff in 1557. Influenced by her husband Philip II, Mary Tudor declared war upon France in that year. On an urgent appeal from Paris, the Regent called on her Council to retaliate by an answering declaration of war upon England. Though refused, she assembled a large army at Kelso and eagerly recommended invasion. Châtellerault, Huntly, Argyll, and other nobles declared themselves ready to fight for the defence of Scotland, but for no aggressive purpose, and in anger the Regent disbanded them.

The year 1558 offered compensation for these disappoint-
Marriage of ments. In April the youthful Mary Stewart was
Mary Stew- married at Paris to her boy husband, afterwards
art, 1558 Francis II, 'with great solemnity, triumph,
and banqueting.' Some days before, she had been influenced,
certainly by her Guise uncles, to sign three secret documents
conveying her kingdom, in default of heirs of her body, to
the King of France; constituting him master of Scotland
till the cost of her maintenance in France had been refunded;
and declaring the agreement binding on the two kingdoms
against all others inconsistent with its tenor to which she
might have put her hand. Seven months later the
death of Mary Tudor enabled Mary and her husband to
assume the arms of England and Ireland and in July 1559
Henry II's sudden death prematurely set them on the throne
of France. The year 1559 was thus ordained by events outside the kingdom to be critical in Scotland's history. Nothing
less was at stake than her independence and the victory or
defeat of a religion already making compelling appeal to
her conscience.

As an advancing cause the Reformation dates from Knox's
visit to Scotland in 1555. Of his early life little
The Reforma- is known. He was born in 1515, two years after
tion Flodden, of Lothian stock. In 1540 he was a
papal notary and in priest's orders; in 1545 tutor to the sons
of the lairds of Ormiston and Longniddry, in attendance on
Wishart when the martyr was arrested, and already a convert to his preaching. Beaton's assassination in 1546 moving
him 'merrily,' he joined the Protestant garrison beleaguered
in St Andrews as preacher. Released from the French galleys
early in 1549 he spent four years in England, was offered
and refused preferment, and again passed into exile when
Mary Tudor became queen in 1553. His contact with Calvin
and Geneva fixed the principles of his faith and taught him
that alliance between England and Scotland on the basis
of their common Protestantism was essential to the general

success of the Reformation. He was the most violent of the
Reformers, without fear, outspoken, stern, rugged, and
evolved a religion impressed with the intellectual character-
istics of the people he served. His visit to Scotland lasted
from September 1555 till July 1556. The Regent had been
installed for more than a year. But Knox was allowed unexpected freedom and preached widely throughout the
country, looking, he admitted to the Regent, 'rather for sentence of death' than licence. In the Mearns the lairds bound
themselves to maintain the true preaching of the Evangel,
and converts or adherents were found among the nobility,
notably Lord James Stewart (later Earl of Moray and
Regent), the Earls of Argyll and Glencairn, Erskine of Dun,
and Maitland of Lethington. The value of their support was
apparent in May 1556 when Knox was summoned before an
ecclesiastical court. At the last moment his accusers' hearts
failed them, and Knox returned to Geneva, leaving his
enemies the vain satisfaction of burning his effigy.

A party among the nobility being now openly identified
with the Protestant movement, its progress was
rapid. In December 1557 the first Covenant was   *The Consigned, pledging its signatories 'to maintain,   gregation*
set forward, and establish the most blessed word of God.'
The 'Congregation of Jesus Christ,' or 'Lords of the Congregation,' as the new organization came to be called, forthwith sent an urgent summons to Knox, demanded the
introduction into Scotland of the second Prayer-book of
Edward VI, and, pending the institution of public preaching,
asked permission to expound and discuss Scripture in private.
Meanwhile a Court of Elders was elected, and at Dundee
the first Reformed church in Scotland was forthwith
set up.

Emboldened by success, the Congregation demanded the
immediate reform of the Church and liberty to worship
publicly according to the reformed ritual. But the marriage
of her daughter to the Dauphin encouraged the Regent to

resist. She proposed a settlement which the Congregation could not accept, and sent to the stake Walter Mill, an old man of 'decrepit' age, a renegade priest. The last of the Protestant martyrs, his death was a challenge to the Congregation, who now declared their intention to worship God after their own manner, to defend themselves if attacked, and 'if it sall chance that Abusses be violentlie reformed,' imputed the blame in advance to those who refused a just reformation. Coincidently (November 1558) the death of Mary Tudor changed the situation to their advantage. Elizabeth mounted her sister's throne, and, menaced by the open rivalry of Mary Stewart, could not neglect the weapon Scotland's Protestant revolt offered to her hand. In May 1559 Knox was again in Scotland: the prospect of English support loomed hopefully, and both sides rallied for an encounter which brought down the Roman Church and French alliance in ruin together.

Assured of French support, the Regent took a firmer stand—the preachers must cease to preach or leave the country; 'albeit they preached as truly as ever did St Paul' she would banish them. She summoned them to appear before her at Stirling in May 1559, and the Congregation made their quarrel its own. Asserting them to be lawful ministers, duly called in accordance with Scriptural order, the Lords assembled at Perth to accompany the accused to the Regent's presence. Anxious to avoid a meeting which promised an explosion, Mary agreed to postpone sentence, but broke her word, and on the appointed date declared the preachers outlaws *in absentia*. On the morrow Knox preached in the Parish Church at Perth. When he ended, a courageous priest began the Office of the Mass at one of the altars. At the sight an ill-mannered boy flung a stone at the celebrant. The priest gave him 'a grit blowe,' and immediately, in Knox's words, 'the haill multitude that war about cast Stanes.' The houses of the Black Friars, Grey Friars, and Carthusians were pillaged and gutted, and by the evening of the next day,

Knox records with satisfaction, 'the Wallis onlie did remane of all these grit Edificatiounes.'

The issue now lay patently with the sword. Both sides summoned their dependents, and before the end of June the Congregation was installed in Edinburgh. But success was short-lived, and Knox was dispatched to England to invite support. Elizabeth, however, neither dared alienate her English Catholics nor was disposed to aid rebellion against a sister sovereign. Moreover she was at peace with France, whom open war in Scotland would certainly provoke. She therefore preferred to lavish promises, even to send money, but only in the last resort to aid with arms. But the desperate fortunes of the Congregation forced her hand. A new contingent from France swelled the Regent's forces and Lethington was dispatched urgently to Elizabeth. In the last days of December the Duke of Norfolk reached the Border, where a large army was to be mobilized. In February 1560, he signed at Berwick an agreement with the Protestant lords which took Scotland, her liberties and rights, under English protection. A month later his army was over the Border and the Regent sought shelter in Edinburgh Castle. On June 11 she died, a valiant, lonely woman. Three weeks later the Treaty of Edinburgh negotiated with *Treaty of* the French by Elizabeth's minister, scattered *Edinburgh* Guise ambition like a pack of cards. The French *1560* troops, excepting 120, were to quit Scotland; Mary and Francis to desist from using the arms of England; no Frenchman to hold an important office. Pending the sovereign's return a Council of twelve persons would administer the kingdom. No word was said about religion. But the issue was not in doubt. On every point English aid had made the Congregation victorious and not only in Britain but in western Europe Protestantism was assured.

In August 1560, after French and English had withdrawn, the Estates assembled to sanction the reformation of religion on which a determined minority was set. Their first request

was to Knox and his brother ministers, to formulate a
statement of Protestant doctrine. In four days
Confession of Faith, 1560 Knox's committee achieved the task and drew
up 'The Confession of Faith professed and
believed by the Protestants within the Realm of Scotland.'
With few dissentient voices it was accepted as 'hailsome and
sound doctrin.' A week later the Estates in three successive
Acts swept the Church of the past away. The first abolished
the Pope's authority over the realm and the jurisdiction of
all Catholic prelates. The second annulled Acts of Parliament
supporting doctrines and practices contrary to the new Confession. The third forbade the saying, hearing, or being
present at Mass. Passed on August 24, 1560, the three Acts
substituted Calvinistic Protestantism for Rome's system and
doctrine.

The authors of the Confession were now asked to draw up
First Book of Discipline, 1561 a constitution for the new Church, and in
January 1561 laid before the Estates the 'First
Book of Discipline.' For the Church's government it proposed Kirk-Sessions, Synods, and General Assemblies. As office-bearers it recognized Ministers, Teachers,
Elders, Deacons, Superintendents (overseers of districts cor-
responding roughly to the episcopal dioceses), and Readers
(needed to supplement the ordained ministers, who were
few at the outset). Upon these proposals there was unanimity
and the Scottish Protestant Church assumed the Presbyterian constitution it has since maintained. For the Church's
ministers the Book of Discipline demanded a liberal sus-
tenance, objecting that otherwise the service of God would
lack fitting instruments. The new Church, it was contended, had indisputable right to the endowments of its
predecessor. But Knox and his fellow ministers were disappointed to discover the zeal of their lay colleagues to pull
Endowments down the old fabric exceeding their enthusiasm
to endow the new one. Their hope to secure the
whole of the Church's wealth was unrealized. After long

debate it was left to the Privy Council to resolve the matter. By a transaction known as 'the assumption of thirds of benefices,' one-third of the ecclesiastical revenues was attached to the Crown for public purposes, including the sustentation of the Presbyterian ministry. The remaining two-thirds was assigned to the Catholic clergy.

Rejecting Edward VI's Prayer-book, which satisfied the Congregation in 1557, the Book of Discipline recommended for general use 'The Book of *Book of Common Order* Common Order,' used by Knox's congregation at Geneva and generally known as 'Knox's Liturgy.' It was accepted until 1637, when Archbishop Laud's attempt to supersede it plunged Scotland into the Bishops' Wars.

Thus rapidly were the system and doctrine of the old Church thrown down and its successor set up. But the victory was won rather than secured, and Knox and his colleagues were fearful lest their work should be undone. Elizabeth was not prepared to go as far as they hoped in identifying their interests with her own. It is probable also that three to one of the entire population were still Papist at heart. They would have welcomed reform of the old abuses, but were estranged by the wholesale reconstruction of the Church's fabric. Also the sovereign was a Catholic. The revolution had been carried in her despite and lacked her sanction. She represented the old ally, and already, as we know, had sold her people to France. Her determination to uproot the Kirk was not in doubt. In December 1560 death disposed of Francis II, and eight months later his widow trod the soil of Scotland after thirteen years' absence. The critical chapter of the Reformation opened.

CHAPTER IX

MARY STEWART

IN August 1561, almost exactly a year after the overthrow of the Mass, Mary landed at Leith out of France. The skies were dark, sea-fog hung upon the shore, no welcome awaited her, and at sight of the sorry equipage provided to carry her to Holyrood she wept. She came back a widow, but still a girl, accomplished, tall, like her French mother, endowed with great charm of manner rather than physical beauty, of courage indomitable and ever prompt to act with sure decision. Had her heart been as manageable an organ as her cousin Elizabeth's her reign might have recorded a not dissimilar success. But Bothwell crossed her path, tempting her to permit and condone an atrocious crime which destroyed herself and the Catholic cause she championed. One axe felled both at Fotheringay.

On the first Sunday after her return Mary heard Mass in her private chapel, while Protestant fanatics without were barely restrained by her half-brother Moray from breaking in to wreak their hatred on the 'idolatrous' priest. Though Knox, installed as minister in St Giles', at her palace door, thundered menaces, she claimed for herself and her household the liberty to follow their consciences which she hastened to accord to her Protestant subjects. Indeed, compromise was necessary, both to preserve her authority between the contending Churches, and also to permit her to press her right to recognition as Elizabeth's heir. On that purpose her policy bent unyieldingly until, early in 1565, Darnley entered her life. To secure Elizabeth's recognition she could offer assent to the Treaty of Edinburgh, which stipulated her disuse of the English title and arms: and though the

English succession was settled by law and little likely to be altered on Elizabeth's initiative, the strong Catholic feeling of the North of England, and the possibility of Mary's appeal to it, were considerations which Elizabeth could not afford to neglect.

Because he imperilled her dearest hopes to unite the British kingdoms it was the Earl of Huntly, her principal Catholic subject, who first felt the weight of Mary's royal authority. Seated in his castle *Corrichie, 1562* of Strathbogie, with Aberdeen as his port and capital, he boasted something of the independence of the old Earls of Moray, whose territories he possessed, and was little less than king of a wide region in which the old faith was rooted and ineradicable. Before Mary returned to France he had offered her his sword to restore the Roman Church, a proposal she then rejected. Partly to purge herself of suspected collusion with his schemes, partly to allay rising feeling among her Protestant subjects stirred by her leniency towards her co-religionists, partly at the instigation of her half-brother Lord James Stewart, who coveted the territories and title of the Moray earldom, vacant for nearly twenty years, Mary, in the summer of 1562, took the field and at Corrichie, near Aberdeen, made Huntly prisoner. His sudden death saved him from a judicial process: sentence of treason and forfeiture was pronounced in Parliament over his dead body, and Lord James received the Moray earldom.

Mary's difficulties began with Huntly's fall. Her consent to his undoing, her tolerance to the Protestants, had been won in the belief that no *Marriage Proposals* other means could extract from Elizabeth the recognition so eagerly desired. But concessions brought Mary no nearer to the English throne, and disappointment drove her on another course. Where she should bestow her hand had fluttered European Courts since her French boy-husband died. In the summer of 1564 a match with Don Carlos, son of Philip II of Spain, was hinted, to the equal

alarm of Elizabeth, who feared to see Scotland absorbed in
Spain's fierce hatred of her Protestant realm, and Knox,
who thundered against his queen's union with the most
powerful Catholic prince in Europe. Perturbed by the throng
of Catholic suitors round Mary, Elizabeth half-heartedly
suggested her favourite, Robert Earl of Dudley, who professed to be a Protestant. Mary entertained the proposal
only as a means to secure her cousin's recognition. Before
the end of the year it was known that Elizabeth, who dared
not commit herself to a Catholic heir, refused the condition.
Dudley was therefore added to the lengthening procession of
rejected suitors and Darnley comes upon the scene. His
mother, Lady Margaret, was daughter of Margaret Tudor,
sometime Queen of Scotland, by her Douglas husband, and
was the hope of the English Catholics. His father, the fourth
Earl of Lennox, shared his wife's ambitions for their son; for
twenty years the couple had plotted to set him on the two
British thrones to which he could advance a claim. His marriage with Mary undoubtedly would please the English
Catholics, who saw in it the means to preserve the British
Isles from foreign meddlers, assure the union of the realms,
and preserve the old faith.

At Wemyss Castle, in February 1565, Mary and Darnley
Darnley met for the first time. He stood before her, a
youth of twenty, three years her junior, 'the
properest and best proportioned long man that ever I saw,'
she reported him. But Darnley, though personable, was
vicious, dull, cubbish, 'lusty, beardless, and lady-faced.' His
attraction for her was in the prospects marriage offered.
None but he could win her what Moray had offered and
Elizabeth withheld. But her choice snapped her relations
with Moray, while the Kirk, thundering against a Catholic
consort, demanded abolition of the 'blasphemous Mass' and
compulsory attendance of all at Protestant worship. Elizabeth uttered threats and warnings, and, finding remonstrance
useless, encouraged Mary's enemies with advice and money.

In April Moray left her. In May Darnley received the Earldom of Ross, and a Convention of notables approved his marriage with the sovereign. In July Mary denounced the reports of 'evill gevin personis' that she intended to impede their religion and conscience. A fortnight later (July 29, 1565) she married Darnley 'with all the solemnities of the popish time.'

Mary tied herself deliberately to the worst of the Stewarts. At the outset his enemies were few. Besides *The Round-* Moray and Châtellerault they numbered chiefly *about Raid,* the foes of Lennox and the extremer Calvinists. 1565 Darnley's Douglas connexion secured him the Earl of Morton, Lords Lindsay and Ruthven, his relatives, and the Catholic faction among the nobility. Young Huntly and Bothwell, both of whom had a private quarrel with Moray, were restored, the one to his dignities, the other to the Lieutenancy of the Marches. The Catholic Atholl also returned to the sovereign's councils. Moray was impotent against so considerable a body. Towards the end of August he attempted to raise the Protestant flag in the capital, but, coldly received, fell back on the Border. Having passed sentence of outlawry upon him and his associates, Mary pursued with unrelenting vigour, and in the Roundabout or Chaseabout Raid drove them to Carlisle. Châtellerault visited his French estates. Argyll fled to his Highland strengths. Mary's triumph was thorough; the Congregation was at her feet.

Within six months of their wedding the relations of Mary and her husband were intolerable. Darnley was *Rizzio* pressing for the Matrimonial Crown, such as Francis II had worn, which Mary was unwilling to grant. The slight to his offended dignity demanded expiation and provoked a tragedy. Searching for a victim Darnley found David Rizzio, an Italian, once the queen's singing master, now her private secretary and in her confidence. To excuse his assassination a motive more respectable than Darnley could honestly allege was preferable. He therefore stooped to accuse his wife, now nearing her confinement, of familiarity with her Italian secretary. Others abetted Darnley to secure their own ends. The Protestant exiles in England had strong inducement to welcome a *coup d'état*; the Estates, soon to meet, could be expected to pass sentence of forfeiture on them. But Darnley's revolt offered a way of escape. They could guarantee him the Crown Matrimonial, sacrifice the queen to his ends and their own, and exact restoration as their reward. Moreover, Rizzio was held to be the arch promoter of Catholic intrigue and in close communication with Philip II—by whom in fact his name was not known. His death promised to advantage the cause of religion.

Parliament was summoned for March 12, 1566. Moray rode northward to Berwick on March 9, ready at a sign to enter Edinburgh. The same evening, about seven o'clock, the conspirators burst into the queen's apartments at Holyrood, the Earl of Morton and others from the main gallery, Darnley and Ruthven by the privy stair from the king's room beneath. Mary was at supper, Rizzio and a small household in attendance. Ruthven summoned the Italian forth to speak with him, and struck at his victim cowering behind Mary's back. There was much confusion, the supper table was overthrown, violent hands were outstretched, and Rizzio, stabbed at over the queen's shoulder, was dragged resisting to the outer chamber. There he was dispatched and left, with Darnley's dagger sticking in his mangled body.

From Darnley Mary wormed the details of his plot, dominated his weak purpose, and bent him to her own. Moray, presenting himself after the crime, was graciously received. Under cover of night Mary rode to Dunbar, with Darnley at her side, pausing at Rizzio's fresh turned grave to threaten that 'a fatter man than he should lie as low ere the year was out.' In bitter wrath against Darnley, she drew round her those he had betrayed. Joseph Rizzio succeeded David as her secretary, nursing vengeance for his brother's death.

Scowling faces met Darnley on every hand. To Mary, in her
own words, it was 'a heart break' to have him as her husband. Her son James' birth in June invited reconciliation,
but though she had forgiven, she told him she could never
forget. In September Darnley nervously planned to 'go beyond sea.' He was dissuaded and encountered on all hands
'dishonourable disdain.'

Meanwhile in Mary other passions worked. Since her marriage the Earl of Bothwell had been always in   *Bothwell*
her company and now possessed her heart.
Some six years older than herself, she met him first in France
in early widowhood, when his unfailing loyalty to her mother,
Protestant though he was, commended him to her as one on
whom she might rely. Their common love of France also
made strong appeal to her regard. He was cultured, beyond
the standard of his unlettered class, handsome, loyal and
reckless, a man of the world to whom a young queen might
lose her heart. She came to love him passionately. To
his feelings for her nothing gives a clue beyond his one
criminal service.

Events hurried to the approaching tragedy. Towards the
end of November the Court was at Craigmillar
Castle, near Edinburgh. Maitland of Lethington   *The Craig-*
proposed divorce from Darnley, and Moray,   *millar Band*
Bothwell, Huntly, and Argyll approved. The inevitable
'band' was prepared and signed. A month later Morton,
Ruthven, and other participants in Rizzio's death received
their pardons and returned. Bothwell, it must be supposed,
was already resolved upon his plan to win his mistress.
Realising his insecurity, Darnley retreated to Glasgow, where
he joined his father. There he fell ill, apparently of small-
pox. Visiting the sick man, Mary found him recovered,
and suggested Craigmillar for his convalescence, Holyrood
being denied him for fear of infecting his son.   *Kirk o' Field*
Disliking Craigmillar, the queen's country seat,
Kirk o' Field was named, a small building close to the

city wall of Edinburgh, in the most desolate part of the town. On the last day of January 1567 the dismal mansion received its victim. For the next ten days the queen assiduously nursed her invalid. Gunpowder was stored, and the night of February 9, when festivities at the Palace were arranged, was chosen for the crime. About two o'clock in the morning the house was shattered by an explosion. Darnley's body and that of his servant were found in the garden, untouched by gunpowder; strangled, it is alleged.

Public opinion fastened upon Bothwell as author of the *The Bothwell* crime. Though Lennox demanded judgment, *Marriage,* Mary refused to prosecute, and permitted Both-*1567* well to overawe the Court. Parliament, which had not met since her marriage, assembled and did him honour. On the evening of its rising a number of lords entered into a 'band' to maintain his innocence and procure his marriage with the queen. Five days later, intercepting her as she rode from visiting her son at Stirling, he carried her to Dunbar, while he procured divorce from his wife. It was granted on May 3. On May 12 Mary created Bothwell Duke of Orkney and Zetland, and three days later married him, 'not with the Mass, but with preaching.' She had the husband of her choice and wrecked her career.

In Scotland Mary's marriage to the man universally held *Mary abdi-* her husband's assassin produced a revulsion of *cates, 1567* feeling. Only the Hamiltons, out of hatred of Lennox, and the other Stewarts stood by her. At Carberry Hill (June 15), under a banner showing Darnley's infant son praying for vengeance beside his father, dead beneath a tree, the insurgent lords confronted her. Bothwell rode from the field and out of her life while she was brought to Edinburgh, where 'the common people' assailed her with vile names. Thence she was removed to Lochleven, and for nearly eleven months remained a prisoner. Meanwhile opinion hardened against her. One of Bothwell's men was captured in possession of a silver casket containing her

letters to the earl, which, it was told, proved her clear complicity in Darnley's death and justified her deposition. Knox
denounced her from the pulpit. She was openly called a
murderess. Feeling ran violently against her and on July 24,
1567, she was forced to sign her abdication. Five days later
James VI was crowned. Moray, fresh returned from France,
was named Regent. His sister's cause was lost. The Pope
refused to have relations with her. Only from Elizabeth,
moved by womanly concern, came a word of sympathy.
Mary turned hopefully to the unlooked-for gleam. In May
1568 she broke prison at Lochleven. Hamiltons and others
rallied to her, and at Langside, now Glasgow, in considerable
force she faced her brother (May 13). Routed after a short
encounter she rode for the Border, crossed the Solway, and
looked on Scotland for the last time.

The twenty years (1568–87) of Mary's exile in England
coincided with the active period of the Counter-
Reformation. The Inquisition and Society of **James VI, 1567-1625**
Jesus were its instruments, the Guises and
Philip II its captains, Mary Stewart its most precious
asset. She claimed her 'bastard' cousin's English
crown and had the devotion of no mean part of *The Counter-Reformation*
her subjects. Once eradicated from Britain,
heresy would perish utterly elsewhere. As in 1559, mutual
danger drew the British governments to close accord, till
Mary's death in 1587 and the Armada's humiliating failure
in 1588 conserved their independence, assured their common
faith, and established Protestantism irrevocably in the countries in which it had taken root.

Mary's arrival in England presented a dilemma to Elizabeth. If she offered hospitality Mary might
seduce the English Catholics and with their *The Casket Letters*
support rally Scotland. If she passed to France
she had equal opportunity to marshal forces there favouring
her candidature for the British crowns. Restored to Scotland
she would destroy those whom Elizabeth held her friends.

Mary was therefore allowed to understand that before she could be received by her cousin she must clear herself of the aspersions on her character. Moray, too, was required to justify his treatment of his sovereign. Both were invited to stand an inquisition in England upon the circumstances of Darnley's death. Neither dared reject the invitation, and at York, in October 1568, Commissioners representing all parties assembled. Moray was unwilling to advance an open charge of murder until he had an assurance that Mary, if proved guilty, would be delivered to her former subjects' custody, or be detained in England out of mischief. To impress the English Commissioners with the evidence in his possession, the Casket Letters were unofficially exhibited. Their effect being as he desired, Moray proceeded to prefer a charge of murder against his sister. Mary answered passionately, alleging the accusation calumnious, and importuned her cousin to accord her a personal interview. It was denied; for the proceedings at York, transferred to Hampton Court, had fulfilled Elizabeth's purpose. Her cousin's reputation was irreparably smirched and her credit as an agent of the Catholic enemies of England's State and Church seemingly undermined. In January 1569 Elizabeth conveniently exonerated both sides from their conflicting charges, but showed her evident intention not to restore her cousin to the throne in which her infant son now sat. Till her death, eighteen years later, Mary remained a prisoner on English soil.

Scotland meanwhile was plunged into disorder. Before James reached man's estate four Regents in succession held authority and three came to violent ends. Returning from England early in 1569 Moray found the North, where Huntly's power lay, and the West, dominated by Argyll and the Hamiltons, on whom Mary chiefly relied, in open revolt. In February Châtellerault arrived with Mary's commission as her Lieutenant and the rival parties prepared a test of arms. In March,

Moray Regent

Moray gathered his levies at Glasgow in the Hamilton country. Outnumbered, the duke made submission and Huntly and Argyll followed his example. But elsewhere Mary's spells worked with effect. Her arrival in England stimulated the Catholics there. Philip II's diplomacy was active; Mary promised restoration of the Mass within three months if Spanish help was forthcoming. The Earls of Northumberland and Westmorland were eager to strike, and the Catholic Duke of Norfolk, opportunely a widower, was ready to make Mary his wife. In November the northern Earls broke into rebellion, heard Mass in Durham Cathedral, burned the English Bible and Book of Common Prayer, and advanced towards Tutbury Castle, where Mary was confined. Had she fallen to their power, or Scotland been obedient to her partisans, the issue might have been other than it was. Informed in time, Mary's guards removed her, while Moray guarded the Borders. Taken between two fires the rebellion collapsed. It was Moray's last service against the 'abominable Mass.' In January 1570, he was assassinated by James Hamilton of Bothwellhaugh, nephew of the Archbishop. Like other personalities in this contentious period Moray's character is disputed. His opportune disappearances at moments of crisis, avarice, and meanness, cannot obscure his statesmanlike qualities, directed upon two absorbing purposes, the triumph of the Protestant faith, and union of the British kingdoms.

Moray's death was a sore blow to Elizabeth and to the young king's party, which as yet had little support outside the Protestant ministers and the *Lennox Regent* commonalty. In February, too, Pius V at length issued his Bull depriving Elizabeth of her 'pretended' right to the English crown, a decree which made it impossible henceforth to reconcile favour of Mary's succession with loyalty to Elizabeth's person. Scotland had become in effect an outpost in the international war of religion. By the middle of May 1570 English troops were in Edinburgh. Lennox and the king's party, thus strengthened, drove Châtellerault from Glasgow, sacked the Hamilton country, and burned Hamilton Palace. The Marians were dispersed and impotent. In July Lennox was named Regent, an appointment which threatened the instigators of his son's assassination.

With hopes dashed by events in Scotland, Mary resumed her interrupted intrigues with Norfolk, lately released from the Tower, and committed her plans to Roberto Ridolfi, a Florentine banker acting in London as the Pope's agent. His master and Philip were soon involved in a plot which contemplated England's invasion, Elizabeth's assassination, Mary's union with Norfolk, and her accession to the English throne. In March 1571 Ridolfi left London to make preparations, whose details were soon revealed to the English ministers. Meanwhile in Scotland civil strife continued. In April 1571 an act of splendid daring deprived the Marians of Dumbarton, their port of entry out of France, and yielded prisoner Archbishop Hamilton, who was hanged forthwith as accessory to Darnley's and Moray's murders. Edinburgh Castle remained the only stronghold of the queen's party. Châtellerault threw himself within its walls and Lennox vainly attempted its reduction. Towards the end of August he summoned to Stirling a Parliament over which the six-year old king presided and to which he uttered an unrehearsed oracular remark. Pointing to a flaw in the roof he said, 'There is a hole in this Parliament.' A few days later Huntly led a sortie from Edinburgh, surprised the king's nobles at Stirling, and was not driven from the town before Lennox, the 'sillie Regent,' was pistolled and dead, consummating a career of treachery and ambition.

The Ridolfi Plot, 1571

Lennox's office as Regent was assumed by the Earl of Mar, who had held Edinburgh Castle against the Congregation in 1554. His brief Regency is chiefly memorable for a scheme, promoted by Morton, calculated to relieve the king's party's straits for money, for

Mar, Regent

lack of which troops scarcely could be paid. The settlement of 1560 left to the surviving ecclesiastics of the Roman Church the larger part of its wealth. Morton's avarice and the necessities of the Exchequer recommended a plan which proposed to restore the titles Archbishop, Bishop, Abbot, Prior, abolished by the First Book of Discipline; approximate the functions of Bishop and Superintendent, the prelate being subject to the Assembly and associated with a clerical Chapter in each diocesan centre, whose advice he should accept for the admission of ministers and generally in his spiritual functions; and divert to secular uses the endowments of the rehabilitated Sees. Thus, a witty preacher distinguished three sorts of bishops: 'My lord bishop was in the Papistry. My lord's bishop is now when my lord gets the benefice and the bishop serves for nothing. The Lord's bishop is the true minister of the Gospel.' *Tulchan Bishops* To 'my lord's bishop' the name 'Tulchan' was found appropriate, the tulchan being a mock or changeling calf exhibited to cows recently calved to induce a flow of milk. The institution initiated a passionate controversy.

While Morton's proposals were being debated, Mary's fortunes developed to another crisis. In January 1572 Norfolk was brought to trial for complicity in Ridolfi's plot, whose intricacies had been unravelled. Mary's guilt was extracted from her agent, the Bishop of Ross. Her execution was clamoured for by both Houses of Parliament, and her exclusion from the succession was demanded. In September communications were opened with Mar for her surrender, trial, and execution in Scotland. They were not concluded in October when Mar died, and were abandoned when Morton's firm hand at length made the Kirk secure. Edinburgh Castle, in May 1573, surrendered to an English force. Huntly and the Hamiltons already had accepted a pacification and recognized the king's authority. Mary's cause was irrevocably lost and Protestantism in Scotland as firmly assured.

Morton, third of the four Regents, ruled with vigour and
ability and gave the country peace. To do justice
*Morton
Regent*
to all men and heap up great treasure, a contemporary said, was the double purpose of his
rule. He tamed the Borders; the Raid of Reidswire in 1575 was
the last notable encounter between the two nations on their
common frontier. The Kirk felt his firm, rapacious, hand in
a re-allocation of the one-third of the ancient Church's revenues assigned to the Crown and the ministers. The latter
had benefited little from the fund. Morton, pretending a
remedy, constituted himself collector of the 'thirds' and
their distributor among a ministry whose numbers he arbitrarily restricted in order to reduce his contribution to their
maintenance after satisfying his own rapacity. The sham
Episcopacy established in 1572 was notorious; his bastard
children were in large measure supported by pensions charged
against episcopal revenues. The commons groaned under his
exactions, the nobles under his iron rule. Early in 1578 their
intrigues came to a head. The young king was in hands
hostile to Morton, whose intention to abduct his sovereign,
in the Douglas manner, was suspected. In March 1578 his
Regency was proclaimed at an end.

Morton's overthrow filled Elizabeth with concern and facili-
Esmé Stewart
tated a new move in the Counter-Reformation's
patient effort to subject Scotland to its purposes. In March 1578, within a few days of Morton's fall,
James lost his grandmother, Lady Lennox, who died in
England. To continue the title and acquire its English properties James called out of France in September 1579 his
father's first cousin Esmé Stewart, Sieur d'Aubigny, James'
senior in years, whose influence proved wholesome neither
to his precocious character nor to his policy. He was a
courtier, a Catholic, accomplished, a man of the world, 'of
comlie proportioun, civile behaviour, red-beardit.' Six months
after his arrival, the favourite received the Earldom of
Lennox, a title subsequently (1581) advanced to a dukedom.

In him, and Arran after him, the Catholic Powers had their agent within James' secret counsels.

Ever since Mary's flight to England in 1568 Elizabeth had kept close touch with Scotland. It was now broken, and at a critical moment. Morton, who alone could restore it, succumbed to Lennox's enmity. With cunning craft the favourite attended sermons, professed himself an earnest Protestant, and boasted his call to 'a knowledge of salvation.' He was named High Chamberlain and received command of a bodyguard of nobles which gave him custody of the king. In December 1580, on a charge of implication in Darnley's murder, Morton was arrested at the instance of James Stewart of Bothwellmuir, a soldier of fortune in the king's bodyguard, whom James rewarded with the Earldom of Arran. In June 1581 a jury of his peers pronounced Morton guilty 'art and part of concealing the king's father's murder.' He was guillotined by 'the Maiden,' last of Darnley's murderers, a true type of his unruly house, whose attachment to the Kirk and the English alliance gives him a place among the statesmen of his generation.

Upon Morton's death, Lennox revealed himself the envoy of the Counter-Reformation. In February 1582 a Papal mission elicited from him a pledge to procure James' conversion, rouse the English *The Ruthven Raid*, 1582 Catholics, and restore England to Rome. Guise was ready to invade England, Spaniards to land in Scotland: Elizabeth's assassination was a detail in the design. But the Kirk's ministers suspected Lennox's purposes. Elizabeth put herself in touch with the remnants of Morton's English party. Money was distributed, a 'band' was formed for Lennox's ejection, and a plot was contrived to snatch the king from his keeping and extricate him from Guise and the Jesuits. On a day in August 1582, as James rode out of Perth, the Earl of Gowrie, with others of the English party, surrounded him, conducted him to Gowrie's Ruthven Castle, and thence to Stirling for security. James cried for anger, but was com-

pelled to issue proclamations admitting his favourite's dealings with Spanish and Papal agents. Lennox transferred
himself to Edinburgh Castle, whence he viewed public signs
of satisfaction at his fall, and stealing away to Dumbarton
sailed thence to France. James meanwhile found restraint
intolerable. In June 1583, with a single attendant, he rode
to St Andrews. Huntly and the Gordons drew a cordon round
him. Montrose and other Catholics flocked to him. The
Ruthven raiders held an empty cage.

Of James, now entering his eighteenth year, an observing
Frenchman flashes a brilliant portrait: 'The

James VI   king is for his age one of the most remarkable
princes that ever lived. I venture to say that in languages,
sciences, and affairs of state, he has more learning than any
man in Scotland. In short, he is wonderfully clever, and has
an excellent opinion of himself. He dislikes dances, and
music, and amorous talk, and curiosity of dress, and courtly
trivialities. He has an especial detestation for ear-rings.
From want of instruction, his manners are rough and un-
couth. He speaks, eats, dresses, and plays like a boor, and
he is no better in the company of women. He is never still
for a moment, but walks perpetually up and down the room,
and his gait is sprawling and awkward. His voice is loud, and
his words sententious. He prefers hunting to all other amuse-
ments, and will be six hours together on horseback, galloping
over hill and dale. His body is feeble, yet he is not delicate.
In a word, he is an old young man. He is prodigiously con-
ceited. He irritates his subjects by indiscreet and violent
attachments. He is idle and careless, too easy, and too much
given to pleasure, particularly to the chase, leaving his
affairs to be managed by Arran and his secretary.' At bottom
James throughout his life remained opinionated, self-con-
fident, meddlesome, endowed with native shrewdness which
the circumstances of his upbringing intensified.

By conviction James was a Protestant. His interests,
moreover, clashed with Rome's, and at no time was he

seriously disposed to change his creed. His one clear purpose was to secure his succession to the English crown, which, it was said with little exaggeration, he was ready to take from the devil himself. He resented the hectoring tones of the Kirk, envied Elizabeth's easy control over an episcopal system, was resolved to give the Scottish crown an equal advantage and, pursuing a middle course, to rule as 'universal king,' in hope one day to unite the British realms.

The Kirk, which James now resolved to subject to his purposes, had developed menacing power. Mary's dramatic fall procured for the Acts of 1560 Parliamentary approval (1567) till then withheld, and in the *The Kirk* General Assembly of 1575 Andrew Melville, returned from Geneva to become the head of Glasgow University, raised a controversy which divided Scotland for generations—Had the bishop's office the authority of Scripture? He held it unlawful, and in 1580 the Kirk confirmed his opinion. Next year, the Assembly at Glasgow formally instituted the Courts known as Presbyteries, after which Scottish Protestantism has its name. Thus, in 1584, the Kirk's organization, from Kirk Session upwards through Presbyteries, Provincial Synods, to the General Assembly, focussed power which no other institution excelled. Its Assembly was representative, included the most prominent laity as well as the clergy, exercised the jurisdiction of the old Church Courts over questions touching moral conduct, and assumed their dread powers of excommunication.

The Kirk's claim to withdraw itself from the authority of the State, and from behind its own inviolable barrier to scold, threaten, and defy the civil *The Black Acts, 1584* magistrate, was intolerable. In May 1584 Parliament passed a series of measures, styled the 'Black Acts,' which asserted the royal power and authority 'over all states as well spiritual as temporal within this realm,' withdrew the legislative and judicial functions which the Kirk's courts arrogated, and forbade the convoking of ecclesiastical Assemblies without royal licence. The Acts riveted the Crown's headship upon the Kirk, maintained its patronage of the Episcopal bench, and closed the pulpit as a platform for 'treasonable, seditious, and contumelious speeches' on public affairs. Nor were the new measures merely declaratory of royal policy. In December 1584 James gave orders for every beneficed minister between Berwick and Stirling forthwith to accept them and obey episcopal authority. Deprivation was the penalty of refusal. The stubborn conflict between Kirk and State was fairly joined.

Master of the Kirk, James' inclination was to offer Elizabeth Scotland's alliance against his mother's friends abroad, in hope to receive her recognition of himself as her successor. His overtures divided Elizabeth's Council. But the assassination of William of Orange, in July 1584, pointed the value of Scotland's friendship. In August 1584 Elizabeth professed her willingness to discuss the relations of the two countries and agreed to receive as James' ambassador the Master of Gray, an accomplished, treacherous, handsome youth, a Catholic in the confidence of Mary and the Guises, in whose service he had come to Scotland. He spent the winter in England as James' ambassador, and fulfilled a discreditable part. His ostensible mission was to secure a defensive alliance between the two Courts. But his private intention was to advance his own fortunes. He coveted Arran's influence with James and aspired to fill his place. By betraying Mary Stewart he won Elizabeth's favour. In January 1585 he returned to Scotland and reported his success. Mary Stewart was removed to the dismal isolation of Tutbury, a position where she could no longer conspire.

The European situation rapidly moved to serve James' purpose. In January 1585 the Guises united their Holy League with Philip of Spain to exclude the Protestant Henry of Navarre from the throne of France. Every Protestant crown was menaced, and in April Elizabeth invited a counter-association with James. In July an offensive and defensive union against the common Catholic enemy was ratified by the Estates and James promised to be guided by Elizabeth in his marriage. His title to the English succession was tacitly recognized; his mother was not mentioned. Arran's ruin followed consequently and swiftly; he was in correspondence with and trusted by the Guises. Elizabeth demanded his surrender by James, who 'shed tears like a child newly beaten' at the demand, put him under guard, but soon released him: in November he fled. James was again in the hands of the Protestant lords, and a Catholic faction which had distracted Scotland since Morton's death at length was dissipated.

The treaty with England, confirmed at Berwick in July 1586, and the disappearance of Arran, set James firmly upon his new course. With Mary he had conclusively broken. In her bitterness she wrote *Death of Mary Stewart, 1587* to Elizabeth (May 1585) threatening to disown, curse, and disinherit her son. A year later she fulfilled her threat and made over to Philip of Spain all her rights and claims. In the spring of 1586 her English adherents, eager to advance Philip's halting enterprise, desperately evolved a plot for the assassination of Elizabeth and her ministers. Anthony Babington and five other assassins undertook to rescue Mary after their bloody deed was accomplished. Mary incautiously communicated with Babington in terms which revealed foreknowledge of what he proposed to do. Spies intercepted and copied her correspondence, by which means Elizabeth was reluctantly convinced that her rival's death alone could relieve the realm and its religion of an implacable enemy. In October 1586 Mary was indicted under the Act for the surety of the Queen's person passed in the preceding autumn. In February 1587, at Fotheringay, she met death with the undaunted courage which supported her throughout her life.

Mary's execution stirred Scotland with concern for one

who was but a memory to a generation grown to manhood since her flight. But there was little disposition to translate emotion into action, which, unless France and Spain supported it, had no likelihood of success. Neither James nor his people were inclined to sacrifice the advantages of the recent treaty with England. And though a dramatic moment occurred in Parliament in July 1587, when the lords present fell on their knees and placed lands, lives, and goods at the sovereign's disposal 'touching a revenge for the death of the queen,' public indignation was neither deep nor durable.

Only in Philip II did sympathy display itself in action. He was Mary's heir and proposed at once to avenge her, establish the triumph of his faith, and win the crown she had never worn. For years he had been preparing the great Armada which, in May 1588, set out upon its heavy course. But of Philip's galleons Scotland saw none but battered wrecks: *Flavit Deus et dissipati sunt* England inscribed on her medals of victory. With the Armada's shattering the cause for which Mary schemed and died sank also to its doom. Protestant Elizabeth sat securely on a throne whose foundations the Counter-Reformation had failed to move, and within twenty years the son whom Mary disinherited held the sovereignty of the kingdoms her Church failed to recover.

The Armada, 1588

CHAPTER X

KING AND KIRK

W HEN Philip launched the Armada at these islands,
the Kirk, though powerful and established, was not
yet supreme. One-third of the nobility still professed the
faith of their fathers. On the Borders the Roman Church
retained Dumfries and Wigtown, shires in which, a century
later, the stern creed of the Covenanter found its sternest
disciples. Caithness and Sutherland, at the northern extreme,
also remained strongholds of the Catholic cause. From Aberdeen and Moray westward through Elgin, Inverness, to Skye
and the Hebrides, Protestantism was little regarded. Of the
north-eastern provinces Huntly was almost sovereign. But
everywhere the Mass was proscribed and the belief and ritual
of centuries rested under the anathema of a recent creed.
Without assistance Huntly could not overawe the State or
establish the liberty of his Church. But he looked on the
North Sea and offered a door of entry to the Catholic Powers.
Their activities, the revolt of the Catholic population against
Presbyterian tyranny, the Kirk's suspicion of James' collusion, and its own fiery warfare with the Crown, fill the years
which intervened between the Armada and James' departure
to his English kingdom.

James was not blind to the activities of Catholic emissaries
and was in friendly correspondence with the sovereign on
whom they leaned. It was to his interest to present a sympathetic demeanour; for it promised to relieve him of Spain's
hostility. On the other hand, being the sport of feudal turbulence, lacking an adequate guard to protect his person,
bearded in his very palace by brawling nobles, he could
not afford to make an enemy of the Kirk, whose extravagant pretensions on occasion might usefully serve his ends.

Between two extremes he preserved a middle course, seeing his goal clear ahead and destruction the consequence of deviation to either side.

As the massacre of St Bartholomew, so the attempted invasion of 1588 played into the hands of the Protestant stalwarts, who raised petitions in the Parliament of 1592 urging the annulling of the Black Acts of 1584, transference of the ancient Church's patrimony to its successor, and exclusion from Parliament of prelates not exercising power or commission from the Courts of the Kirk. James was unwilling to recall the Acts of 1584 or to approve the Presbyterian polity which the Second Book of Discipline set up, having little reason to misjudge the manner in which the Kirk would use its liberty. But Huntly's murder of the 'bonnie' Earl of Moray, holder of a title dear in the recollection of the Kirk, increased the clamour against the sovereign and prompted concessions. Hence, James gave assent to a statute which has been styled the 'Golden Act' and 'Magna Carta of the Church of Scotland.' It superseded the Act of 1584 authorizing an episcopal hierarchy and legalized the General Assembly and subordinate Courts, but with a condition, designed to protect the royal authority, upon which the Kirk in the following century waged eager warfare: the Act stipulated the presence of the king or his Commissioner in the Assembly, and prescribed that, before dissolving, the time and place of its next meeting should be named by royal authority. The laws against the Mass, harbouring of Jesuits, seminary priests and papists were at the same time confirmed, an act of war upon the religion they threatened which prompted its last and futile revolt against the Kirk.

The Golden Act, 1592

The last days of 1592 disclosed a plot in which the Catholic Earls of Huntly, Errol, and Angus were involved. A report to Philip exposed their motives: 'The people generally outside the cities are inclined to the Catholic faith, and hate the ministers, who dis-

The Spanish Blanks, 1592

turb the country with their excommunications. The nobles and people are sick of this tyranny, and are yearning for a remedy. They are looking to his Majesty [Philip] for his support for the restoration of the Catholic faith.' As invariably, the English secret service winded the plot and a hint to Andrew Knox, minister of Paisley, put him on the road to detect it. Boarding a ship in the Clyde he arrested George Ker, a Border Catholic of position, and found inside the sleeves of a sailor's shirt incriminating documents, including eight blank sheets bearing the signatures of the earls and Sir Patrick Gordon of Auchindoune. The Blanks, eight in number, had neither designation, address, nor writing thereon other than the concluding courtesy customary in letters addressed to royalty—*de vostre majestie tres humble et tres obeisant serviteur*—followed by a signature. Two were signed by Angus and Errol jointly, two by Huntly, one by Angus, one by Errol, and two (in Latin) by the three earls and Auchindoune. Torture elicited an explanation from Ker. The arch-contriver of the plot was Father William Crichton, an active Jesuit, implicated in Orange's assassination in 1584, and lately domiciled in Spain. He had persuaded Philip to attempt another invasion, relying on the Scottish Catholics instead of those of England, who were represented as having failed him in 1588. It was proposed to land a Spanish army 30,000 strong in Scotland and, after restoring the old faith, advance into England to exact vengeance for Mary Stewart's execution. James' assumed regard for his mother's memory was relied on to win his co-operation. To encourage or confirm Philip's resolution Crichton demanded a number of Blanks, bearing the signatures of prominent Scottish Catholics, to be filled in by himself when his negotiations with Philip were complete. Two of the Blanks were intended for use as proclamations and bore the seals of all four conspirators.

The discovery of the Blanks placed James under suspicion, and his obstinate leniency towards the earls increased it. They were cited to appear before the Estates in July 1593, but James declared the evidence of their guilt inadequate. Preachers prayed God to send 'sanctified plagues' to correct his obduracy. The Fife Synod summarily excommunicated the offenders and invited the Kirk to devise measures for the defence of religion. Alarmed by these evidences of public concern, the earls, presenting themselves before James, consented to stand a trial and meanwhile to be confined at Perth, an arrangement which fanned the Kirk's apprehensions; for the accused would have the backing of their retainers at Perth and already were summoning them to force toleration for their religion. Hence, in November 1593, ministers and others convened at Edinburgh required James to postpone the trial until they were in a position to prosecute the 'treasonable apostates.' Otherwise they proposed to 'pursue' the defendants 'to the uttermost.' The threat portended civil war and James intervened. The earls were called on to 'satisfy the Kirk' and conform by February 1, 1594, submit to Presbyterian instruction, and prepare for subscription to the Confession of Faith by the appointed date, or alternatively leave the country. Their choice was to be declared by the first day of the approaching New Year. None of the accused made submission by the appointed date. They were ordered to confine themselves in separate castles. Not one gave obedience.

James assured the Estates that he had 'used plaister and medicine hitherto in dealing with the rebellious lords, but, that not availing, he was now to use fire, as the last remedy.' The earls put it out of his power to refrain. In July 1594 Father James Gordon, their envoy to Rome, arrived at Aberdeen accompanied by a Papal Nuncio bearing an exhortation to James to embrace the Roman faith, and money for the Catholic insurgents. Upon the ship's arrival the magistrates seized the Nuncio, money, and letters, nor surrendered them until the earls, assembling in force, threatened to fire the city. The challenge could not pass disregarded.

The shire levies were summoned, and the youthful Argyll, acting under a commission of Lieutenancy, led the Campbells and Forbeses northward upon an inglorious campaign terminated by Huntly's defeat of them at Glenrinnes, or Glenlivet, in October 1594. James himself advanced to Aberdeen, destroyed Strathbogie and Slains, the seats of Huntly and Errol, but made an agreement with them which permitted them to depart the realm, leaving their wives to administer their estates, with secret encouragement to return when Presbyterian rancour had cooled. In the spring of 1595 Huntly and Errol went abroad till the following year, when the prospect of their return engaged Kirk and Crown in a critical struggle.

The fiction of Spain's invincibility survived its exposure by the Armada. Neither Elizabeth, nor James, nor the timid Kirk realized that her sun had set. In the summer of 1595, petty raids on the Cornish coast excited fears of a new Armada, and in the autumn came news of Philip's intention to launch a greater force even than the ill-fated fleet of 1588. Upon a situation of tense apprehension, therefore, the memorable year 1596 opened in Scotland. Rumours of Spanish armaments, of the machinations of Errol and Huntly, of James' alleged communications with Rome and Madrid, excited popular fears and moved the Kirk to action.

The General Assembly met at Edinburgh in March 1596, a memorable body, the last, it was recalled, of the Assemblies of the Kirk enjoying 'liberty of the Gospel under the free government of Christ,' *The Octavians* that is, free from the over-riding authority of the civil power. It was not impressed by James' measures to thwart the Spanish menace. He was held to have connived at the earls' escape from the death their enemies demanded. Even their forfeitures were nullified by permission to their wives to nurse their estates. That he awaited opportunity to recall them was suspected; meanwhile they were imagined deep in Philip's counsels. Another suspicious circumstance was remarked. Chancellor Thirlestane, whom the Kirk associated with its Golden Act, died at the close of 1595. James did not replace him, preferring to appoint eight Commissioners, whom the country named the 'Octavians,' 'hollow Papists' whom the preachers viewed askance as portending a 'great alteration in the Kirk.' Their most prominent member, Sir Alexander Seton, later Earl of Dunfermline, the son of Mary Stewart's devoted servant, and educated at Rome, was particularly obnoxious.

These reflexions induced an angry mood in the Assembly *James and* of 1596. But towards the practical purpose *the English* which summoned it it contributed no more than *Succession* a demand that the recusancy laws should be executed rigorously and the estates of Huntly and Errol be sold to equip levies to confront the Spaniard. James paid little heed to these counsels. He was pursuing his own tortuous paths, influenced by a controversy in England which menaced his peaceful succession to her throne. The Jesuit Robert Parsons *alias* Doleman had published in 1594 a treatise in which he passed in review the several candidates. Against James he objected that Henry VIII's will preferred the House of Suffolk to the descendants of Margaret Tudor, and concluded that his mother's conspiracies forfeited James' claim. The controversy seriously alarmed James, inspired his apparent zeal against the Spaniard in hope to capture Elizabeth's favour, nerved him to his imminent challenge of the loud-voiced Kirk, with a view to closer approximation of the Protestant Churches of the island, and stiffened his resolution to deal leniently with his Catholic exiles.

Anxious not to alienate the English Catholics by severity, *Andrew* James summoned the Estates in September *Melville* 1596 to consider Huntly's petition for the quashing of his banishment. Andrew Melville presented himself unsummoned and 'with plaine speeche and mightie force of zeale' protested against the return of men who

'sought to betray their citie and native countrie to the cruell
Spaniard, with the overthrow of Christ's kingdom.' His protest was unregarded: the recall of the earls was immediately
approved, and in high dudgeon Melville confronted the
king. Shaking him by the sleeve he called James 'God's
sillie vassall' and, amid hot interruptions, laid down the
Kirk's doctrine of the relations of Church and State: 'Sir,
as diverse tymes before, so now again I must tell you, there
are two kings and two kingdomes in Scotland: there is Christ
Jesus, and his kingdome the Kirk, whose subject King James
the Sixt is, and of whose kingdome not a king, nor a head,
nor a lord, but a member. And they whom Christ has called,
and commanded to watche over his Kirk, and governe his
spirituall kingdome, have sufficient power of him, and autho-
ritie so to doe, both together and severallie, the which no
Christian king nor prince sould controll and discharge, but
fortifie and assist, otherwise, not faithful subjects, nor
members of Christ.'

Determined that Huntly and his fellows should 'conform'
before they were restored to estates and liberty, the ministers
gathered for a conclusive conflict with the Crown. A 'Council
of the Kirk' sat daily in Edinburgh with the Presbytery of
the capital. Late in October 1596, David Black, minister at
St Andrews, vented from the pulpit 'spite' against James,
'a devil's bairn,' and spoke of Elizabeth as 'an atheist, a
woman of no religion.' The English ambassador complained
to James, who summoned Black before the Council. Black
denied the competence of a civil tribunal to call his pulpit
utterances in question. His contumacy sounded a challenge
which James could not evade. He dissolved the Kirk's
Council and banished Black 'benorth the North Water,' on
pain of outlawry if he disobeyed. The Edinburgh Presbytery
took up his banner. Excitement rose to frenzy and burst on
December 17, when a mob surged round the Tolbooth, where
James was employed with the Lords of Session, demanding
surrender of the Octavians as 'inbringers of the Popish lords.'

The hubbub died down but accomplished an unexpected result—James removed the Court and Lords of Session to Linlithgow. Within a twelvemonth he had curbed Presbyterian indiscipline and vindicated the authority of the State. As one sadly wrote, December 17, 1596, was an 'accursed wrathful day to the Kirk' and its extravagant pretensions.

The year 1597 proved 'God's sillie vassal' master of the *The Perth* Kirk. In February he convened a General As-
Assembly, sembly at Perth, a centre in touch with a district
1597 well-disposed towards Episcopacy. In unusual numbers northern ministers attended his invitation 'to have the Policy of the Church so cleared, as a pleasant Harmony might be settled betwixt him and the Ministry,' and approved his intention to restrict the Kirk to its spiritual sphere. He was empowered to modify 'the external government' of the Church; the convention of General Assemblies without his authority was forbidden; the license of the pulpit was restricted. On his side James approved the terms proposed by the Assembly for 'reconciling' the Catholic lords to acknowledge the Kirk to be a 'true' Church and become members of it. He warned the earls that his interests required their submission. In June Huntly and Errol were received into the Kirk at Aberdeen. Angus made submission elsewhere. In November their forfeitures were revoked. Their apostasy was a sore blow to the Church they foreswore, and contributed to the permanent weakening of the ancient faith in one of its most stubborn strongholds.

Meanwhile James adventured a covert reintroduction of *The First* Episcopacy. In December 1597, an Act was
Estate re- passed by the Estates providing that ministers
stored to whom the king appointed to the dignity of
Parliament bishop, abbot, or other prelacy should vote in Parliament as freely as at any past time. A General Assembly at Dundee in March 1598 confirmed the Act, by a narrow majority, and settled the number of ministers to sit in Parliament at fifty-one 'or thereby,' a representation which

promised them a generous proportion of its membership.
The title Bishop was eschewed: that of 'Commissioner of
such or such a place' was recommended.

Until the call to England came in 1603 James was truly
master of his house. He had conciliated the *Death of*
Catholics by leniency, dragooned the Kirk into *Elizabeth,*
obedience, and set up an episcopate which pro- *1603*
mised to assimilate the British Churches when the day of
union arrived. To that prospect his every thought was
directed. Elizabeth was ageing. Her intentions seemed friendly.
But Henry VIII's will was unrepealed and under it Lord
Beauchamp, father of Arabella Stewart's future husband,
was heir. Early in 1603 it was known that Elizabeth's end
approached. On March 23 her councillors gathered round
her death-bed to learn her wishes for the succession. They
named the King of France; she made no sign. They named
the King of Scots; she did not stir. Only when they named
Lord Beauchamp she broke out with her old spirit: 'I will
have no rascal's son to sit in my seat, but one worthy to
be a king.' Already the Council had prepared for James'
proclamation when, in the early hours of March 25, the
queen expired. In less than three days, riding hard, Sir
Robert Carey brought the news to Holyrood. Two days
later official intimation of James' proclamation followed.
On April 5 he set out to his new kingdom, promising to
revisit Scotland every three years. He saw it once again.

A portrait of James as he appeared to his English subjects
has come down to us: 'He was of a middle
stature, more corpulent through his cloathes *James I of*
than in his body, yet fat enough; his cloathes *England*
ever being made large and easie, the Doublets quilted for
stiletto proofe; his Breeches full stuffed. He was naturally
of a timerous disposition, which was the reason of his quilted
Doublets. His eyes large, ever rowling after any stranger
came in his presence, in so much as many for shame have
left the roome, as being out of countenance. His Beard was

very thin; his tongue too large for his mouth, which ever
made him speake full in the mouth, and made him drinke
very uncomely, as if eating his drinke, which came out into
the cup of each side of his mouth. His skin was as soft as
Taffeta Sarsnet, which felt so because hee never washt his
hands, only rub'd his fingers ends sleightly with the wet
end of a Naptkin. His legs were so very weake, that weak-
nesse made him ever leaning on other men's shoulders. His
walke was ever circular. He was very temperate in his
exercises and dyet, and not intemperate in his drinkings.
In his Dyet, Apparell, and Journeys he was very constant.
In his Apparell so constant, as by his good will he would
never change his cloathes till very ragges, his fashion never.
His Dyet and Journeys were so constant that the best
observing Courtier of our time was wont to say, was he
asleep seven yeares, and then awakened, he would tell where
the King every day had been, and every dish he had had
at his Table. He was very witty, and had as many ready
witty jests as any man living, at which he would not smile
himselfe, but deliver them in a grave and serious manner.
In a word, take him altogether and not in peeces, such a
King I wish this Kingdome have never any worse, on the
condition, not any better; for he lived in peace, dyed in
peace, and left all his Kingdomes in a peaceable condition,
with his own Motto: *Beati Pacifici.*'

Upon Scotland's political development the union of 1603
had an effect altogether prejudicial. Immature already in
her constitutional apparatus, the Court's departure subordinated her every institution to a distant authority. 'This
I must say for Scotland,' James told his English Parliament
in 1607; 'here I sit and govern it with my pen. I write and
it is done, and by a Clerk of the Council I govern Scotland
now, which others could not do by the sword.' The instrument of his authority was the Privy Council, whose functions
were at once administrative and judicial, and whose members
were his nominees. The Scottish Parliament possessed neither

power nor inclination to oppose its sovereign. Only the
nobles were fully represented in it, and only on four occasions
before 1661 did more than forty-four of their order attend.
Its powers were practically usurped by the Committee of
the Articles, a manageable body which comprised an equal
number, usually eight, of each Estate, along with certain
high Officers of State. Their election made the Committee
the tool of the Crown: the Nobles chose the Bishops, the
Bishops chose the Nobles, and both together chose the
county Barons and town Burgesses. Moreover, Parliament
adjourned during the Committee's deliberations and merely
reassembled to ratify the legislation it had prepared. The
General Assembly was equally at James' orders. It met only
with his permission, its membership was manipulated, its
procedure was regulated, and its disciplinary powers were
transferred to Courts of High Commission of an English
pattern. Opposition to the sovereign was powerless and only
the insane provocations of Charles I revived it.

Before attempting to bring the Scottish Kirk into harmony
with the English Establishment James broached a project
in which he was deeply interested. His first Speech to the
English Parliament, in March 1604, invited a political union
of his two realms. His insistence so far prevailed that Commissioners were appointed by both Parliaments,   *Union Ne-*
who in December 1604 signed Articles of Union.   *gotiations,*
They enumerated for repeal ten English and   1604
fourteen Scottish hostile laws made by England against
Scotland, or by Scotland against England. They recommended
the establishment of free trade between the two countries.
They proposed that persons born after the demise of Elizabeth should be entitled to possess property and receive
offices, ecclesiastical and civil, under the Crown in either
kingdom as freely as in that of their birth. Fearing that
naturalisation of *Post-nati*, as such persons were termed,
would permit James unduly to promote Scotsmen to offices
of position and profit, the English Parliament rejected the

Commissioners' proposals in their entirety, with the exception of the abrogation of hostile laws. Determined, however, to procure the status of English citizenship for *Post-nati*, James encouraged a collusive action before the Court of Exchequer in the name of Robert Colvill, an infant born at Edinburgh in 1605, who claimed to be deemed a natural English subject. Ten of twelve Judges upheld Colvill's petition and decided the status of *Post-nati* as James desired. The Scottish Estates (August 1607) received the Commissioners' report in more amicable mood and on it framed an Act of Union, but made its operation conditional upon England's acceptance of reciprocal conditions. Consequently the expunging of the hostile laws and recognition of the common citizenship of *Post-nati* were the sole positive results of James' proposal. The project of union revived half a century later.

While negotiations for political union pursued their fruit-*Bishops as* less course, James was following a purpose which *Constant* lay as near his heart, the assimilation of the *Moderators* Kirk to an Anglican model. The design required a diocesan episcopate, involved disturbance of Presbyterian discipline, and threatened the established forms of public worship. In 1606, by two notable measures, the Estates assembled at Perth materially advanced James' policy. One confirmed his prerogative over all estates, persons, and causes, ecclesiastical as well as civil, and so conferred an authority which the Kirk categorically denied. The second restored to the bishops the revenues of their Sees which, by the Act of 1587, had been annexed to the Crown. Provided at length with an adequate endowment, it remained only to clothe the bishops, whose number now equalled that of the pre-Reformation Church, with diocesan and administrative functions.

As a step towards that end, James summoned in December 1606 a number of ministers and laymen whose conclusions were subsequently vested with the authority of a General Assembly. Taking advantage of complaints alleging activity among the Catholics that needed to be watched, James recommended that over every Presbytery one of its most experienced and authoritative ministers should preside and bear the title Constant (*i.e.* perpetual) Moderator with an annual revenue; and that a similar official should preside over the Synods. Every bishop would act as Moderator of the Presbytery in which he resided and would also preside *ex officio* as Constant Moderator of his Synod. Thus the bishops obtained a status within the Presbyterian organization of the Kirk. But notwithstanding James' judicious association of Constant Moderators with the observation and correction of Papists, the attempt to set the bishops over the Synods excited much disorder, especially in Fife and Lothian.

James now urged the bishops to take upon them the administration of all Church affairs. But, unwilling to make any change without the sanction of the Church's established authority, they desired the convention of a General Assembly, which met at Glasgow in June 1610. As steps were taken to assure the presence of sympathetic persons, its conclusions were agreeable to James' purposes. The dependence of the Kirk's Assemblies on the Crown was asserted; Synods under the bishops' presidency were directed to sit twice annually; sentences of excommunication or absolution were forbidden without their sanction; presentations to vacant livings were henceforth at their disposal. These sweeping changes were accompanied by the institution of Courts of High Commission, subsequently united (1615), in each of the two archbishoprics, with disciplinary powers. Their erection completed the process by which James imposed Episcopacy upon a Presbyterian polity. But his episcopate lacked spiritual authority. To recover it the Archbishop of Glasgow and the Bishops of Brechin and Galloway were summoned to London in October 1610 to receive consecration from three English bishops. Upon their return they consecrated the other holders of Scottish sees. James' purpose was fulfilled: the ratification

of the Assembly's conclusions by Parliament in 1612 gave
Scotland the ecclesiastical organization he required.

A lull preceded James' adventure upon his more pro-
The Five vocative attempt to harmonize the worship of
Articles, his two Churches. After six years' interval a
1618 General Assembly met in the summer of 1616
at Aberdeen, whose episcopal atmosphere and remoteness
from the Presbyterian south made it an appropriate platform from which to announce the further reforms James
contemplated. He proposed five Articles to be accepted as
Canons of the Church. They prescribed that (1) the Holy
Communion should be received kneeling, and (2) might be
administered to the sick in their homes; that (3) the Sacra-
ment of Baptism should not be deferred beyond the Sunday
after the child's birth and might be administered in private
houses; that (4) the Festivals of Christmas, Easter, Ascen-
sion, Whitsunday, and also Good Friday must be observed;
and that (5) young children should be presented to the
bishops for confirmation, after instruction by their parish
minister. Even the bishops objected the impossibility of
summarily establishing the Five Acts as binding Canons.
James, in consequence, revisited Scotland in 1617, accompanied by the future Archbishop Laud, proposing to secure
recognition of his prerogative, 'with advice of the archbishops
and bishops,' to legislate for the Kirk. Once more the bishops
represented to their testy sovereign the wisdom of caution.
James angrily threatened his displeasure, but in 1618, after
his return to England, submitted his proposals to a General
Assembly at Perth and, by a majority of more than two to
one of a membership carefully regulated beforehand, secured approval of the Five Articles. Three years later (1621)
he summoned the last Parliament of his reign to fortify
them with constitutional sanction. James had his way; but
his criticism of Laud is not less apt applied to himself:
'he knew not the stomach' of his people, else he had turned
aside from a course of provocative folly. His successor

followed it with greater unwisdom, and reaped his reward in revolution.

James' efforts to unite his kingdoms and harmonize their Churches did not exhaust the tireless interest of a sovereign whose serious view of his office and earnest endeavour to promote the prosperity of his native country are patent as his errors of judgment. His passion for public order directed him to the state of the Highlands, Islands, and Borders; they were pre-eminently the 'peccant parts' of the kingdom. In the Highlands and Isles, where *Highlands* Presbyterianism had not penetrated and Catholic *and Islands* missionaries were infrequent, there was little authority to curb the natural propensity of the clans to pursue private vendettas and harry their neighbours. None exceeded in disorderliness the Macgregors, a 'wicked and unhappy race.' James decreed their unruly stock unworthy to exist, ordered the abolition of their name, and with remorseless vendetta pursued the 'nameless clan,' of whom but a remnant survived. In 1608 a punitive effort was projected against the inhabitants of the Inner Hebrides, who in the following year accepted the Statutes of Icolmkill [Iona], binding the chiefs to profess and support the Reformed religion, establish inns and hostelries for travellers, send the eldest son or daughter of every yeoman to school in the Lowlands to acquire English, and surrender firearms even for sporting purposes. The Orkneys were another disturbed area. The earl's oppressions were proverbial, his power considerable. The earldom was permanently annexed to the Crown in 1612, and in 1615 the earl and his son were executed.

The pacification of the Borders naturally followed the union of the British Crowns. Having for centuries *The Borders* turies followed their lawless courses on the circumference they now became the 'heart' of a united Empire. Hence, while the two Parliaments were considering the problem of union, James took steps to establish law and order throughout the 'Middle Shires,' as the Borders were now styled. In 1605 a mixed Commission from each kingdom was appointed to disarm the population and deal summarily with the unruly. A company of mounted police was at its disposal, whose ' Jeddart Justice'—hang first, try afterwards —passed into a proverb. By 1609 the work was effectually accomplished, and by the end of James' reign the Borders, like the Highlands and Islands, were on the road to quietude.

James' wider authority as 'King of Great Britain' permitted him to introduce his native subjects to two new fields of activity. For generations Scotland's poverty had driven her sons into the service of foreign States. In 1609, following an abortive rebellion, the six Irish counties of Tyrone, Donegal, Armagh, Coleraine, Cavan, and Fermanagh escheated to the Crown, and for their settlement James adopted an experiment of colonization already followed in the Lewis. English and Scottish settlers were invited to purchase parcels of land torn from the Irish, upon the condition that a fortified castle should be erected on each property and the land be neither alienated to Irishmen nor cultivated by them as tenants. In the autumn of 1610 fifty-nine Scotsmen took up some 80,000 acres in Ulster, which the provocations of Stewart ecclesiastical policy made, like New England, a refuge for Calvinism, and consequently impressed upon the province a character which it never lost.

Plantation of Ulster, 1610

A desire to admit Scotland to the colonial activities of her neighbours caused James in 1621 to grant to Sir William Alexander the 'isle and continent of Norumbega,' or Acadia, on the St Lawrence, to the peninsular portion of which the name Nova Scotia was attached, a designation it never lost in spite of Alexander's failure to colonize it. He was authorized to divide his concession into a thousand allotments and to offer the dignity of a baronetcy to all who provided money or labour. But the attempt had no success: in 1632 Acadia was restored to France. Scotland awaited the Union of 1707 for

Nova Scotia

the colonial heritage of England to be thrown open to her profit.

In March 1625 James' long reign ended. It presents a remarkable record of success in circumstances of peculiar difficulty. He had brought his nobility to heel, averted the tyranny of the Kirk, introduced order into regions hitherto turbulent, transformed an ineffectual monarchy into a paternal despotism, and enlarged the commercial welfare of the kingdom. He is, admittedly, one of the oddest figures encountered in the pages of history. But he was able, knew his people, was sincerely devoted to what he held their interests, though neither nice nor scrupulous in his state-craft, and vastly more sensible than his son and grandsons who followed him on the throne.

CHAPTER XI

THE COVENANT

F OR the first time since Robert III's death in 1406 Scotland received a sovereign who did not step from the nursery to his throne. Charles I was in his twenty-fifth year

Charles I, 1625–49

when his father's death gave him the British crowns. His inclination to despotic government was the result of daily and hourly contact with James, whom in some respects he resembled. His bent was serious—his brother once threatened to name him Archbishop of Canterbury. He inherited his father's interest in theology, and possessed a nature which found its surest consolation in the offices of religion. Anglican episcopacy and the ceremonialism of the English Church satisfied his nature and convictions. A profound belief in the divine right of his office also was his father's legacy, and from him he inherited a preference for subterfuge and disingenuous action which made men think him insincere and even dishonest, though in his private relationships there was none more honourable. His personality was reserved, even chilling, too confident in its own rectitude to be patient with the standpoint of opponents. Such a man, aiming to complete the policy of harmonization his father had bequeathed to him, stirred a revolution which a shrewder knowledge of his northern kingdom might have averted.

The first eight years of Charles' reign in England moved rapidly towards revolution. In Scotland he pursued his father's aims, but without displaying hasty intention to extend them. The Five Articles had been presented to the Estates in 1621 as James' last word in ecclesiastical innovation. They remained the law of the Church and continued to excite meetings of protest. An angry spirit was abroad which Charles' provocations in 1633 eventually goaded into action.

The basis of James' success had been in the good relations he maintained with the nobility. Charles, less wise, opened his reign with measures which made *The Nobility* their order his most determined enemy. In March 1626 he completely transformed the composition of his Privy Council, introduced five of the bishops into it, and gave Archbishop Spottiswoode, the Primate, precedence even of the Lord High Chancellor. It was Charles' deliberate purpose to remove from the Council the opposition of his lay nobility and to rely on the bishops' votes to carry the measures on which he was set. Their numerical strength upon it was gradually increased, and early in 1635 Spottiswoode was appointed Chancellor. The advancement of his order stirred deep prejudices: as bishops they were obnoxious to Presbyterian prejudices: as clergymen they were deemed interlopers by the secular nobility whom they displaced.

By another measure Charles still further alienated his nobles from the Crown, snapped its alliance *Act of* with their order which alone had enabled *Revocation,* James to bring the Kirk to his feet, and *1625* united them heartily with it on a common platform of opposition in the Covenant of 1638. Charles was the first of a sequence of eight sovereigns whose reign did not begin with a minority which afforded the nobility ready opportunity to enrich themselves at its expense. Under customary circumstances Acts of Revocation recalling to the Crown properties alienated from it during the sovereign's minority were both necessary and usual. But in 1625 Charles ordained an Act of Revocation of quite exceptional character: it recalled to the Crown's possession all properties alienated from it since the death of James V in 1542. Over so extended a period the amount of landed property involved was enormous and included the bulk of the endowments of the pre-

Reformation Church annexed to the royal domain by the Act of 1587 and since alienated from it. Transactions more than eighty years old were, in some cases, now revoked, the prescriptive rights of individuals long possessed of the lands in question were denied, and almost every family of consequence in the kingdom was threatened. Dismay and indignation were general.

But accompanying Charles' measure was a purpose alto-
Teinds and Superiorities gether laudable, whose accomplishment promised to rally to him the interests of another class. A large part of the revenues of the old Church was in the form of tithes, or 'teinds,' a tenth of the harvest of the land. In the confusion of the Reformation these revenues fell into the hands of lay owners, with the result that, while the land itself (temporality) passed into the possession of *A* and his heirs, the teinds upon it might be owned by *B* and his heirs, who, known as 'titulars of the teinds,' enjoyed the 'spirituality' of the property, *i.e.* the fund it had contributed to the clergy's maintenance. At harvest time the titulars levied their tithes with a rapacity and inconsiderateness which the Roman Church never exhibited. As Charles declared, they 'did use and practice the uttermost of that severity which the law alloweth them.' Announcing his desire that 'the said teinds may no longer be, as they have been heretofore, the cause of blood, oppressions, enmities, and of enforced dependencies,' Charles proposed to give every landowner (heritor) power to purchase his tithes from the titular 'upon reasonable conditions.' By that means the landowner would be freed from the annoyance of the tithe-collector, and the Church could hope that the teinds once more would be devoted to their historical use.

So loud was the chorus of remonstrance from the owners of superiorities and teinds that Charles agreed to temper his original proposals. In January 1627 he set up a 'Commission for Surrenders of Superiorities and Teinds,' representing the bishops, nobles, minor landowners, and burghs, with a view to settlement on a basis of compromise. Provided that its feudal superiority over the alienated Church lands was established, and its purposes in regard to the teinds were realized, the Crown offered to abandon a policy of confiscation and compound with lords of erections and titulars on equitable terms. Meanwhile the interested parties were invited to execute a 'submission' of their claims to the king's arbitration and decision. After long and tedious investigation the four groups concerned in the complicated transaction—the superiors or lords of erections, the burghs possessed of Church lands, the bishops and clergy, and the titulars of the teinds—agreed to a submission of their claims to the king's decision.

In September 1629 Charles gave his award. Church lands were suffered to remain in possession of their then owners. But the Crown demanded a moderate purchase price equivalent to ten years' rental of them. The teinds were dealt with in a more complicated manner. Their value was declared at one-fifth of the rental of the land on which they were levied, whose owner was empowered to purchase them from the titular at nine years' purchase. If the heritor failed to exercise his option of purchase the teind was settled as an annual charge upon the property, burdened with (1) a fixed payment to the parish minister, and (2) another to the Crown. The transaction has been praised as the greatest economic revolution in Scottish history, the one successful action of Charles' reign. But while the Kirk eventually acknowledged the Act as having secured to it adequate and permanent endowment of its clergy, the nobles were alienated by the transaction and were rendered suspicious of the king's intentions. The Act of Revocation consequently cost the Crown the support it formerly received from their order against the ministers and other classes. The nobles became Protestants to get the Church property, Covenanters to keep it.

So soon as the principles of the Act of Revocation were

determined, the nobles, anxious that its legality should be established on Parliament's approval, urged Charles to celebrate his long delayed coronation and meet his Estates. After various delays, Charles paid his first visit to Scotland since 1604. Laud, who once more accompanied his sovereign, had recently been promoted to the See of London and his imminent translation to the arch-diocese of Canterbury was anticipated. More than twice Charles' age, their common opinions, his experience and ability, enabled him to exert over his master large influence. He was as honest in his convictions, as narrow in his outlook, shared his antipathy for Presbyterianism and his desire to reform the Scottish ritual of worship to the standards of the English establishment. Already he contemplated a Prayer-book for Scottish use, and the passing of the Revocation Act suggested the moment opportune for further ecclesiastical innovations. In the summer of 1633 the king and his minister arrived in Edinburgh. The coronation was celebrated with a ceremonial which 'bred gret feir of inbringing of Poperie,' while the bishops appeared clothed once more in the ancient vestments of their office, a sight which Scotland had not witnessed since the Reformation. Parliament, summoned immediately after the coronation, amply fulfilled Charles' purposes. The bishops again sat upon the Committee of Articles, the Five Articles and other ecclesiastical measures of the late reign were confirmed, and Charles received power to settle the official apparel of the clergy. Laud enlarged in sermons upon the beauty and propriety of ecclesiastical uniformity, while Charles made public his intention to replace Knox's Liturgy by another, and ordered the bishops to busy themselves in its production.

The Corona-tion, 1633

Upon his return to England Charles pressed forward his intention to augment the political authority of the Scottish bishops and to harmonize the public worship of his two Churches. Edinburgh was constituted the seat of a new bishopric: order was

Further Innovations

made directing the archbishops of St Andrews and Glasgow and the bishops to wear the vestments they had presented themselves in at the coronation: the lower clergy were permitted to preach in black gowns, but were directed to wear surplices ('whites') for the other portions of divine service, an order which accentuated the bitterness of Presbyterian feeling. At the same time, the English Prayer-book was ordered to be used in the Chapel Royal and University of St Andrews. Before the end of 1634 a new Court of High Commission was set up to ensure the adoption of the innovations already announced and still to come. The latter were revealed in the form of 'Canons and Constitutions Ecclesiastical' introduced into Scotland in 1636. They affirmed the royal authority over ecclesiastical causes and authorities, upheld the episcopal office, ordered the Holy Table to be set up at the east end of the churches, directed the communicant to kneel—heretofore he sat—at the celebration of the Lord's Supper, enjoined the use of the English Authorized Version of the Bible, and the adoption of a new Liturgy shortly to be issued.

In May 1637 the long threatened Service-book, popularly styled 'Laud's Liturgy,' was issued by the King's Printer at Edinburgh. At the moment *Laud's* when it was imposed upon the Kirk Sunday *Liturgy* worship followed a uniform ritual: first, set prayers, followed sometimes by the Decalogue and Creed; large portions of the Psalter, followed by the 'Gloria'; chapters from the Old and New Testaments; the Sermon, preceded by an extempore prayer and the Lord's Prayer, and concluded by a set prayer from Knox's Liturgy for special seasons, a psalm, and the Benediction. A simpler Liturgy than the English, it allowed larger latitude to the minister and derived its sanction from ecclesiastical authority. Objections to the new one were not inspired by hostility to a Liturgy *quâ* Liturgy but by other considerations. It was substantially the work of Laud. Only a minority of the bishops favoured it and many of them most

opposed to it did not see it before publication. A few altera-
tions distinguished it from its English original, *e.g.* the substitution of 'presbyter' for 'priest.' But these emendations
were counterbalanced by changes of a character to suggest
the Book a revision of the English Prayer-book in a ritualistic
direction, and that Scotland was to be made the *corpus vile*
of an experiment which, if successful, would encourage an
effort to restore Popery in England as well. In typographical
detail, too, the Book was reminiscent of the Missals of the
old Church. It was printed partly in Gothic black letter,
obsolete for nearly eighty years. It outraged Scottish suspicion of illustration in books of devotion by including
pictorial capitals, though the latter were quite innocent of
innuendo. A contemporary styled the Liturgy a 'Popish-
Inglish-Scottish-Masse-Service-Booke.' The Book came from
England, was imposed by royal authority, and had not been
submitted to the approval of the Kirk. On every ground it
was obnoxious.

The first reading of the Prayer-book was appointed for
Sunday, July 23, 1637, and its fate was decided by its reception at Edinburgh. The Primate was present in St Giles',
the new Bishop of Edinburgh was announced to preach, and
the sermon was to be preceded by the new Order for Morning
Prayer. That opposition was organized is probable. Serving
women occupying stools in waiting for their mistresses are
credited with the disturbance that arose when the Dean read
the opening sentences. 'The Mass,' they shouted, 'is entered
amongst us.' 'False thief,' said one to a devouter neighbour,
'dost thou say Mass at my ear?' A stool was flung with such
precision at the quavering Dean that the 'devouter sex'
were suspected to be youths in disguise. Legend fashioned
a mythical Jenny Geddes, leader of the fray. The Primate
called on the magistrates to clear the rioters from the
Church. The disorderly body, gathering outside, flung stones
at the windows, amid the crash of which the service proceeded to its close. At Glasgow the introduction of the

Liturgy was attended by disorder. Opposition to it was reported on every hand, and, on the Presbyterian frontier,
the Bishop of Brechin read the service with pistols on his
desk and his wife and servants armed for action.

Petitions poured in on the Privy Council from all classes,
parishes, and Presbyteries against the 'fearful
innovation' of the Liturgy and Canons. Alex-   *The Suppli-
ander Henderson, minister of Leuchars, disputed   *cants*
the king's warrant to enforce the Service-book, contending
that 'in material points' it drew near to the Church of Rome,
was authorized neither by Assembly nor Parliament, and
was an invasion of the people's right to determine their
religion. Letters from the provinces proved that in few
places the Prayer-book had been read, and the Council, of
whom the larger number were half hearted in its champion-
ship, made abject surrender. On August 24 they decided
that the obligation to use the Service-book was confined to
the buying of it and no further. Still unsatisfied, petitions
were addressed to London from groups of Supplicants, as
they were styled, who thronged the capital and patiently
awaited the king's reply. On October 17 it was published.
It ordered all strangers to leave Edinburgh within twenty-
four hours on pain of outlawry, and directed the removal of
the Court of Session to Linlithgow and thence to Dundee,
a step which James VI had found efficacious to overcome
resistance.

The Supplicants, disobeying the royal command and con-
ducting themselves as a Convention of the
nation, now occupied the Parliament House   *The Cove-
and, separating into the four classes they re- *nant, 1638*
presented—nobles, county lairds, burghs, and clergy—elected
four of each to form a committee, popularly known as The
Tables, to act for the general body, who were now free to
return to their distant homes. Only in Aberdeen, among the
principal burghs, was their party in a minority, and Charles
was warned that a powerful army would be required to

enforce the Liturgy. But he remained obdurate, and the recent decision of the English judges affirming the legality of Ship-money strengthened his determination not to yield to popular ferment. The Tables, affecting to believe that the Privy Council, on which the bishops sat, did not accurately reflect or report the sovereign's will, continued their protests, and towards the end of February 1638 summoned 'all who love the cause of God' to repair once more to Edinburgh to prosecute the 'intended Reformation' on which their leaders were set. Within a week the rebellion they had in mind to accomplish was consecrated by a popular 'band' or 'covenant' with God.

The authors of the Covenant of 1638 realized their inability to frame a confession of faith to which all shades of Presbyterian opinion could assent, and foresaw that the cry 'No Popery' would rally their ranks to a degree no other watchword could afford. Without the concurrence of moderate opinion they could anticipate little chance of success: a revived crusade against Rome, allegedly co-operating with Laud and his master, would capture the support of a valuable and numerous body and promised victory. Nearly sixty years ago (1581), at a moment when her Protestant belief seemed in acute danger, James VI and his people had signed a Confession of Faith denouncing Rome in violent terms, pledging its subscribers to renounce Popery, and to defend the true Kirk according to their power. The leaders of the Tables concluded to revive this stern document, whose resurrection suggested that a similar crisis to that of 1581 again menaced Scottish Protestantism. It had the advantage also of confronting Charles with his father's profession of faith and signature. Additions were necessary to bring present events within its scope. By February 27 they were complete and were submitted to some three hundred ministers whom the crisis brought to the capital. On March 2, laid out upon a tombstone in Grey Friars Kirkyard, it was signed by a thronging multitude. Copies were made and carried throughout the Lowlands. Almost everywhere it evoked passionate assent. Every shire, all the burghs except three, and every Protestant noble but five, gave it their signatures. The bishops, suddenly a Church invisible, fled or made 'solemn recantations.' 'All that we have been doing these thirty years,' said Spottiswoode bitterly and truly, 'is thrown down at once.'

The document to which the nation so unanimously pledged its assent, after rehearsing the Confession of 1581, the Acts which confirmed it, and recent events, concluded with an oath of obligation to support the king in defence of 'true reformed religion,' reject the 'novations' recently introduced till Parliament and Assembly had 'tried and allowed' them, and 'by all means lawful to recover the purity and liberty of the Gospel.' Alleging that the innovations of which their Supplications and Protestations complained had 'no warrant of the Word of God,' and 'do sensibly tend to the re-establishing of the Popish religion and tyranny,' the signatories concluded arbitrarily that the innovations now challenged were as much to be held Popish as though they had been specifically scheduled in the Confession itself. They insisted: 'we have no intention or desire to attempt anything that may turn to the diminution of the King's greatness and authority; but, on the contrary, we promise and swear that we shall, to the utmost of our power, with our means and lives, stand to the defence of our dread Sovereign, the King's Majesty, his person and authority.' None the less, the Covenant challenged the Crown's authority, and so Charles understood it. 'So long as this Covenant is in force,' he wrote, 'I have no more power in Scotland than as a duke of Venice, which I will rather die than suffer.'

Being without material force to coerce rebellion, Charles played for delay, proposing to push his preparations before the Covenanters—the name now supplanted Tables and Supplicants—were ready to strike. 'Anything to win time' was his positive instruction to the Marquess of Hamilton, whom he dispatched to Scotland in June 1638 as his High Commissioner to view the situation on the spot. Hamilton brought with him two forms of a declaration, one or the other of which he was commanded to make public according to the circumstances that faced him. One categorically required withdrawal of the Covenant. The other merely rated the Covenanters for their disobedience and suspicions and protested Charles' intention to enforce Canons and Liturgy only in a 'fair and legal way.' But Hamilton found a situation to which even the more conciliatory message was inapplicable. Nothing short of the withdrawal of Canons, Articles, High Commission, Liturgy, and instant summons of an Assembly and Parliament would satisfy the Covenanters. Hamilton reported the demand as 'impertinent and damnable.' But only instant surrender could avert a conflict for which Charles was unprepared. Hamilton therefore communicated his master's decision to revoke the offending measures, summon an exclusively clerical General Assembly in November, and Parliament on a later date.

A General Assembly had not met for twenty years. In *The Glasgow Assembly, 1638* convoking a new one Charles expected to bring together such a manageable body as had assisted his father: to abandon Episcopacy was the last thing he had in mind to do. The Tables, on the other hand, were as resolved to give the Assembly the widest representation and popular authority. Lay as well as clerical members were summoned from every Presbytery and burgh, and means were taken to exclude all but whole-hearted subscribers of the Covenant. From such a body Charles had nothing to expect. On November 21, 1638, the Assembly met in Glasgow Cathedral, the only one of the great fanes of the ancient Church spared by the Knoxian fury. Directly it was formally constituted a document signed by certain of the bishops challenged its constitution and authority. Hamilton, presiding as High Commissioner, added his protest: his master was willing to submit the bishops, their

office and authority, to an Assembly legally constituted:
the present one, in which laymen had a seat, he could not
recognize. He therefore declared it dissolved, ordered its
members to disperse, and himself withdrew. Heedless of his
orders, the Assembly voted its competence to continue and
for three weeks remained in active session. When it rose it
had swept away Service-book, Canons, Articles, deposed
and excommunicated the bishops, annulled the Acts by
which Charles and his father had established Episcopacy,
and restored to the Kirk its Presbyterian constitution. 'We
have now cast down the walls of Jericho,' said the Moderator
in his closing address. They had also brought two kingdoms
to the brink of revolution and civil war.

Both sides realized that the proceedings at Glasgow invited a military struggle. Charles mustered
the trained bands of the North of England, *The First
Bishops' War*
proposing to land a force under Hamilton at
Aberdeen to cooperate with Huntly. The Covenanters,
ranged, in spite of their professions, against constituted
authority, needed to improvise an army and a revenue.
Eight collectors were appointed in every shire to raise a
'voluntary' contribution. The creation of a military organization was undertaken by a committee of laymen at Edinburgh superintending parochial committees in every shire
and Presbytery. The provision of experienced officers was
not difficult, though for nearly one hundred years Scotland
had enjoyed peace. At least one hundred Scotsmen held
Swedish commissions in 1632, one of whom, Alexander
Leslie—illegitimate son of the Aberdeenshire Leslies of
Balquhain—attained to the rank of Field-Marshal and the
direction of the Swedish armies after Gustavus' death in
that year. In the summer of 1638 he came home to 'settle
himself,' an 'old little crooked soldier' of sixty years, not
brilliant, but tactful and experienced. His opportune arrival
met the difficulty of selecting a commander from the
Covenanting Lords, and while he never showed himself a

commanding figure, his shrewdness and authority inclined them to be guided by him 'as if he had been great Solyman.'

In March 1639 hostilities opened in the North, where the bishops had their chief support. On the last day of the month Leslie and the Earl of Montrose entered Aberdeen, under flags bearing the legend 'For Religion, the Covenant, and the Country.' The rank and file wore a blue scarf across the breast and under the left arm called 'the Covenanter's ribbon,' Montrose's device to answer the royal red rosette Huntly's men disported in their hats. Enticed to Aberdeen by Montrose, Huntly was scurvily arrested and put under lock and key in Edinburgh Castle. In the south the castles of Edinburgh and Dumbarton were seized, and by May a force of 20,000 men, mobilized under Leslie, formally commissioned to command it 'for the defence of the Covenant, for religion, crown, and country,' watched the Borders, to which Charles was slowly approaching with an army of inferior quality some 21,000 strong. Hesitating between negotiation and war, on May 14, from Newcastle, he issued a proclamation of his intention 'to give his good people of Scotland all just satisfaction in Parliament, as soon as the present disorders and tumultuous proceedings of some are quieted,' and on the 30th encamped near Berwick. On June 5 Leslie established himself on Duns Law, some twelve miles distant, ready to negotiate, if peaceful counsels prevailed, or to be 'on their backs' if his enemy advanced upon Edinburgh.

With the royal standard fluttering almost within sight of their lines, the Covenanting leaders were moved seriously to ponder the consequences of an encounter. Their success was not certain, and a rout of the royal army undoubtedly would excite a desire for 'revenge' in England. Charles was as little disposed to risk an engagement: the situation was unpromising in Scotland: the English ranks had little enthusiasm for the cause in which they were employed: and

the City exhibited considerable chariness in providing the
royal treasury. On June 11, upon the overture of   *Treaty of*
the Covenanting leaders, a conference was held   *Berwick,*
in the English camp near Berwick. A week later   1639
terms were agreed. The Scots undertook to disband their
forces, dissolve the Tables, restore the captured castles, and
carry themselves as obedient subjects. Charles bound himself to withdraw his army and convene once more a General
Assembly, to be followed by a meeting of Parliament. On
that inconclusive note the first Bishops' War ended.

Charles had not undertaken to abandon Episcopacy and
nothing less would satisfy his opponents. The promised
Assembly met in August 1639 and, as at Glasgow, care was
taken to exclude all but uncompromising Covenanters. Once
again the innovations of Charles and his father were condemned as alien to the constitution of the Church of Scotland. Now, in the flush of victory, the Assembly demanded
that the Covenant should be made binding on all, an act as
tyrannous as those challenged in the Crown and destructive
of the unity which to this point opposed it. The Estates
followed the Assembly and reflected its demeanour. As
before, Charles appeared to yield, but actually awaited an
opportunity to secure his ends by force. For that reason he
refused to expunge from the Statute book Acts of Parliament
which confirmed the proceedings of the alleged 'corrupt'
Assemblies of 1606–18, which, he wrote for private information, 'may hereafter be of so great use to us.' Amid loud
protests Parliament was dissolved.

Charles' demeanour left little doubt that he contemplated
another appeal to arms. The Covenanting leaders consequently were moved to invoke the memory of the Ancient
League and invite the mediation of France. Their action, opportunely revealed to Charles, supported his contention that
the Covenant cloaked treasonable political designs. Parliament was summoned to Westminster to receive the evidence
of Scottish disloyalty and, Charles hoped, vote adequate

supplies for its punishment. In April 1640 the Short Parliament met, but refused to accept Charles' denunciation of Scottish treasons, denied him the subsidies he asked for, and but for sudden dissolution (May 5) would have urged him to satisfy his Scottish subjects. Fully apprised of the king's intentions, the Scottish Estates assembled a month later (June 2). In a mood of defiance they made the Covenant compulsory on all citizens under civil penalties, passed an Act establishing triennial Parliaments, and appointed a permanent Committee to act when Parliament was not sitting. Already Leslie's commission had been renewed, a war fund raised, and experienced officers set to drill a force not less numerous and better equipped than that of 1639. Argyll was charged to watch the western coasts against invasion from Ireland, and the Earl Marischal was appointed to deal with the loyalists of the north about Aberdeen.

The campaign upon which Scotland was about to embark differed in character from its predecessor. In *Second Bishops' War* 1639 Leslie was content to await Charles' arrival in Scotland. In August 1640 he boldly plunged into England and for a year remained in occupation of its northern counties. Such a step hardly could have been taken had not those who authorized it known that the English Puritans were agreeable to the advent of an army which could be employed to gain their own ends. On their side, the Scots were not unwilling to lay on broader shoulders the considerable expense of an army raised for their own purposes. The boldness of the design gave it success. It forced Charles to summon the Long Parliament, converted a Scottish into an Anglo-Scottish question, and laid the burden of the army upon the English ally who paid for it and the English counties that provisioned it.

On August 20, 1640, Leslie sent his army across the Tweed. Charles left London for the north on the same day. As Lord Conway, the English commander, had at his disposal forces inadequate to hold Newcastle and the fords of Tyne, Leslie marched unchecked through Northumberland, forced the Tyne at Newburn on August 28, and put Conway to 'the most shameful and confounding flight that was ever heard of.' Newcastle opened its gates to Leslie, and the brief campaign was at an end.

Charles was at York with an army whose numbers justified a stroke against the invader. But it was badly furnished and its leaders were unreliable. Therefore, vainly seeking a line of compromise, Charles summoned a Council of Peers to York at the end of September, and invited counsel upon his attitude towards the invaders. To his annoyance the peers urged an accommodation and named sixteen of their number to negotiate with the Scots. Early in October representatives of both nations met at Ripon, and, after long and uneasy debate, agreed to a cessation of arms. The Scots demanded £850 a day for the maintenance of their army on English soil pending a settlement *Treaty of Ripon, 1640* in Parliament of the questions which brought them into England. Charles, whose exchequer was empty, was forced to concede the condition, and the controversy was withdrawn to London, where, on November 3, the Long Parliament met.

The discussions interrupted at Ripon were taken up by the English Parliament. While it pursued Strafford and Laud and other instruments of Charles' tyranny, the Scots asked for a similar procedure, demanding that his advisers during the recent troubles should be called for trial at the bar of the Estates. Charles gave a categorical refusal: but conceded that he would not favour persons whom the Estates might condemn. He counted, not without reason, on a division in the ranks of his enemies so soon as Parliament was faced with the cost of Scotland's 'brotherly assistance.' In January 1641 it was presented, and amounted to £514,000, in regard to which the Scots offered to bear such a proportion 'as the Parliament should find reasonable or us able.' More urgent were the expenses the army was still incurring: they already amounted to over £80,000. Even to their well-wishers a proposal to saddle England with two-thirds of the charges of an army raised to pursue Scotland's quarrel was bold. But in spite of complainings from the English forces still unpaid in the north, a sum of £300,000 was voted for Scotland's Brotherly Assistance, apart from the debt her army's maintenance was steadily augmenting.

Encouraged by growing signs of ill-feeling between his English and Scottish adversaries, Charles spied an opportunity to increase it to his advantage by paying a second visit to the land of his birth, whence he was receiving heartening encouragement. The Marquess of Montrose, who had sworn the Covenant and led its armies, already realized the dangerous situation which Scotland's defiance of her sovereign threatened. In Scotland the Crown had abdicated to the noisy Kirk and the Marquess of Argyll, its lay leader. In England it was as humiliatingly debased by the proceedings of the Long Parliament. Montrose urged his master to show himself in Scotland, abandon his ill-judged attack upon her religion, summon a free Parliament, and trust himself to the fundamental loyalty of his ancient kingdom. Charles approved the advice. In August 1641 he ratified the treaty with Scotland which assured to her payment of her Brotherly Assistance. Three days later he reviewed at Newcastle the army to whose presence on English soil he owed his discomfiture. It followed in his wake as he rode on to Scotland and was disbanded on the anniversary eve of Newburn Fight. At the cost of a few shot and a single skirmish it had carried a revolution in two kingdoms.

Montrose's advice

CHAPTER XII

THE SOLEMN LEAGUE

CHARLES came to Scotland in August 1641 to secure the service of Leslie's army against his English Parliament. That he would obtain it was not an extravagant hope. Scotland's Brotherly Assistance kindled little gratitude in English breasts: her long occupation of northern England irritated its inhabitants and to the general public appeared impertinent and unsolicited. The financial burden of her alliance was disagreeable. Moreover, she was already beginning to urge England to follow her upon a Presbyterian course and overturn her Episcopal establishment, though Presbyterian discipline was disagreeable to those on whom it was pressed. On her side Scotland remarked with some dismay the king's humiliation at Westminster which her army's occupation of English soil made possible. She herself had taken arms to preserve religion in purity and her civil liberties in peace, whereas in England the very monarchy was now menaced. The nobles were gravely alarmed at the clerical tyranny of the victorious Kirk and some *The Cum-* of their number, including Montrose, had al- *bernauld* ready (1640) subscribed a 'band' at Cumber- *Band,* 1640 nauld to counteract it. His open antagonism to Argyll led to Montrose's imprisonment in Edinburgh Castle, where he lay when Charles came to Holyrood.

In a mood of conciliation therefore Charles met his Scottish subjects. He submitted to Presbyterian pulpit admonitions, employed neither Liturgy nor ceremonies in his Chapel, and in Parliament hastened to ratify the Acts which gave a Presbyterian Establishment security. With reluctance, and only after a 'tough dispute,' he even surrendered his prerogative of appointment to the executive offices of State, Privy Council, and Court of Session and conceded that, for the future, those officials should be appointed only with the advice of Parliament. But the effect of his concessions was wholly dissipated by an untoward event which increased the suspicion with which his past conduct caused him to be disregarded. In October 1640 one of his Catholic supporters among the nobility formed or broached a plan to abduct Argyll and other persons obnoxious to the royalists. Popular credulity associated the king with the plot, and the Incident, as the event was named at the time, seeming to confirm his character for insincerity, deprived him instantly of the advantage which his judicious concessions were beginning to win for him. Its result was to establish Argyll and the Kirk party more firmly, though Charles stipulated for Montrose's release. In November 1640 he left Scotland for ever.

The Incident, 1640

His failure to enlist Scotland on his side left Charles alone to face his English opposition. In his absence Parliament had drafted the Grand Remonstrance, a detailed indictment of his rule presented to him on his return, with a demand for the exclusion of bishops from Parliament and appointment of counsellors agreeable to that body. A month later (January 1642) he swooped upon Pym, Hampden and their fellow leaders, intending, in words attributed to the queen, to 'pull these rogues out by the ears.' In February the bishops' exclusion from Parliament was voted. In March Charles withdrew himself to York with an eye on Hull as a port of entry from the Continent. In April he was denied entrance there, and on August 22, 1642, at Nottingham, at length raised his Standard. For eighteen years to come, with intervals, the British kingdoms were torn by civil strife.

Civil War in England

From the moment war was seen to be inevitable both sides sought Scotland's alliance. The course of the campaign of 1642 made it clear that the conflict would not prove to be the short struggle the English Parliament anticipated, and events inexorably drove it to seek Scotland's military alliance. In the summer of 1643 a deputation reached Edinburgh to solicit an army of 11,000 men. Scotland was willing to enter the conflict, but for her own purposes alone. Her hope was to assure her own Presbyterian establishment by forcing a similar settlement upon England. The English Puritans, on the other hand, though they had followed Scotland's example in condemning Episcopacy, were not prepared to submit to the intolerable inquisition of Presbyterian courts and aimed, rather, at establishing an 'Independent' or 'Congregational' system which was as stoutly opposed to Presbyterian as to Episcopal discipline. Civil liberty was the boon for which the English Parliament had taken the sword. But to secure it Scotland's assistance had become imperative. The pressure of military compulsion was inexorable. The north of England already had been won for Charles. The fall of Bristol gave him the West and brought Parliament a suppliant to Scotland's feet. She prescribed her own conditions, and bound her English ally to fight at her side for an object impossible of attainment and ruinous, in the long run, to the alliance mutually pledged to achieve it.

In accordance with Scottish custom the new alliance was cast in the form of a Band or Covenant. It pledged the allies to maintain the Church of Scotland in doctrine, worship, discipline and government, and to endeavour the reformation *The Solemn League and Covenant, 1643* of the Church of England according to 'the example of the best reformed Churches,' a phrase which each side interpreted in its own way. In August the Estates, with shrewd caution, named £30,000 a month as the price of their military assistance and demanded three months' payment in advance before their army could be permitted to move. In September the House of Commons gave the Solemn League and

Covenant its sanction. A month later the House of Lords followed its leading. In November a separate treaty adjusted the material details of the partnership. The Estates agreed to furnish an army of 18,000 foot, 2000 horse, 1000 dragoons, and a train of artillery. Parliament guaranteed a subsidy of £30,000 a month, a sum increased to £31,000 by a supplementary agreement. Leslie, now Earl of Leven, was again placed in command. 'The play is begun,' wrote an onlooker, 'the good Lord give it a happy end.'

When Scotland entered the war the North of England, with a great wedge of territory between the Mersey and Humber southward to Derby and Nottingham and including the fortress of Newark, was held for Charles. Its reduction, and, in particular, recovery of the Newcastle coal-field and the north-eastern ports of communication with the Continent, was the immediate service looked for at the hands of Parliament's ally. In January 1644, in bitter weather, Leven's cavalry crossed the Tweed. Newcastle, into which the royal commander, the Marquess of Newcastle, had thrown himself, offered resistance. Lacking material for its reduction, Leven swept along the coast, joined hands with the Army of the Eastern Association, and with it sat down to the siege of York. Prince Rupert's defeat at Marston Moor in July, to which the Scottish infantry materially contributed, was followed by the fall of the city. In six months the North of England had been almost purged of its royalist garrisons. In August Leven drew his lines round Newcastle and in October received its surrender. Carlisle and a few insignificant garrisons alone stood for Charles at the close of a campaign which Scotland could regard with satisfaction: the king's power was confined to Wales, Devonshire, Cornwall, and the western counties. In 1645 Leven was invited to participate with Parliament's New Model in their reduction. The fall of Carlisle in June enabled him with less misgiving to venture so far from Scotland. Late in July he moved to invest Hereford. But in August Montrose's victory at Kilsyth destroyed Scotland's home army and created a situation of utmost peril. David Leslie and the cavalry were dispatched in all haste northward, and Leven, abandoning the siege of Hereford, returned to the North of England in readiness to enter Scotland should events demand his presence. Opportunely David Leslie overthrew Montrose at Philiphaugh in September, and Leven consented to reduce Newark, the only considerable strength remaining to Charles in the Midlands. The siege was still in progress when, on May 5, 1646, Charles, whose sinking fortunes demanded a desperate measure, rode into the Scottish camp. Next day, at his bidding, Newark surrendered, and Leven withdrew northwards with his royal prize. The Army of the Solemn League and Covenant had done its last service.

Meanwhile, more heroic warfare had been waged in Scotland, where Montrose, then with the king at Oxford, was appointed Lieutenant-General (February 1644). Early in March 1644 he joined *Montrose in Scotland* the Marquess of Newcastle at Durham, picked up recruits a few hundred strong, and was at Dumfries in the middle of April. There he raised his master's Standard for the defence, he made proclamation, of 'the true Protestant religion, his Majesty's just and sacred authority, the fundamental laws and privileges of Parliaments.' Not a sword joined him. Falling back on Carlisle, which still flew the royal flag, he harried Leven's communications in Northumberland and, on Prince Rupert's arrival in the north, rode southward to solicit reinforcements, proposing to cut his way home to Scotland. Rupert could not spare him even a musket. So, while his pack-horses and servants jogged southward to the king, Montrose himself, in the guise of a groom rode northward again behind two companions garbed as Leven's troopers, and after four days' hazardous adventure was among friends near Perth, his year of victories before him.

Montrose's Year opened discouragingly. The Gordons were

watching the hereditary foes of their house, and the Lowland gentry of Angus and the Mearns timidly withheld encouragement. Opportunely Alastair Macdonald brought some
2000 of his name from Islay and Kintyre, the diminished
Irish force Montrose and his master so long had expected.
Montrose met him at Blair Atholl and raised the king's
Standard. Argyll was marching from the west. Lord Balfour
watched at Aberdeen, and Lord Elcho guarded the Tay
valley at Perth. Montrose struck swiftly at his nearest foe,
routed Elcho at Tippermuir, near Perth, on September 1,
1644, and by nightfall was master of Perth. A week later
(September 13) Balfour was in flight after a stubborn contest
and Aberdeen a prize. Argyll and a larger force, lumbering
in Montrose's rear, followed his elusive quarry backwards
and forwards through the autumnal Grampians. In December
Montrose returned to Blair Atholl and Argyll to Edinburgh,
where he had 'small thanks' for his conduct of a campaign
which demonstrated his inferiority as a soldier.

The clans loved a fighter now as later they followed
Dundee, and flocked to Atholl eager to strike at Argyll,
their common foe. As Christmas approached, Montrose led
them thither and wreaked vengeance on the Campbell clan.
By the end of January 1645 the work of destruction was
complete and Montrose struck northward. Argyll followed
hard in his rear and took station at Inverlochy on Loch Eil,
where, on February 2, Montrose exterminated two-thirds
of his force. He had 'let the world see that Argyll was not
the man his Highlandmen believed him to be,' had beaten
him 'in his own Highlands,' and was 'in the fairest hopes of
reducing this kingdom to your Majesty's obedience,' he
wrote to Charles. Meanwhile, the Kirk thundered excommunication against him and the Estates added their male-
diction; henceforth he was 'that excommunicated traitor
James Graham.' But Montrose was not awed. At Auldearn
(May 9), Alford (July 2), Kilsyth (August 15), he increased
his tale of victories and vanquished every opponent. In

Scotland the Covenant was at his feet. Edinburgh and the south accepted him as Charles' Viceroy and released the Covenant's prisoners. He summoned Parliament to meet at Glasgow in October. It never met. Three weeks after Kilsyth David Leslie, hot-foot from England with 4000 horse, surprised Montrose's scanty force at Philiphaugh, near Selkirk (September 13). Fighting desperately, Montrose cut his way to freedom. Charles, Leven's prisoner-guest, sent a command in May 1646 to abandon a hopeless enterprise. A few weeks later Montrose said farewell to the remnants of his heroic band and passed into a foreign exile.

When Charles surrendered to Leven in May 1646 the enthusiasm which brought Scotland into the war in 1644 had evaporated. None but a visionary could anticipate England's conversion *Anglo-Scottish dissension* to Presbyterian discipline. The war, indeed, had given birth to the army of the New Model, fixed to uphold liberty of conscience against episcopal and presbyterian uniformity alike. Other causes contributed to dissolve the partnership of 1643. England taunted the Scots with inefficiency, complained that their army accomplished little after the fall of Newcastle in October 1644, alleged forced levies and billetings upon the counties through which it passed, and suspected its intention to compile as imposing a bill of costs as possible. Scotland retorted that her army was unclothed, unfed, unpaid; that she had magnanimously thrown herself into England's quarrel, and thereby exposed herself to Montrose's harrying. Circumstances, too, were obviously heading towards a struggle between the English Parliament and the New Model, whose officers and rank and file were firm to resist any attempt to bind their consciences, from whatever quarter it might come. Upon the Presbyterian benches, therefore, the termination of the Scottish alliance was beginning to be favourably regarded as the condition which alone made it possible to disband the New Model, the chief strength of the Independents.

Hoping to take advantage of these complicated relation-
Charles joins ships Charles, on May 5, 1646, rode into the
the Scots, Scottish lines at Southwell. Newark surrendered
1646 on the 6th and Leven ordered an instant retreat. A week later he brought the king to Newcastle, where
the last scene of the Solemn League was enacted.

To his indignation Charles found himself a prisoner at
Newcastle. His usage, he complained to the queen, was
'barbarous'; 'I cannot call for any of my old servants nor
chuse any new without leave.' Ministers descended from
Scotland to expound the iniquity of Episcopacy, and the
Assembly dispatched a deputation to 'let his Majesty know
what the Kirk censure is' if he refused the Covenant. On
July 24 the last ultimatum of the Solemn League was presented to him and required him to establish ecclesiastical
uniformity between his two kingdoms. After his manner,
he evaded a decided negative, and desired permission to
return to London, counting on his opportunity to play off
against each other the jealous interests that strove to win
him. On August 12 Scotland intimated a desire to withdraw
her army from a fruitless alliance. The resolution involved
surrender of the king's person. Late in September the
Houses directed a Committee to examine the situation, and
the Independents in the Commons carried a resolution
asserting the exclusive right of the English Parliament to
dispose of the king so long as he remained on English territory. It placed the Scots in a position of difficulty; they
were, one wrote, 'reduced either to commit the unheard-of
dastardly act of delivering up their king, or to be brought
into conflict with all the army of the Independents.' It was
a dilemma which material considerations rather than national
The King's chivalry were permitted to resolve. Scotland
surrender, asked for £600,000, and in the result accepted
1647 £400,000 in full discharge of her claims under
the treaty of 1643. The payment of the first half of the
amount was completed on February 3, 1647. On the same

day Charles was delivered to Parliament's Commissioners at Newcastle and set out with them for Holdenby. Leven already had begun the evacuation of the North of England and before Charles reached his new prison it was complete. 'I do not know what will be the result of the bargain that the English have just concluded with the Scots,' a Frenchman wrote shrewdly to his master on the eve of Charles' departure; 'but it seems to me that it will be very difficult for the enmity that is between these peoples to remain long without breaking out.'

Public sentiment in Scotland was already moving in Charles' favour when Cornet Joyce kidnapped the king at Holdenby (June 1647) and made him prisoner of the English New Model Army. Neither generosity nor national pride could approve the somewhat sordid transaction at Newcastle which surrendered a Scottish king to an English prison. England's evident resentment of Scotland's interference between the king and his English subjects was galling, and the pathos of his situation was evident, despite his wrong-headedness. Moreover, jealousy of the bishops and anxiety over the Act of Revocation had long since been allayed: even if Charles were restored it was inconceivable that he should repeat his provocations. The futility of the lapsed alliance with the English Parliament itself made converts to his cause. Joyce's act stirred a deeper revulsion of feeling: on the morrow of it the New Model in a 'Solemn Engagement,' whose very title challenged the League of 1643, bound itself to impose an ecclesiastical settlement whose broad tolerance offended the Kirk and its partisans. It refused to enforce the Covenant or the Book of Common Prayer or to coerce the conscience of individuals. Having entered the lists against Charles to force the Covenant upon the three British kingdoms, Scotland now witnessed the triumph of Independency in England. A Scottish army had entered England in 1644 to enforce Presbyterian uniformity. Conceivably an

The Engagement, 1648

English army might, and later did, enter Scotland to enforce uniformity of another kind. The situation was one of anxiety. Hamilton and his brother the Earl of Lanark set themselves to rally opinion in Scotland in Charles' favour, and in November 1647 put themselves in communication with him. Alleging his life to be in danger, Charles had recently escaped from the New Model's custody to the Isle of Wight, whence he might reach France if circumstances compelled that course. His visitors had no mandate from the Kirk, whose leaders still stood out for the letter of the treaty of 1643. But they spoke for a growing body of royalist opinion which promised to provide Charles with the army he needed. Late in December 1647, at Carisbrooke, he signed the 'Engagement' with the Scottish Commissioners.

The Engagement bound Charles to confirm the Solemn League by Acts of Parliament in both kingdoms, with the stipulation that it should not bind objecting consciences. He undertook to sanction 'Presbyterial government' in England for a probation of three years, the subsequent settlement being expressly reserved for future consideration. He concurred with Scottish feeling against the New Model in an undertaking to suppress a formidable category of Independent sects. He declared his willingness to confirm the Acts passed in the last Scottish Parliaments. On these terms the Commissioners engaged their countrymen to support his demand for liberty to negotiate a treaty with the New Model at London, and in case the demand was not conceded, to launch an army into England 'for defence of his Majesty's person and authority, and restoring him to his government.' As the publication of these conditions would expose Scotland to instant invasion, the Engagement was wrapped in lead and buried in the garden of Carisbrooke Castle. Lanark and his colleagues hastened to Scotland to announce it.

In March 1648 Parliament assembled at Edinburgh to determine the national policy towards England in view of recent happenings there. Though the ministers in the General Assembly bitterly denounced association with an uncovenanted king, it was clear that the old alliance between Crown and nobility which supported James VI in his early contests with the Kirk had been revived. Nobles who deserted Charles in 1637 to confound the bishops were now his friends to humble the Kirk and vindicate Scotland's legitimate concern in the fortunes of her sovereign. Of their order nearly five out of six approved the Engagement and supported military intervention. The shires and burghs sounded a less certain note; they were closely divided. But of the whole House the majority favoured war. On April 11, 1648, the Estates delivered an ultimatum to the English Parliament and its masters in the New Model. Charles' liberation, the Army's disbanding, establishment of Presbyterian discipline, and suppression of the Book of Common Prayer, were demanded.

The ultimatum was disingenuous; under a cloak of zeal for the Covenant it concealed a purpose which *Defeat of the* at bottom was political, and vainly angled for *Engagers,* ministerial support. The clergy thundered 'solemn 1648 curses' from their pulpits upon the enterprise, obstructed its levies, and refused to associate with English 'Malignants' to restore a sovereign whose enmity to the Covenant was declared. Supplications against the Engagement poured in from the Presbyteries. The Covenanters of Clydesdale, Kyle, and Cunningham assembled at Mauchline in armed protest and were dispersed with bloodshed. But the army of Engagers proved contemptible in numbers, raw, undisciplined. Instead of 30,000 men few more than a third of that strength mustered when, on July 8, 1648, Hamilton crossed the Border into England. Cromwell, whom the crisis summoned from South Wales, burst upon him near Preston, and, pursuing a maimed quarry, dispatched him on August 25 at Uttoxeter, in Staffordshire, where Hamilton made his surrender.

Hamilton's misadventure delivered Scotland bound hand

and foot to the Kirk, in the teeth of whose opposition he
had moved to his disaster, and cheated Charles of his last
hope of rescue from Cromwell and the Independents. Early
in 1649 a new Parliament assembled at Edinburgh whose
composition gave Argyll and the Kirk secure predominance.
Such peers as were present supported them to a man.
A few weeks earlier Cromwell had administered Pride's
Purge to Parliament at Westminster. The Covenanted Kirk
demanded a similar expulsion of royalists and Engagers
from offices of public trust. The Estates complying passed an 'Act of Classes' which expelled
from the public service all who had actively or
passively promoted the Engagement, supported Montrose,
or been already denounced as Malignants: and ostracized all
persons in public positions guilty of swearing, drunkenness,
profanity, and neglect of public worship. Those who came
within the Act's displeasure were expelled from their
appointments for periods of varying duration, the most
notorious backsliders for life.

*Act of
Classes*, 1649

The Act of Classes placed Scotland under the Kirk's angry
heel. Seven days after it was approved Charles
ended his uneasy reign on the scaffold at White-
hall. Once more a Scottish sovereign had been
done to death by an English tribunal in Scotland's despite.
The country was profoundly stirred. That the dead king's
son would repeat his father's stubborn hatred of the Covenant
and Solemn League was improbable in view of his forlorn
condition and dependence upon Scotland's loyalty. Hence,
instantly upon the news of Charles I's death the Estates,
careless even to restrict the declaration to their own kingdom, proclaimed his son King of Great Britain, France, and
Ireland.

*Execution of
Charles I,
1649*

Charles II was barely nineteen when his father's death
brought him upon a stormy stage. 'Very tall of
his age, with a beautiful head, a brown complexion, and a very tolerable personality,' the young prince

Charles II

since the summer of 1648 had been the guest of his brother-in-law the Prince of Orange at the Hague. Late in March 1649 Commissioners of the Scottish Estates and Kirk presented themselves before him to offer Scotland's allegiance on their own imperative terms. Montrose counselled him to eschew the Covenant's humiliating conditions and trust himself to the fundamental loyalty of his subjects. Yielding to his insistence Charles dispatched him to Scotland as his Lieutenant-Governor, an adventure which ended in the hero's rout at Carbisdale and execution (May 21, 1650) at Edinburgh. He had fought for the *Carbisdale, 1650* Covenant and against it, but for one ideal—to release Scotland from the tyranny of Church, Crown, or Nobility. His loss and Cromwell's merciless vengeance on Ireland dashed Charles' prospects in the only fields of promise open to him. Four days after Montrose's capture, he bartered his conscience for the throne the Kirk offered him, accepted the Covenant, promised to impose it upon England and Ireland, and confirmed the ostracism of his partisans whom the Act of Classes condemned. On June 23, 1650, he arrived at Speymouth and swore to the two Covenants, a hateful obligation till then postponed. As a Covenanted sovereign he landed to invite the loyalty of a suspicious people.

The apparition of a Covenanted Stewart in Scotland was a challenge England could not disregard. Measures were devised to restrain royalist sym- *Charles II in Scotland* pathisers, money was raised on the lands of Malignants, and Cromwell was named to command a punitive expedition to confine Stewart and Covenant to the farther side of the Border. On July 22, 1650, with an army 16,000 strong, he entered Scotland. The country was prepared to meet the challenge; 18,000 foot and 8,000 horse had been raised under David Leslie's command. But the battle was lost before it was joined. With the enemy at its gates the Kirk clamoured to purge the army and entrust the Covenant's banners to none but its uncompromising professors. Denounced as the chief Malignant, his sincerity contemptuously questioned, Charles himself was banished beyond Forth, ejected from an army assembled to defend his throne. He was summoned, in a new declaration presented for his signature, to profess shame for his mother's idolatry, his father's blood-guiltiness; to confirm his unhappy pledge to prosecute the reformation of the English Church in accordance with the Covenant. Facing alternatives varyingly disagreeable—hypocritical surrender to ease uneasy consciences, or loss of the one army at his service to gain the English throne—Charles preferred the former. Resolving ' to swallow the pill before further chewing it,' he signed a document which, he said bitterly enough, prevented him from looking his mother in the face again. Meanwhile the army's purging proceeded. Engagers, Malignants, men of lukewarm attachment to the extremer Presbyterian cult, were sifted and expelled. Between 3000 and 4000 officers and men were dismissed as unworthy to *Battle of* fight for a cause which their ejectors had no *Dunbar, 1650* other means to defend. On September 3, 1650, the zealots did their last disservice, and forced David Leslie to engage Cromwell at Dunbar in circumstances which ordained his overwhelming defeat.

The disaster, reviving the shameful memories of Flodden and Solway Moss, was attributable to the Covenant which had embroiled Scotland with the Independents now dominant in England. It shook the hold of the zealots and opened the door to moderate counsels whose eventual victory set the Scottish Kirk upon a less extravagant foundation. While the extremists of the south-western counties presented a *Remonstrants* Remonstrance or Protest denouncing their alle-*and Resolu-* giance to the sovereign until by evident acts *tioners* he dissevered himself from persons and interests whose loyalty to the Covenants was suspect, the Moderates replied in a Resolution denouncing the Remonstrance as 'scandalous and injurious' to the kingdom by making the Covenants the test of public service. They spoke for the majority and won the cautious approval of Argyll. On January 1, 1651, the Marquess himself crowned Charles at Scone: the Act of Classes was repealed six months later: and all were invited to rally round the sovereign and free Scotland from the invader. But Charles's hopes were fixed above everything on winning the English throne. He convinced himself that his arrival among them would rally the English royalists, and in August 1651, evading Cromwell, put himself upon Hamilton's track. But few partisans joined him in England, where the Scots were unpopular and Charles' tactless association with the Lancashire Roman Catholics revived the suspicions which had assailed his father. On September 3, 1651, *Worcester Fight, 1651* Cromwell overtook him at Worcester and won his 'crowning mercy,' the last battle of the civil wars. Charles escaped to the Continent to await a more hopeful summons.

Worcester fight submitted Scotland to an unforeseen experience, a sudden experiment in the relations of the British kingdoms which endured for barely eight years. For a similar period Scotland had striven to impose upon England ecclesiastical uniformity. England, retaliating after Worcester, enforced upon Scotland ecclesiastical toleration and political union as well. Her degradation *The Cromwellian Union* was such as she had not known since Edward I struck her down. Her government was extinguished, her Committee of Estates captive, her armies overthrown, her king in exile. Only her Regalia, deep hidden in Dunottar Castle, preserved her sovereignty inviolate. The first purpose of her victor was to incorporate so much of Scotland as his armies occupied into the territory of the English Commonwealth. Abandoning that resolve the Long Parliament, in December 1651, announced its intention to unite Scotland with England in a single Commonwealth and 'to advance the power of true holiness' there, a phrase of ominous suggestion to Covenanted Presbyterianism. Early in 1652 the Scottish monarchy was formally annulled and delegates were summoned to Dalkeith from the shires and burghs to accept the English 'tender of union.' Very generally it was accepted: the means to resist it, indeed, were absent. Thereafter Scottish representatives journeyed to Westminster to assist Parliament in framing an Act of Union, whose details were finally promulgated in the Instrument of Government (December 1653). It fixed Scotland's representation in the United Parliament of England, Scotland, and Ireland at thirty members, abolished the Stewart monarchy and Scottish Estates, and established free trade between England and Scotland. In the House of Lords, subsequently restored (1657) by the Humble Petition and Advice, Scotland was allotted four seats.

Undisturbed save by the Earl of Glencairn's abortive rising in 1654, the Cromwellian Union held Scotland in firm, unrelaxing grip. The Highlands, where loyalty to the fallen Stewarts especially survived, were reduced by General Monk. A Scottish Council of State was set up in 1655, Justice of Peace Courts were appointed throughout the Lowlands, and the whole country experienced impartial government and even-handed justice. The arrogant and exclusive rule of Covenanted Presbyterianism was curbed, congregations of Independents were encouraged, and the General Assembly was summarily (1653) refused permission to meet without the authority of the civil power: it did not meet again for thirty-seven years after that year. On the other hand, true to its tolerant creed, Cromwell's government permitted the subordinate courts of the Presbyterian organization to continue, regulating impartially, however, the patronage of Church benefices.

Scotland may regard the Cromwellian Union with respect and even admiration. Like James VI the Protector aimed to incorporate two kingdoms in 'one worship of God, one

Kingdom entirely governed, one uniformity of law.' Like
his predecessor he quashed the General Assembly. Like
James he left the Church's Synods and Presbyteries undisturbed, willing to allow the Kirk liberty in its proper
sphere. Like James he dangled the prospect of free trade
with richer England before the poorer nation. He remodelled
its legal and judicial system, but wisely did not attempt to
harmonize English and Scots law. Like James he proposed
to undermine the antiquated polity of Highland Scotland.
And he gave the kingdom quiet. With little exaggeration it
was boasted that a man might ride over Lowland Scotland
with a switch in his hand and a hundred pounds in his
pocket, yet have no hurt. But the unity he conferred was
hollow and evanescent. Remarkable and admirable as the
experiment was, it was founded on Scotland's defeats at
Preston, Dunbar and Worcester, wounded the pride of a
proud people, and vanished with its author, respected, but
without regret.

Though the Restoration had its beginning in England,
Monk and his English army in Scotland directly
brought it about. The cry in England was for *The Restora-*
the cessation of military rule. That a free Par- *tion, 1660*
liament would abolish the Commonwealth and restore the
Monarchy was understood. Whether from conviction or ambition, Monk concluded to champion Parliamentary authority,
and, a fortnight after the dissolution of the Rump in October
1659, launched an enterprise which Scotsmen hoped would
also restore their king and independence. Summoning the
constituencies to send representatives to Edinburgh on 'an
especial occasion,' he announced his intention immediately
to return to England to assert the liberty of Parliaments,
protect the people of the three nations from tyrannical
military usurpation, and establish 'a godly ministry.' Com-
mitting the maintenance óf order in his absence to those
whom he addressed, he crossed the frontier, on January
1, 1660, a month later was in London, and restored the

Rump. At its fourth sitting it voted to set up the ancient constitution, a conclusion which restored to Scotland her independence and her monarchy. On May 14, 1660, Charles was proclaimed, a second time, at Edinburgh amid every token of satisfaction. His first act restored the Committee of Estates, dormant since 1651. On the first day of 1661 Parliament itself came together in its accustomed place and Scotland passed out of bondage.

CHAPTER XIII

THE LAST STEWARTS

CHARLES made no promises to Scotland preliminary to his return. Yet his restoration was welcomed in a spirit of extravagant joy. For nearly a quarter of a century the ancient constitution of the kingdom had been in abeyance while a generation grew to manhood which had not experienced the Cove- **Charles II, 1660–85** nants' emotions, and yet witnessed the consequences of their intolerance—a shattered monarchy, a Kirk torn by dissension, a bitter civil war. One hundred years spanned the interval between the Reformation and Charles' return: but the later event found Scottish Presbyterianism cloven into two bodies. The Whiggamore Protesters or Remonstrants, who rejected Charles in 1650, thought him as insincere now as then, a body whose principles, stubbornly rooted in the Covenants, raised the banner of rebellion at Rullion Green, Bothwell Bridge, and Drumclog. The Protesters, however, or Covenanters, as they are more generally styled, were a small, assertive minority, whose adherents were chiefly, but not exclusively, found in the south-western shires. The main body of Presbyterian feeling was represented by the Resolutioners, who accepted Charles as their sovereign in 1649 and were careless, now as then, to bind him to the Covenants, antiquated documents no longer congruous to circumstances, provided he gave the Kirk a Presbyterian constitution. Within their ranks were not a few inclined to moderate Episcopacy, and all anticipated the new sovereign's favour in recognition of their past fidelity to him. Of gratitude Charles was utterly devoid. He came back from his travels, a man of thirty, good tempered, indolent, versatile, clever, but with no sense of religion. He frankly admitted his preference for a Church ready to accept his authority as infallible, secretly bound himself to the Church of Rome therefore, and in Scotland restored Episcopacy, following a course prescribed by convenience and not by conscience. Whether Scotland, chastened by her experiences in the interval, would permit her sovereign to succeed where his father and grandfather had failed was the problem of the generation that followed the Restoration.

The new king's earliest acts declared his refusal to have *Lauderdale* dealings with the Covenanters, at whose hands he once had suffered deep humiliation. Glencairn, who raised the royal standard in 1654, was named Chancellor; the Earl of Middleton, a hard drinking soldier, Glencairn's associate in 1654, was appointed commander-in-chief and High Commissioner for holding Parliament. Other nobles who had suffered in the king's cause received the Treasury and Presidency of the Council, while the Secretaryship of State was given to the Earl of Lauderdale, one of the signatories of the Engagement, who had fought at Worcester and suffered imprisonment, a heavy, ungainly man, of brilliant attainments, a settled Presbyterian at heart, but contemptuous of principles where his interests and lust of power were involved. His office kept him at the king's side at Court and permitted him to dictate or control his policy. For twenty years he ruled Scotland.

On January 1, 1661, after an interval of nine years, Par-*The Restora-* liament assembled at Edinburgh. The con-*tion Settle-* stituencies having been carefully nursed, nobles *ment*, 1661 and commoners gathered in a mood of obsequiousness beyond the ordinary, sat for six months, and restored at a stroke the autocracy of James VI and his son. The appointment of Officers of State was declared an inherent privilege of the Crown and an undoubted part of the royal prerogative, while the power to hold, prorogue, and dissolve Parliaments was proclaimed to reside solely in the King's Majesty. Further Acts placed the control of the

Militia, making of peace and war, conclusion of treaties or leagues with foreign states, exclusively within the royal prerogative, while an Act Rescissory expunged from the Statute Book all measures subsequent to the Parliament of 1633, and consequently made Episcopacy automatically the government of the Church 'as it is settled by law.' An annual grant of £40,000 put it in Charles' power to maintain a standing force in Scotland, an engine of discipline which none of his predecessors had possessed.

The Act Rescissory deprived the Presbyterian Church of a constitutional status. What should replace it *James Sharp* was not revealed until the following September. Meanwhile, Glencairn proceeded to London, in company with James Sharp, minister of Crail, the leader of the Resolutioners for ten years past—'Sharp of that Ilk,' Cromwell called him, admiring his supple intelligence. Though his opinions were not rigid, he looked back on the late 'troubles' with dismay, convinced that the new generation had no love for Presbytery, and that, as he expressed himself, 'were it putt [to] the vote [in Parliament] within ten dayes episcopacy would [be] sett up.' That his opposition to Episcopacy would have been effectual cannot be alleged. To impeach him as the traitor within a fortress otherwise impregnable exaggerates his influence and opportunity. He was ambitious, not ill-meaning, a weak man at bottom, disposed to join the stronger side, and loosely grounded in Puritan principles. But his correspondence convicts him of persistent duplicity. On the eve of his departure in 1661 he announced to a friend his employment on a 'new toil,' and added, 'but I tell you it is not in order to a change of the Church.' Before the end of the year he was a bishop!

Meanwhile in Scotland the Privy Council was set up, to which, in August 1661, Glencairn reported the king's resolution to restore the Scottish Church *Episcopacy restored, 1662* to its government by bishops as it was by law before the late troubles. The Council was directed to recover the endowments of the revived Sees and repress public protests against the royal order. In September Charles' decision was proclaimed and cheerful acquiescence was commanded. It needed only Parliamentary ratification. In May 1662, the Estates restored their 'ancient constitution.' Sharp and eight other ministers, having received episcopal consecration, forthwith took their places in Parliament and upon the Committee of Articles. A fortnight later they were confirmed in their former dignities, privileges, jurisdictions, and power of ordination. To complete their authority a further Act (June 1662) directed all ministers who, by virtue of the Act of 1649 abolishing lay patronage, were holding their charges on the appointment of congregations or Presbyteries, to obtain presentation from the lawful patron and admission by their diocesan bishop before September 20 following. The Act effectually purged the Church of its Covenanter wing. Of the whole body of clergy something less than one-third, preferring to 'suffer rather than sin,' gave up their livings. The Universities were submitted to similar winnowing, and all persons in public trust were ordered to abjure the Covenant.

Thus Episcopacy was again erected. But Charles' system lacked the provocations of his father's. Kirk Sessions, Presbyteries, and Synods continued to function as they had done without interruption since 1638. The ritual of Presbyterian worship was not disturbed. 'Conceived,' that is, extempore prayers and the Psalter provided the apparatus of public devotion. The Perth Articles were ignored: there was no altar, no surplice, no liturgy, no kneeling at Communion. But the bishops, surrounded by sinister associations, were again in their accustomed seats, clothed both with political and ecclesiastical authority. Their restoration, besides, was open to a charge of treachery and of ingratitude to the majority of a Presbyterian body who had welcomed the sovereign's restoration and were disposed to yield more to him than to either of his immediate predecessors. Moreover

the Covenants provided martyrs. Chief among them was
Argyll, unfairly condemned to death for compliance with
Cromwell's rule. An Act of Indemnity, tardily conceded
(September 1662), excepted some eight hundred   *Fall of*
persons, among whom Middleton strove to in-   *Middleton,*
clude Lauderdale himself. He paid the penalty   1663
of his daring and was recalled. With his fall the recon-
structive work of the Restoration was complete (March
1663).

Middleton's place as the Crown's Viceroy in Scotland was
taken by the Earl of Rothes, son of the famous Covenanter,
a genial drunkard who defended his lax morals on the logical
plea that his office represented the king's person. Sharp, as
Archbishop of St Andrews, and his colleague Alexander
Burnet, Archbishop of Glasgow, were added to the Council,
and along with Rothes were responsible for a repressive
policy which reaped its sowing in the Pentland Rising.

Parliament assembled under the new Commissioner in
June 1663, and, having restored the mode of electing the
Committee of the Articles which made the bishops its master,
passed (July 1663) an Act fruitful in disquiet   *The Bishops'*
hereafter. The measure, entitled an 'Act against   *Drag-net,*
separation and disobedience to ecclesiastical   1663
authority,' popularly known as the 'Bishops' Drag-net,'
subjected all persons who absented themselves wilfully from
their parish churches to fines and such 'corporal punishment'
as the Council might ordain. The purpose of the Act was
to compel conformity; it put into the hands of the Council
a weapon of discipline whose employment shortly drove the
Covenanted population of south-west Scotland to revolt.
While the rest of Scotland submitted quietly to the restoration of Episcopacy and lay patronage, the ministers within
the Synods of Dumfries, Glasgow and Ayr, and Galloway
vacated their livings almost to a man. To replace them was
difficult, but from the Universities and conforming Synods
a number of ministers, contemptuously styled 'Bishops'

Curates,' were introduced who vainly sought to serve their parishioners. Church doors were locked against them, bell clappers were detached and secreted to excuse the obligation of church-going, and 'bare walls and nobody to preach unto' was the common experience of the interlopers, whose parishioners preferred the ministrations of their 'outed'

Beginning of Conventicleism (ejected) pastors, and resorted to them in conventicles held in the open fields. The practice began in the Presbytery of Dumfries, became general in the south-west, and invited the Council's angry reprisals. Nonconforming ministers were bidden remove themselves at least twenty miles from their former parishes: a High Commission, styled 'Crail Court' by its enemies, on which the bishops preponderated, was set up to deal with nonconformity, and Sir James Turner, a soldier 'naturally fierce, but mad when he was drunk, and often so,' was given a force of cavalry charged to fine absentees from church. Towards the end of 1664 he was instructed to exact fines from persons named in the Act of Indemnity and also to disarm the troublesome south-western shires, the government being apprehensive of collusion between them and the Dutch, with whom England at that time was at war. More troops were raised, to a strength of about 3000, an establishment strange to Scotland's experience in time of peace, whose charges were met by the Indemnity fines, an added reason for their savage enforcement. Landlords were arbitrarily held responsible for the conduct of their tenants, and all were searched suspiciously for possession of arms. The whole area seethed with disaffection till a sudden scuffle blazed into rebellion.

On November 13, 1666, a party of nonconformists at

The Pentland Rising, 1666 Dalry, near Dumfries, came upon some of Turner's troopers threatening a prisoner who refused to pay his church fines. A scuffle followed: the soldiers drew their swords and one of their number fell, 'barbarously shot in the body with a great many pieces of tobacco pipes, ten whereof afterward were by the surgeon's care taken out.' Turner was at Dumfries and instant reprisals could be looked for. Sending out a hasty summons, the Whigs named a rendezvous at Irongray next day, proposing a dash on Dumfries. Early on the 15th about fifty horse rode into the town, abducted Turner in his night-gown, nightcap, drawers and socks, and impounded his papers and money. Having gone too far to retreat, they resolved to beat for recruits in Ayrshire, rendezvoused on the 21st near Bridge of Doon, about seven hundred strong, and had a valuable recruit in James Wallace, who gave competent military guidance to a force otherwise deficient in it. An advance on Glasgow was mooted and abandoned on the news that Sir Thomas Dalziel, an officer lately in Russian service, was gathering his forces there, preparatory to an advance. Edinburgh was reported friendly, and the prospect of supporting action by the Dutch fleet lured the Whigs towards the capital. In weather vile and most de-pressing the weary march was continued to Lanark where the whole force, about 1200 strong, renewed the Covenant. Unofficial overtures promised pardon if they would lay down their arms. But their hearts were high, and the ad-vance proceeded. At Colinton on the 28th the vanity of their hopes was patent; Edinburgh was close guarded and Dalziel hot on their track. Before nightfall he forced an action at Rullion Green on the Pentlands and brought the rash adven-ture to an end. About fifty of the insurgents were left dead on the field. More were made prisoners.

The brief rebellion alarmed the government and goaded it to severity. Dalziel reported that the country would not obtain quiet until 'that damned crew' in the Whig counties had been destroyed or removed. Rothes clamoured for them to be 'totally ruined.' A Commission of Justiciary was forth-with set up to aid the military: the criminal Courts were overworked. At Edinburgh and Glasgow offenders were hanged, their dissevered arms being exposed at Lanark where they had been held up to swear the Covenant. But milder counsels gradually prevailed. Sharp, disappointed of the Chancellorship, was ordered to confine himself to his own diocese: Rothes was dismissed: the standing forces were considerably reduced, and in October 1667 an Act of Indemnity, though clogged with exception of the ringleaders, was offered to all engaged in the recent rebellion. Charles' policy, guided by Lauderdale was now upon 'measures of moderation and comprehension,' realizing the unwisdom of the provocations which had goaded a minority of the Presbyterian body to revolt.

Not for long did the government stand upon its new course. The disbanding of the army and Act of Indemnity encouraged marked increase in the number of house-conventicles, and a spirit was abroad which revealed itself in July 1668, when a youth named James Mitchell shot a brace of bullets into Sharp's coach in full daylight in an Edinburgh street and narrowly missed his intended victim. A year later Lauderdale launched an insidious policy which, in the result, achieved the ends repression had failed to *The First* accomplish and rent Covenanted Presbyterianism *Indulgence,* to the foundations. In July 1669 the Privy 1669   Council was instructed to announce a measure, hereafter distinguished as the First Indulgence, which proposed to restore to their churches, manses, and stipends such ministers 'outed' in 1662 as since had lived 'peaceably and orderly,' provided their old livings were vacant and they accepted episcopal induction. To those who refused that condition manse and glebe were offered, with such a sum for maintenance as the Council might contribute from the revenue of vacant benefices. All who were restored were pledged to attend Presbyteries and Sessions, confine their ministrations to their own parishes, and refrain from seditious discourse or expressions in the pulpit. About forty-two ministers availed themselves of conditions which, the Council declared hopefully, removed 'all pretences for Conventicles.'

Their surrender compromised the essential principle of Presbyterianism—the Church's independence of secular authority—and divided the Covenant's once irresistible ranks. By their old parishioners they were treated with something of the contempt which the Bishops' Curates had received. 'King's Curates,' 'Council's Curates,' 'dumb dogs that can not bark,' were names hurled at them in contumely.

The Indulgence, conflicting with the legislation of 1662, which forbade persons not collated by their diocesan bishop to preach, was for that reason not agreeable to the bishops. Burnet of Glasgow thundered so strong a denunciation of it that, in punishment, he was bidden confine himself to his city. An assertion of the royal prerogative therefore was necessary to enable the Crown to carry its purposes against a bench no longer wholly sympathetic. But the Assertory Act (November 1669) declaring the *Assertory Act, 1669* king's 'supreme authority and supremacy over all persons and in all causes ecclesiastical within this his kingdom' was extravagant in its scope. It alleged the Crown's unqualified right to control the Church's administration, meetings, and officers, and declared null and void all laws and customs inconsistent with the supremacy thus declared. 'You may now dispose of Bishops and Ministers, and remove and transplant them as you please (which I doubt you can not do in England),' Lauderdale reported triumphantly to Charles. On the same day the Estates passed an Act authorizing the raising of a militia of 22,000 to replace the army disbanded in 1667, a force declared liable to serve in 'any part of his Majesty's dominions.' 'If you command it,' Lauderdale wrote joyously to his master, 'not only this Militia, but all the fensible men in Scotland, shall march when and where you shall please to command, for never was King so absolute as you are in poor old Scotland.' Such was Lauderdale's work. It restored to the monarchy the autocracy which the Civil Wars had disturbed, secured his

master's favour for ten years, but laid a foundation upon
which James VII built to his undoing.

While he remained constant in his resolution to make
himself the minister of an absolute monarch, cir-
The 'Clank-
ing Act,' 1670   cumstances caused Lauderdale again to modify
his policy towards the nonconformists. In 1669
he revived an earlier intimacy with Elizabeth Countess of
Dysart, a woman of brilliant ability, ambitious, and un-
principled. Lauderdale, who married her, became in consequence, a contemporary remarked, 'quite another sort of
man than he had been in all the former parts of his life.'
Presbyterian though he was, his mood towards the nonconformists changed to severity, influenced also by a disconcerting revival of field-conventicles to which, refusing
the ministrations of the established and indulged ministers,
bands of nonconforming Whigs resorted in arms. Even
outside the Whig area, notably in Lothian and Fifeshire,
field-conventicles began to be held. The government suspecting that another rebellion was being hatched, Lauderdale,
in August 1670, obtained from Parliament what he termed
'a Clanking Act' against Conventicles. Unlicensed ministers
and others attending house prayer-meetings or preachings
where more than the family were present were made liable
to severe penalties. Field-conventicles were declared treasonable and, for the preacher, punishable with death. By other
Acts 'outed' ministers were forbidden to baptize, and persons absenting themselves from their parish church on three
successive Sundays incurred heavy fines. Still, Conventicleism increased. Fiery zealots, rabbling the houses of conforming ministers, robbed and wounded them. Lauderdale,
moved to fury almost ungovernable, prayed for a rebellion
which should permit him to bring over the Irish 'to cut all
their throats.' Meanwhile the outbreak of the Dutch War
afforded opportunity to enlarge the lengthening list of Acts
against nonconformity. Illegal ordinations were made punishable by confiscation of goods and banishment. Fines were

imposed on persons failing to have their children baptized by their parish minister, and the 'Clanking Act' of 1670 was continued for three years beyond its approaching expiry in 1673. In September 1672, to divide the Presbyterian ranks still further, the Council issued a Second In- *The Second* dulgence to about eighty ministers ejected in *Indulgence,* 1662, who were now offered livings, chiefly in *1672* the diocese of Glasgow, upon the conditions of the First Indulgence. The offer worked its subtle poison. 'The Presbyterians, who before this had been very much of a piece, did now divide'; those who conformed held it reasonable to accept livings from which they had been unlawfully excluded; the extremists scouted the Indulgence as an act of unlawful secular authority.

Encouraged by success in dividing its enemies, the government neither feared nor scrupled to pro- *The Highland* ceed vigorously against the irreconcilables, *Host, 1678* stirred to activity by the defection of so many of their leaders. House- and field-conventicles became as general in Fife, Perth, the Merse, as below the Forth. Nonconforming ministers, preaching to large audiences, sometimes in the fields, sometimes in vacant churches, even in Edinburgh itself, provoked the Council to revive a discipline formerly imposed upon the Roman Catholics. In June 1674 landlords and masters were bound in damages to restrain their tenants and servants from attending house- and field-conventicles, and rewards were offered for the apprehension of ministers frequenting them. A year later (August 1675), 'unsatisfied with this small game of picking up a minister here and there,' the Council issued 'letters of intercommuning' against more than one hundred persons, a process which made those who entertained or conversed with them art and part in their offence. Troops patrolled the disturbed districts, local garrisons were quartered in private houses, but failed to enforce the irksome obligation. Hence, in February 1678, at the ploughing season, eight or nine thousand Highlanders and Lowland militia were distributed throughout Ayrshire to enforce the bond and disarm the county. The Highland Host behaved with 'exorbitant rudeness and insolence,' exacted free quarters from an indignant population, and after a month withdrew, laden with spoil as if from a battlefield.

Lauderdale's measures deliberately provoked rebellion. 'There was no pre-concert, but the oppressed people gradually fell into the rising by a chain of things making it some way necessary to them.' Its beginning was as unpremeditated as that of 1666. On May 3, 1679, lurking on Magus Muir near St Andrews to apprehend one of Sharp's agents, certain outlawed Whigs falling in with the archbishop himself travelling with his daughter from Edinburgh, pistolled and hacked him to death before her eyes. Three weeks later a larger band, the archbishop's murderers among them, entered Rutherglen, burned the Acts since 1661 which established and supported Episcopacy, and withdrew after affixing their Declaration or Testimony. Similar signs of active dissent had recently (1678) caused the raising of three new troops of horse, to the command of one of which John Graham of Claverhouse, lately in service in the Low Countries, had been promoted. Encounters had already taken place with the Whigs, whose leaders, Claverhouse inferred, were accustoming them to face regular troops. It fell to him to track the authors of the Rutherglen defiance. On June 1, 1679, he came upon them at Drumclog, near Strathavon, in superior numbers and a position not easily accessible. Eager to distinguish himself on the threshold of his career, he engaged and was repulsed. 'This may be counted the beginning of the rebellion,' was his report to his superiors.

Drumclog was a trumpet-call to the persecuted. They flocked in hundreds to Hamilton, a devoted mob prating of 'testimonies' but at fierce issue upon the terms of them. Had James Wallace, who headed the revolt of 1666, been

Drumclog, 1679

present, another story might have been told. Robert Hamilton, whom social position marked out for leadership, had no other qualification. While the forces of the government fell back on Stirling to await reinforcement, the insurgents occupied Glasgow (June 6) and misspent a fortnight in wrangling and indecision. The Moderates affixed their Testimony to Hamilton Cross. The 'honest' or non-Indulged, demanding a stringent testimony against 'the defections and apostacies of the times,' condemned it as inadequate and called for explicit repudiation of the Indulgence.

Meanwhile the government was taking large measures to quell the sudden revolt. The Militia were called out, and reinforcements were dispatched to Berwick by sea. The Duke of Monmouth, *Bothwell Bridge*, 1679 favourite of the English nonconformists, judiciously selected for the command, reached Edinburgh on June 18, 1679. Two days later he advanced towards Hamilton Moor, where the insurgents were encamped. On June 22 the armies faced each other, Bothwell Bridge intervening. By ten in the morning the Whigs were in utter rout with a loss in killed and prisoners of nearly one-third of their strength. The survivors scattered before Monmouth's cavalry. Seven persons were hanged, but of 1400 prisoners most were released. About two hundred, shipped for Barbadoes, were drowned in a storm at sea. Meanwhile, on his return to Court, Monmouth convinced Charles that 'all this madness of field-conventicles' flowed only from the severity against those that were held within doors. His interest procured an Indemnity for the recent rebellion and a third Indulgence (June 1679) which, enforcing the standing laws against field-conventicles, *The Third Indulgence*, 1679 authorized house-conventicles elsewhere than in the immediate neighbourhood of Edinburgh, St Andrews, Glasgow, and Stirling, a concession subsequently withdrawn (May 1680). Meanwhile the rebellion destroyed Lauderdale's credit with his master. Stripped of his honours and offices, he died in 1682. The nonconformists were obnoxious to him as rebellious subjects, not as religious dissidents. Those who followed him treated rebellion as an excuse for religious persecution and doomed the dynasty that authorized it to expulsion from its kingdoms.

Three Indulgences in ten years drew all but a corner of the kingdom into an establishment nominally Episcopal but innocent of the aggravations which invited the Covenant in 1638. The irreconcilables, self-styled 'the godly' and 'the honest' party, continued to denounce the royal supremacy as a deposition of Christ from his proper headship of the Church, assailing the conforming ministers as traitors to the outworn Covenants, and defying the government as the destroyer of 'the Lord's established religion' and setter-up of 'an Erastian [State controlled] synagogue.' This active and violent minority bears the name of one of its two leaders—Richard Cameron and Donald Cargill. The former was in Holland during the Bothwell rising. Returning to Scotland in the spring of 1680 he found the 'honest' party crushed and hopeless, appealed to many non-Indulged pastors to serve the scattered flock as preachers, and, the times being 'so very hazardous,' was refused by all but Donald Cargill, who had fought at Bothwell Bridge. Determined boldly to make their testimony against the evil their consciences condemned, the two men and nineteen other persons on June 22, 1680, the first anniversary of Monmouth's victory, rode into Sanquhar and affixed to the market cross 'a most treasonable and unparalleled paper.' It denounced Charles' 'perjury' to the Covenant, 'usurpation' of Christ's rule over the Kirk, and 'tyranny in matters civil.' 'Considering the great hazard of lying under such a sin any longer,' the small band of Cameronians disowned 'Charles Stuart,' declared war upon him and all others who should betray 'our free reformed mother-Kirk unto the bondage of Antichrist the Pope of Rome.' In particular they named the king's brother

The Came-ronians

the Duke of York, a Papist who lately had followed Monmouth in Scotland to reverse his policy of conciliation.

The Council received this document with horror and
offered 5000 marks for Cameron's arrest, dead
or alive. A month later the irreconcilables met   *Airds Moss,*
the fate their daring invited. In July 1680 their   *1680*
party was surprised at Airds Moss, near Auchinleck in Ayrshire. Cameron was killed on the spot. David Hackston of
Rathillet, one of Sharp's murderers, made prisoner there,
was executed with the barbarities the law prescribed. Of the
leaders only Cargill remained. With undaunted spirit, at
Torwood near Stirling in September, 1680, he pronounced
sentence of excommunication upon the Dukes of York,
Monmouth, and Lauderdale, Rothes, Dalziel, and Sir George
Mackenzie, the Lord Advocate and conductor of the recent
prosecutions. The rodomontade of this surviving pontiff of
a Presbyterian Rump exasperated the government further.
In November a reward was offered for Cargill's apprehension, dead or alive; three of his followers were hanged at the
Market Cross, Edinburgh, in December. The soldiery and
Justiciary courts were active in the south-western counties,
beating energetically for evidence against suspected participants in the Bothwell rising. Cargill, apprehended in
July 1681, boldly upheld the lawfulness of political assassination. He could expect and received no quarter. On July 27,
1681, the day before the Duke of York opened
the last Parliament of the reign, he was exe-   *Cargill exe-*
cuted with four of his adherents. In the following   *cuted, 1681*
October five more sufferers followed the same road. The
Cameronians were headless, as divided from their Presbyterian brethren as from the government that persecuted
them, until in 1683 James Renwick, returning from Holland,
revived them and provoked the Killing Time.

So far the Cameronian Covenanters rallied a meagre host
of supporters. Events were imminent, however, which startled
conformist no less than nonconforming Presbyterianism,

ranged the whole force of public opinion against the monarchy,
and at the Revolution expelled the Stewarts irretrievably.
On July 28, 1681, the Duke of York, as High Commissioner,
opened the last Parliament of his brother's reign. His purpose was at once to secure his own succession to the throne
and at the same time offer safeguards to the Protestant
establishment which the accession of himself, a Roman
Catholic sovereign, seemed to advise. They were provided
by an Act which confirmed the measures of past Parliaments
'made against Popery,' but chiefly by one,
Test Act, hereafter known as the Test Act, which called
1681   upon public authorities to put into sternest
operation the laws against Papists as well as 'all fanatic
separatists' from the established Church. As a test of
orthodoxy a lengthy and contradictory oath was devised
for tender to all persons holding civil and ecclesiastical office,
requiring them to swear fidelity to the Confession of Faith of
1567, accept the royal supremacy in ecclesiastical matters,
and denounce rebellion against the king and his authority.
An oath simultaneously pledging the subscriber to maintain
the Confession of Faith and the royal supremacy which that
docnment explicitly denied deserved ridicule as a medley of
self-contradiction. Moreover, direct repudiation of the Covenants also offended a larger public than the Sanquhar
Declaration spoke for. Many officials in high office refused
the Test, among them Argyll, the son of the first Marquess,
who took it with a qualifying clause, 'as far as it is con-
sistent with itself and the Protestant religion.' Condemned
to death, he escaped to Holland, and there remained till
he headed an abortive rebellion against his Roman Catholic
sovereign in 1685.

Determined to hold the country so securely that nothing
should impede the Duke's succession at his brother's death,
the government wantonly provoked the passive nonconformists, whom at all hazards they should have placated,
by treating them as abettors of the Cameronian fanatics.

Claverhouse, lately appointed Hereditary Sheriff of Wigtown, was sent into the south-west to put the policy into effect and was singularly successful in compelling at least an appearance of conformity. But his duties and the anxieties of his employers were enlarged by renewed Cameronian activity. In the autumn of 1683 *James Renwick, 1683* James Renwick, a precocious youth of twenty lately ordained in Holland, took up Cargill's mantle. A year later (November 1684) he published his 'Apologetical Declaration and Admonitory Vindication,' in which, alleging the 'sinless necessity for self-preservation' and repugnance of the 'hellish principle of killing,' he threatened the government and its officials to withstand them 'according to our power.' The threat was translated instantly into practice. On November 20, 1684, a couple of lifeguardsmen were shot dead in cold blood at Blackburn in Linlithgow. Three weeks later (December 11), in circumstances of peculiar brutality, the conforming minister of Carsphairn in Kirkcudbrightshire was enticed to his door and shot dead as he opened it to four armed men; he was suspected to be an informer. Five days afterwards a band of above one hundred, the Carsphairn murderers among them, raided Kirkcudbright, released the prisoners, seized arms, and rode off with impunity till Claverhouse overtook them at Bridge of Dee (December 18), made three prisoners, and left five of them dead in the track of their flight. The Council rose to the crisis. On November 22, 1684, it prescribed the terms of an oath to be offered by competent authority to any person, requiring him to abjure Renwick's Declaration. The penalty for refusal was summary execution in the presence of two witnesses.

Such was the situation when Charles II expired (February 6, 1685) and James VII and II entered upon his brief sovereignty. The new king was as deter- *James VII, 1685-88* mined as his father to maintain his prerogative against opposition, civil and religious, and as bigoted to settle an ecclesiastical establishment his subjects abhorred. From his early youth he exhibited a spirit of audacity which provoked him to run risks where his inclination was engaged. He was easily led by those who flattered and as obstinate against those who opposed him, having been bred to suppose all who resisted the king rebels at heart. Possessing neither the natural cleverness nor the indolence of his predecessor, he permitted himself to be guided by a dull conscientiousness which drove him to relieve his co-religionists of the Roman Church of the disabilities the Reformation had imposed upon them. In England he discarded his hitherto enforced custom to attend Mass in private. In Scotland he evaded the obligation to take the coronation oath to maintain the Protestant religion. In neither kingdom did he venture at once to raise the question of Roman Catholic relief. But to apprehensive Protestant consciences his very accession consummated 'a deep laid plot of hell and Rome to introduce Popery and slavery.' The Renwickites were stirred to passionate activity and the government paid them in their own coin. The liability to accept the oath rejecting the Apologetical Declaration remained in force: summary execution in the presence of two witnesses was the legal penalty for refusal.

The first three months of the new reign are distinguished as the 'Killing Time.' That its proportions are very grossly exaggerated in popular literature is patent from the discrepancy between the actual and alleged severities of Claverhouse, in the eye of tradition the most savage executant of savage laws. Claverhouse's victims in the Killing Time actually were eight misguided sufferers for Renwick's Declaration, and represent his activities on but four occasions. Five of the eight lives were taken in an armed encounter with the fugitive raiders of Kirkcudbright and murderers of the Carsphairn minister on December 18, 1684. The other three, in May 1685, are cases of summary execution, of which John Brown

The 'Killing Time,' 1685

of Priesthill's is the most familiar but not the most poignant. He was a man well on in years, a carrier by occupation, expressly excluded from the Indemnity in March 1685 as one who refused the oath of allegiance. He had fought at Bothwell Bridge, arms were found underground near his house, and 'treasonable papers' were in his possession. Suspect as a Renwickite, he was offered the Abjuration Oath and refused it. 'I caused shoot him dead, which he suffered very unconcernedly,' Claverhouse reported. Ten days later, by other agents, two women, Margaret Lauchlison or McLachlan and Margaret Wilson, the one over sixty years old, the other under twenty, were drowned at Wigtown as self-convicted Renwickites by their refusal to take the Abjuration Oath. Repugnant to modern consciences, the crime of their death lightly scarred that of a generation whose civilization was disgraced by witch-hunting.

Parliament, which assembled in April 1685, its members elected for the first and only time on the Test Act, showered proofs of loyalty on the new king, anathemas on the Covenanters who denied his authority, and rose unanimously to his invitation 'to rid ourselves of these men and of all who incline to their principles.' Owning and defending the Covenant and Solemn League was made a treasonable offence; preachers at house- or field-conventicles and hearers at field-conventicles were declared liable to death; and a new tender of the Test was ordered. When Parliament rose in the middle of June it had entirely fulfilled James' purposes.

James was now assailed from another quarter. To Argyll, exiled in Holland, he was a mortal enemy whose overthrow alone could restore to him his liberty. Soon after Charles II's death *Argyll's Revolt, 1685* simultaneous rebellions in England and Scotland were concerted: Monmouth, encouraged to assert his legitimacy against his usurping uncle, would try his fortune in England: Argyll, as little a man of war as his father, was to precede him to Scotland by about ten days. His Campbell country was occupied by the Marquess of Atholl at the earliest rumour of his design. His associates, Sir Patrick Home of Polwarth and Sir John Cochrane of Ochiltree, suspected as Malignants, made no appeal to the Renwickites, who alone seemed disposed to deal a stroke against the king. The leaders, moreover, were divided and schism bereft the enterprise of every prospect of success. Leaving Holland on May 1, 1685, the ships touched at Kintyre, where time was spent in launching a Declaration of repellent length denouncing the government's evident purpose 'to bring us back, not only to Popery, but to paganism' at the bidding of 'a notorious apostate and bigot papist.' The indictment was little heeded. Only a meagre three or four hundred of his name rallied to Argyll at Campbeltown, and Sir Duncan Campbell of Auchinbreck joined with eight hundred men. Proposing to recover his Castle of Inveraray, whose garrison was weak, Argyll moved up Loch Fyne. Cochrane and the Lowland contingent insisted that Ayrshire promised more favourable ground and demanded to try their fortune there. Argyll yielded and Cochrane and Polwarth crossed to Greenock. Watched by English frigates, they found an apathetic welcome, and rejoined their chief, who now resumed the interrupted march on Inveraray, leaving his ships and stores under the shelter of Eilean Dearg. But the news that his base was blockaded by English frigates compelled him to retire round Gareloch, heading for the Clyde and Lowland succours. Closely pursued, his dwindling force scattered and he himself was made prisoner in a chance encounter. He was sent to the block a few days later (June 30, 1685) on the old charge and without further trial.

The collapse of his enemies in England and Scotland encouraged James to broach the purpose closest to his heart. In November 1685 he summoned the English Parliament to hear his resolution to employ Roman Catholics despite the Test Act. In Scotland converts in high position already had been made. The Earl

The Dispensing Power

of Perth, Chancellor, and his brother Lord Melfort, one of the Secretaries of State, announced their adoption of James' religion and alleged his instrumentality in their conversion. Ministers whose opposition to the new trend of the king's policy was not concealed were removed and the Catholic Duke of Gordon was admitted without oath to the Captaincy of Edinburgh Castle. Public opinion was deeply stirred: Protestant riots took place in Edinburgh, and the Estates, meeting in April 1686, firmly resisted James' invitation to repeal the penal laws against those of his religion.

In Scotland as in England James fell back upon the dispensing power to achieve his purposes, and used it with particular boldness. Announcing his resolution to establish 'our chapel within our Palace of Holyrood,' he caused its Protestant fittings to be burned to make way for a Catholic equipment. A printing press under Jesuit direction was set up in the Palace and a Jesuit school was established in the same quarters. Bishops were deprived, Privy Councillors ejected, and public officials were dismissed whose consciences would not bend to the king's will. In February 1687 a first Indulgence announced the suspension of all penal laws against Roman Catholics and offered a bribe to Protestant objectors by authorizing house-conventicles, provided no treasonable discourses were uttered in them. The Indulgence, giving the Catholics a footing they had not held since the Reformation, was strongly opposed inside the Council, and failed to purchase the support necessary to give permanence to the work on which James was set. Presbyterian consciences particularly opposed an oath of non-resistance, substituted for the Test, which asserted the royal supremacy and unlawfulness of resistance. In June 1687, therefore, anxious to unite Presbyterian and Roman Catholic in common acceptance of his policy of toleration, James made complete surrender to Presbyterian prejudices: full religious freedom was accorded to nonconformists, except in field-conventicles: it was stipulated that their chapels should be conducted with the authorities' knowledge of their where-abouts and ministers. Only the Cameronians stood out against the insidious bargain, but in February 1688 lost their leader. Captured in hiding, Renwick stubbornly re-fused to acknowledge the king's authority and died affirming the Covenants, the outworn shibboleths of an earlier day.

The birth of an heir to James in June 1688, promising

William of Orange

to perpetuate the provocations of his rule, at once provoked a revolution in England which Scotland contributed nothing to bring about, but from which so much to her lasting benefit resulted. Solicited by the English Whigs William of Orange undertook to appear as the Protestant champion of the kingdom's laws and liberties. So soon as his preparations were known, the Scottish Council, acting in the interests of James, called out the militia of the eastern counties to meet an anticipated landing. Later, when William's course bent towards England, the whole standing military establishment in Scotland, ex-cepting the garrisons of Edinburgh, Stirling, and Dumbarton Castles, was drawn southward to confront the invader. On November 5, 1688, William landed at Torbay and published a Declaration of the purposes of his coming. As to Scotland he announced his resolution to free her 'from all hazard of Popery and arbitrary power for the future,' and to summon Parliament to set the kingdom's civil and ecclesiastical establishments on a basis of national approval.

Despite the Council's care to suppress it, William's Decla-ration was widely published and stirred enthusiasm and hope in Scotland. The archbishops were burned in effigy, Holyrood Chapel was raided, and before the end of the year the Duke of Gordon in Edinburgh Castle alone represented the authority of his sovereign. On December 18 James himself left White-hall for ever, and three weeks later (January 7, 1689) over one hundred Scottish notables presented themselves before the Prince of Orange in St James' Palace to advise him how best to secure Protestant interests in Scotland. They urged the summoning of a Convention in March, and meanwhile invited the Prince to undertake the provisional administration of the kingdom. A month later England showed the way for Scotland's following: on February 13, 1689, William and his consort, the fugitive James' daughter, were proclaimed in London joint sovereigns as William III and Mary II.

The promised Convention sat down at Edinburgh on March 14, 1689. The episcopal bench was full, and James' partisans (Jacobites) were present by their master's permission, headed by Claver- *The Convention, 1689* house, created Viscount of Dundee shortly before James' flight, with a commission to watch his interests in Scotland. From the outset it was clear that William's supporters had a majority: their nominee was preferred as President of the Convention; and a letter from James was only listened to after a resolution had been passed to disobey it if it contained an order to dissolve. The communication showed no sense of the gravity of the situation, peremptorily bade the Convention fulfil its allegiance to its lawful sovereign, and created consternation among the Jacobites by its stubborn disregard of the circumstances. Dundee called at once upon his associates to secede, alleging, not without reason, that their lives were in jeopardy at the hands of angry Cameronians concealed in the city. On March 18, with a single troop of horse, he rode northward to the city whose title he bore: the timid Jacobites withdrew to their homes, leaving behind them in the Convention a solid party to accomplish its purposes.

A week after Dundee's flight the Convention turned to the legislative measures necessary to resolve the crisis. A Committee, from which the bishops were excluded, was set up and, closely following the procedure of the English Parliament, produced a Claim of Right, adopted on April 11, 1689, nearly a month after the Convention's first sitting. It rehearsed the late sovereign's *William II and Mary II, 1689-94*

misdoings and acknowledged William and Mary as King
and Queen of Scotland, with succession to the queen's issue,
whom failing, to the queen's sister Anne and her heirs, whom
failing, to the heirs of William himself. In two particulars
the Act differed from the English Declaration of Right
passed in the previous February. On the ground that James,
'being a professed Papist, did assume the regal power, and
acted as king, without ever taking the oath required by
law,' it declared the crown 'forfeited.' In the second place,
the Act interpolated a resolution, 'that prelacy, and the
superiority of any office in the Church above presbyters, is,
and hath been, a great and insupportable grievance and
trouble to this nation, and contrary to the inclinations of
the generality of the people, ever since the Reformation.'
The motive of this irrelevant declaration was to free William,
already governor of an Episcopal establishment in England,
from the odium of its abolition in Scotland after he became
king. A deputation from the Convention forthwith waited
on him in London on May 11, 1689, and read to him the
Scottish Claim of Right and supplementary Articles of
Grievances. To the clause of the sovereign's oath binding
him to be 'careful to root out all heretics' he demurred, rejecting an obligation to become a persecutor. His apprehensions having been allayed, the new sovereigns took the
oath. As a dynastic settlement the Revolution was complete.
Having given the Stewarts to England eighty-six years before, Scotland followed England in rejecting them. Encouraged by the resources of the larger kingdom, they had
wounded their ancient monarchy in its dearest prejudices
and now paid the penalty.

Easily as the change of sovereign was effected, Dundee
remained to be faced before William's rule could
Killiecrankie, rest securely on the foundations the Convention
1689   had laid. James' prospects were not hopeless.
He himself was rallying his partisans in Ireland. Moreover,
France was closely concerned to shake the throne of William,

xiii]   THE LAST STEWARTS   207

her most dangerous and determined enemy. Relying on the
clans, Dundee proposed a campaign which at least would
divert William from throwing all his resources against James
in Ireland and might create in Scotland a situation of which
James could take advantage when Ireland was at his feet.
On March 30, 1689, suspecting his purposes, the Convention
declared him a rebel and hurried him into action. While
General Hugh Mackay of Scourie, with the Scots Brigade
lately arrived from Holland, was commissioned to deal with
him, Dundee, towards the middle of April, raised the royal
Standard and swept across the Sidlaws. An army had to be
raised, the clans rallied. On May 18 he summoned them to
rendezvous in Glenroy, something short of two thousand in
all. For two months he led his panting enemy round the
Highlands, 'skipping from one hill to another like wildfire,'
said a contemporary newsletter. Towards the middle of July
a single tattered regiment under Colonel Alexander Cannon
arrived from Ireland, the meagre reinforcement that James
could afford. The disappointment was bitter: a stroke
was needed to revive drooping hopes. Mackay gave an
opening by marching to recover Blair Castle, the seat of
Atholl, whom caution had removed to Bath, ostensibly to
'pump his head.' To frustrate Mackay Dundee gave battle
at Killiecrankie on July 27, 1689, and won an encounter
which his death robbed of victory. Cannon took over the
command, for which he was ill suited, and, after an unsuccess-
ful encounter at Dunkeld (August 21), withdrew to Lochaber
for the winter. Now that Dundee's personality was withdrawn the enterprise was hopeless. But early in 1690
Major-General Thomas Buchan was sent by James to
revive it. Surprised at Cromdale, on Speyside, on May Day,
his army dispersed, and the Jacobite challenge to the Revolution collapsed.

Meanwhile one of the most stormy and fruitful Parliaments in Scotland's experience was in session at Edinburgh.
Nothing less than a drastic revolution of the constitution

the last Stewarts had abused was in progress. For four
Abolition of reigns Scotland had been ruled from Whitehall
the Articles, through the Privy Council, while the Committee
1690 of the Articles provided a pliant medium by
whose means the Crown controlled Parliament and its legislation. Already in its Articles of Grievances the Convention
had condemned the Committee and asserted Parliament's
competence to initiate legislation through committees set
up by itself. William, however, was loath to surrender an
apparatus so convenient to the Crown's purposes, and only
after a sharp tussle Parliament carried its will: the Articles
were discharged and abrogated for all time coming: the
House's competence to choose its own committees was
declared: and though high Officers of State were not excluded from them, their inability to vote within them was
affirmed (May 1690). Thus the venerable machinery by
which the Stewarts had bent Parliament to their policy dis-
appeared.

Revolutionary in its constitutional results, the Parlia-
Presbyterian ment of 1690 was not less so in its settlement
Settlement, of the ecclesiastical situation. In his chaplain
1690 William Carstares William had an adviser
who convinced him that, though the majority of Scottish
Protestants had conformed to a prelatical establishment for
the past thirty years, their fundamental inclination was
against Episcopacy, and that a moderate Presbyterian settlement offered the securest guarantee of public quiet. William
also could not fail to be influenced by the fact that the
Scottish Episcopalians showed themselves doggedly Jacobite
—in 1689 nearly two hundred of their ministers were ejected
for refusal to offer public prayers for the new sovereigns.
In July 1689 therefore William consented to abolish
Episcopacy as 'a great and unsupportable grievance to
this nation, and contrary to the inclinations of the generality
of the people, ever since the Reformation.' A year later
(April 1690) the Assertory Act of 1669 establishing the royal

supremacy was repealed as being obnoxious to Presbyterian consciences, and all ministers deprived for nonconformity with prelacy since January 1, 1661, were restored to their churches and manses. Only sixty of them survived—the 'Sixty Bishops'—and to their hands the building of the new Establishment was entrusted. Two further Acts completed the settlement. The first (June 1690) re-established the government of the Church by its Presbyterian Courts and Assembly, vested it in the Sixty and those whom they should admit, and adopted the Westminster Confession of Faith (1647) as that of the new Establishment. Finally (July 1690) private patronage of ecclesiastical benefices was annulled and the right of presentation was transferred to heritors and Kirk Sessions.

Thus, on its constitutional side the Revolution settled Scotland as a limited monarchy served by a Parliament competent at length to fulfil the function of an independent legislature. In its ecclesiastical aspect it broadly conceded the liberty of conscience Cromwell had established. No attempt was made to revive the Covenants: the aim was comprehension. The Presbyterian stalwarts ejected in 1662 and now restored were not less welcome than Episcopal conformists to the settlement of 1689–90. Extremists hovered on either wing: a Cameronian minority which resented the repudiation of the Covenants, and an Episcopal body whose Jacobite principles held it aloof. As in 1662, so in 1690, the State was concerned to confer predominance upon that body of opinion on whose allegiance it could most surely count.

CHAPTER XIV

UNION AND CIVIL WAR

THE settlement achieved in Scotland by the Parliament of 1689–90 was essentially revolutionary and worked fundamental changes. An ecclesiastical system active for the greater part of a century was abandoned for ever: in its room Presbyterianism and a clerical Assembly were established, along with a national Parliament which for the first time proved itself an efficient instrument of legislation and the national will. The controversies of the seventeenth century were at length composed: had the spirit of the Covenants persisted, the Revolution Settlement could not have been permanent. Ever since 1560 religion held first place in Scotland's regard. But after 1690 the Church's discipline ceased to be an absorbing preoccupation to all but the Cameronian rump. Secular interests beckoning to other fields of interest and activity, Scotland ventured upon paths on which England held her an interloper and rival. Throughout William's reign she encountered rebuffs and annoyances which enlarged her suspicion of English policy, stirred her discontent with England's somewhat contemptuous subordination of Scotland's interests to her own, and even excited plans to break the dynastic union which bound two independent kingdoms under a single crown. On her side, the Revolution plunged England into a Continental war in circumstances which made Scotland's unfriendliness, still more her secession, dangerous and unthinkable. The closer political union of 1707 solved the apprehensions of both countries, but was not accomplished until mutual provocations had drawn them to the verge of conflict.

Of these provocations the Glencoe Massacre was the first. Buchan's defeat at Cromdale in May 1690 did not intimidate the rebellious clans. As long as Ireland was in arms, and French succours were anticipated, they remained at the orders of James VII. But in October 1691 the Treaty of Limerick pacified Ireland, while Louis XIV was too preoccupied on the Continent to send aid. To prolong an unaided contest being futile, the chiefs, listening to overtures from the government, generally obeyed a proclamation threatening reprisals against those of their number who had not sworn allegiance to William and Mary by January 1, 1692. The date found Macdonald of Glencoe and Macdonell of Glengarry still delinquents. Glencoe, presenting himself at Fort William in the last days of December, was sent on to the Sheriff at Inveraray, who alone could administer the oath. In bitter weather he travelled thither, and upon January 6 swore his allegiance. Technically he was debarred from the royal amnesty, and the Master of Stair, Lord Advocate, pressed the opportunity to enforce the penalty. In February an armed force occupied Glencoe, lived for a fortnight among its unsuspicious inhabitants, and on the morning of February 13 rose up and slaughtered them. Exploited by the enemies of Stair, and by the Jacobites, the massacre was execrated as an act of English tyranny.

Glencoe Massacre, 1692

During the remaining years of William's reign Scotland was absorbed in an adventure which brought her relations with England to a crisis. The eighteenth century was a period of feverish commercial activity, in which chartered Companies endowed with exclusive monopolies were everywhere held proper pioneers of the State's industrial activities and getters of wealth. Scotland, after the Restoration, passed many measures to promote her industries and commerce, but with little success; for while the Union of 1603 damaged her commercial privileges in France, Charles II's war with

William II, 1689-1702

Holland weakened another of her markets, and the English Navigation Act drew in 1661 a retaliatory measure from her whose provisions recoiled on herself. From this depressing situation the unfathomed prospects of colonial trade were summoned to extricate her. On June 26, 1695, Parliament gave a charter to the Company of Scotland trading to Africa and the Indies, a corporation which received a monopoly of trade with 'any lands, islands, countries, or places in Asia, Africa, or America,' with license to plant colonies, build cities, towns, or forts, in localities not possessed by European sovereigns or states. One-half of the subscribed capital was reserved until August 1, 1696, for 'Scottish men within this kingdom,' after which date Scotsmen and foreigners abroad were to be permitted to become shareholders.

The scheme was drafted by William Paterson, a native of Dumfriesshire, who as Director of the Bank of England had wide experience of finance and considerable authority. But the Act carried a challenge to England which could not fail to be resented. It infringed an English monopoly, engaged the Crown to support the Scottish adventurers, suspended the Navigation Act in the Company's favour, and exempted its commerce from taxation for twenty-one years. When Parliament met in November 1695 an outcry was raised by the English monopoly and its friends. Lords and Commons denounced the Scottish Company as an interloper, insisted that Scotland would supplant England as the emporium of the East Indian trade, complained that the king's obligation to protect the Company at the public charge offered trespassers the English navy's protection, and, had they carried their will, would have impeached the authors of the design. Thoroughly frightened by the storm, most of the London shareholders withdrew from the Company and reduced its English capital to £15,000.

In February 1696 the Company's books were opened at Edinburgh, where before August the sum was subscribed

in full and half the capital was paid up. Excepting the
Covenant, no event since the Reformation so
concentrated the interests of all classes upon a   *Darien*
national undertaking. Meanwhile, as England persisted
in her jealousy, in place of trading with India it was
resolved to establish a settlement upon the Isthmus of
Darien or Panama connecting North and South America.
The territory had been discovered two centuries before by the
Spaniards, who refrained from settling there only because, as
the Scottish adventurers discovered, the climate was fatal
to Europeans. Paterson, however, praised the locality as the
'door of the seas and the key of the universe,' a nearer route
to the Indies than England and Holland followed round the
Cape, and promised its proprietors mastery of two oceans
and to become 'arbitrators of the commercial world.'

After two years spent in acquiring ships in Holland and
materials for barter, the first colonists sailed from Leith in
July 1698 to found New Caledonia, carrying a most unsaleable cargo of periwigs, kid gloves, buttons, blue bonnets,
grey paper, and English Bibles, curiously inappropriate to
a native market. Tweeds, serges, coarse stockings, and
caps were provided for a tropical climate! Eldorado was
reached in November and at once revealed its treacherous
climate. Fever, dysentery, and bad food took a heavy toll
of victims. The leaders quarrelled. No buyers appeared for
the periwigs and kid gloves, and the miserable adventurers
abandoned the depressing spot in June 1699. Few of them
reached Scotland, whence already a supporting expedition
had been dispatched. It arrived in August, found a vacant
wilderness, and withdrew to Jamaica, where most of the
party died. Three months later (November 1699) a third
expedition arrived upon the fatal coast. As before, the supply
of provisions was inadequate, and an unsaleable cargo made
it impossible to augment it. Whether to stay or return was
debated angrily. Upon this black outlook, in February 1700,
a sloop from Scotland appeared opportunely to support the

last effort of the moribund colony. Before the end of the month the Spaniards, indignant at the trespass upon their territory, closed the harbour. In March they mastered the isthmus on which Fort St Andrew flew the flag of Scotland. Decimated by fever and reduced for water to a 'brackish puddle,' its defenders capitulated on honourable terms and turned their backs on New Caledonia. Of the four ships that carried them home only one reached Scotland. In two years the Company had lost most of its fleet, nearly 2000 lives, and about £250,000 sterling.

From north to south Scotland raised a chorus of anger and denunciation, though the fundamental cause of failure was in herself, her inadequate resources, inexperience, and the misadventure which selected for the scene of her colony-building a locality made habitable for Europeans only by the inventiveness of modern science. But of these considerations she was impatient. The brunt of her disappointment was vented on England, with a savage intentness that promised such a national opposition as once faced Charles I.

The Darien fiasco faced Scotland with two imperative alternatives—either to abandon her dearest

Union Proposals ambition, the prospect of commercial prosperity, or, at some sacrifice of national pride, to seek partnership in the trade and colonies of her English neighbour. To England the event exposed the inconvenience of being linked with another independent kingdom under one Crown. So long as Scotland represented a distinct political system, the possibility of war between them, Scotland's alliance with France, and her support of the Jacobite cause, could not be judged unlikely. Such considerations had already prompted reflexion. The invitation to William to assume the provisional administration of Scotland in January 1689 was accompanied by a recommendation of union. William's first communication to the Convention sounded the same note. In a message to the House of Lords expressing deep concern for Scotland's misfortunes (February 12,

1700) he warned his hearers that similar difficulties were likely to embroil the two kingdoms 'unless some way be found out to unite them more nearly and completely.' His last word to the House of Commons (February 28, 1702) expressed the same belief. The fruition of the wish was denied him. Eight days later he died, the first sovereign since James V who consistently adjusted his policy to the idiosyncracies of his Scottish people, a king respected and even popular as the author of the 'Scriptural and Reformation Presbyterian Church government.'

Union, already looming on the horizon of both kingdoms, became an imperative problem from the circumstances under which Anne succeeded her brother-in-law. Childless and like to remain so, *Anne, 1702–14* she was the last of those whom the Revolution named in the succession for both kingdoms. In England, by the Act of Settlement (1701), her successor was *The Succession* James VI's granddaughter and nearest Protestant heir, Sophia, widow of the Elector of Hanover, a vivacious lady of seventy-two. Anne's heir in Scotland had not been determined when, in March 1702, she began her reign. But, in default of a Scottish Act of Parliament to that effect, he would not be the same person as in England, a prospect which English statesmen could not view without anxiety. Nor was the danger remote. Scotland regarded as providential the opportunity, on the morrow of her disappointment over Darien, to prescribe the terms on which union should continue.

Anne's succession was generally welcomed. She was a Stewart, whose elevation to her father's seat *Abortive negotiations for* expiated in some sort Scotland's desertion of *Union, 1702* her ancient princes. In two matters she announced herself William's heir. In May 1702 England declared war on France and Spain, and for twelve years was the mainstay of the Coalition in the War of the Spanish Succession. In such a crisis, though not herself involved,

Scotland could confound English strategy by encouraging France to support a Jacobite restoration. Consequently the war gave England an inclination to union, and caused her for the first time to originate measures to that end. In her first English Speech the Queen desired Parliament to 'consider of proper methods towards attaining an union between England and Scotland.' In the following May 1702, she gave her assent to a Bill empowering her to nominate Commissioners to treat with Scotland on the subject. The Scottish Estates, meeting a month later, invited the Queen to take similar action in their behalf. In October 1702 Commissioners of both kingdoms met at Whitehall but came to no conclusion. Concessions were extracted rather than volunteered by the English, whose deportment suggested their participation in the proceedings to be due to the Queen's insistence rather than their own convictions. It was reserved for the last of Scotland's Parliaments (1703–7) to make her neighbour understand that, failing surrender to her demand for equality of commercial opportunity, she was prepared to break the dynastic union itself.

By a happy stroke Scotland's last Parliament more accurately represented Scottish opinion than any of its predecessors since 1603. Hence it had behind it unusual authority for the momentous act it accomplished. Shortly after their assembling the Estates passed an Act of Security (August 1703) which England could only regard with concern. It provided that, in the event of the queen's death without heirs of her body, or before the Estates had named her successor, they should, within twenty days of her demise, appoint a sovereign of the Stewart line and Protestant religion, but not the holder of the English Crown, unless in the meanwhile 'there be such conditions of government settled and enacted as may secure the religion, liberty, and trade of the nation from English or any foreign interference.' Even more aggressive, since its terms were not conditional, was an Act anent Peace

Act of Security, 1703

and War (August 1703), which stipulated that under no circumstances should it be competent for her sovereign to commit Scotland to war with a foreign state or to make her a party to treaties of alliance without the consent of her Estates.

At first indifferent, England was shaken from her complacency by a mysterious intrigue revealed in *The Queens-* the summer of 1704 by Simon Fraser, after- *berry Plot,* wards Lord Lovat. Called in Scotland the Scots 1704 Plot and in Scotland the Queensberry Plot—the Duke of Queensberry being Scottish Secretary of State—the circumstances indicated that prominent Scotsmen were plotting for the restoration of James VII's son, the Old Pretender, and that they found encouragement in Scotland's deliberate failure to settle her monarchy, like that of England, in the House of Hanover. In the autumn (1704) angry debates filled the House of Lords, addresses passed for raising the northern militia, and in March 1705 an 'Act for the effectual securing the Kingdom of England from the apparent dangers that may *Alien Act,* arise from several Acts lately passed in the 1705 Parliament of Scotland' received the royal assent. Popularly known as the Alien Act, it compelled Scotland to understand that England would not suffer the dynastic union to be broken. As in 1702, but more earnestly, Scotland was invited to negotiate a treaty of union. Otherwise, unless she followed England in naming the Electress Sophia and her Protestant issue to succeed Anne, after December 25, 1705, and until she made such a settlement, no Scotsman except those settled in England would be permitted to hold property there; while Scottish coal, linen, cattle would be excluded from England and English wool from Scotland. The Act sounded a warning: it offered Scotland alternatives: either to confirm the dynastic union concluded in 1603 and renewed in 1689, or to negotiate completer union on terms mutually agreeable. To the latter end the queen was invited to name Commissioners, but not until Scotland had indicated an intention to follow the same course.

The Alien Act brought home to Scotland the critical situation into which she had drifted. When the *Articles of Union*, 1706 Estates met for their third session in June 1705 the young Duke of Argyll, whose father's and grandfather's careers spoke for the soundness of his Whig principles, appeared as Commissioner to move the members to answer England's invitation favourably. Queensberry's deft management as Secretary of State, and the statesmanlike policy of a party which assumed the designation 'Squadrone Volante' and saw in union the alternative to greater inconveniences, smoothed Argyll's task and secured his aims. An Act approving a treaty with England was passed, subject to her withdrawal of the obnoxious Alien Act, and the queen was empowered to name Commissioners, a wise conclusion, since it promised to exclude both Jacobites and hot Presbyterians from discussions in which, above everything, moderate views were needed. England having repealed (November 1705) the sections of the Alien Act to which Scotland took exception, the queen (February 1706) named Commissioners, nearly half of whom had served on the Commission of 1702. The English Commissioners also numbered many who had had that experience. The two bodies met in London in April 1706 and in the space of three months drafted a Treaty of Union.

The Articles of Union, so expeditiously agreed upon, proposed the union of the two kingdoms into a single political system, with the style 'Great Britain,' under the rule of the Electress Sophia and her Protestant heirs, and served by 'one and the same Parliament,' in which Scotland would be represented by forty-five members of the House of Commons and by sixteen peers elected by the holders of Scottish peerages. The trade and colonies of England were thrown open freely to Scotsmen, and in regard to Customs, Excise, and other imposts Scotland accepted the principle of equality. She stipulated, however, that she should not be burdened with England's vastly heavier Public Debt, and, since she would hereafter be taxed to contribute to its service, obtained the promise of an 'Equivalent,' fixed at about £400,000, payable on the day the Union took effect, applicable to the liquidation of her own small Debt and to refund to its shareholders the capital of the Darien Company. Scotland's legal system was to continue, but provision was made for a uniform coinage, a common standard of weights and measures, a common flag, Great Seal, public arms, and Commission of Admiralty. In view of Scotland's economic backwardness, relief from the full brunt of taxation was conceded until the beneficial effects of Union became apparent.

With the careful forethought which marked the government's procedure, the Scottish Parliament was the first to be invited to give a verdict upon the Treaty. *Union* A similarly judicious decision selected the Duke *approved,* of Queensberry to act as Commissioner. By his 1707 ability and conciliatory demeanour he overbore opposition within and without Parliament. In particular, an 'Act for security of the true Protestant religion and government of the Church as by law established' smoothed the fears of those who supposed union dangerous to the Presbyterian Establishment. The Act amply guaranteed to Scotland her Presbyterian Creed, discipline, and government in perpetuity, bound the sovereign by his coronation oath to maintain the Scottish Church in all time coming, and was declared to be an integral part of the Treaty of Union. The Church being thus placated, progress was rapid, and on January 16, 1707, the completed Act of Union, along with the Act of Security, was 'touched' by the Commissioner. Two months later, having passed swiftly through the English Houses, the Act received the Queen's assent on March 6, 1707.

The last scene was enacted with singular lack of circum-

stance. On March 19, 1707, Queensberry communicated the
Act to the Estates under the Great Seal of England. The
Earl of Seafield, Lord Chancellor, received it and handed it
to the Lord Clerk Register with a 'despising and contemptuous remark,' it is alleged, which perhaps covered
emotion—'Now there's ane end of ane auld song.' A week
later (March 25), New Year's Day in Old Style England, the
doors of Parliament House were opened to the Estates for
the last time. In a brief speech Queensberry declared his
conviction that posterity would acclaim the Union now
happily concluded, and adjourned Parliament. It never met
again, and was dissolved on April 25. A week later (May 1)
the Queen attended a thanksgiving service in St Paul's
Cathedral to celebrate the birthday of the United Kingdom
of Great Britain. At Edinburgh the bells of St Giles' chimed
out over a listless city, 'Why should I be sad on my wedding
day?' Two States had been joined in one. But the nations
were preserved.

Scotland soon found reason to quarrel with the Union's
Disappointing working. The material benefits for which she
results of had bartered independence were slow to
Union declare themselves: the burden of taxation
drew her angry protests: the rapacity of English collectors
was a popular theme. The status of the Scottish peerage
was belittled: the Church, in spite of the Act of Security,
was believed to be in grave jeopardy: a series of legislative measures in 1712 so outraged Scottish sentiment
that the repeal of the Union was moved by the very men
who supported it six years before. In such a soil Jacobitism
germinated fruitfully and for half a century after the
Union sought to disrupt it, finding an interested ally in
France, occasional abettors in Sweden and Spain, and its
chief and constant asset in the blind loyalty of the Highland
clans. Had the Pretenders raised a Protestant banner Jacobitism might have worked with other results. But the titular
James VIII grew up in a Catholic atmosphere in France,

preferred his religion to a kingdom, was a pensioner of the
Vatican, and his younger son a Cardinal of the Roman
Church. Jacobitism, therefore, challenged the Protestant
foundation on which the Union was based and so doomed
its efforts to disaster.

Eager to exploit the Jacobites to her advantage, France
saw in Scotland's discontent the opportunity to *France*
embarass England, her chief antagonist in the *and the*
Spanish Succession War. In 1707, shortly before *Jacobites*
the Union came into force, Colonel Nathaniel Hooke was
dispatched to Scotland by Louis XIV to mark the situation.
The Jacobite leaders were cautious; their utmost commit-
ment was a promise to take arms contingent on France's
energetic support. The military situation in Scotland, whose
establishment was quite inadequate, offered some prospect
of success, however, and James' partisans were warned to
expect him immediately after the Union came into effect.
On March 1, 1708, he drafted at Saint-Germain, *The 1708*
near Paris, an elaborate proclamation promis- *attempt*
ing, among other things, to annul the Union
and concede liberty of worship to his Protestant subjects.
A fortnight later he set sail from Dunkirk at the head of a
French squadron carrying some 5000 men. Closely pursued
by Sir George Byng, James made the Firth of Forth on
March 23. His signals to the shore were disregarded and, on
Byng's heaving in sight, the French vessels scattered for
safety. James returned to Dunkirk after a stormy passage.
Seven years elapsed before an opportunity arrived to ob-
literate the memory of a characteristic fiasco.

Meanwhile the Union, as had been foreseen, drew the
Episcopal bodies of the two kingdoms together. *The Green-*
As early as April 1707 the increasing vogue of *shields Case,*
the English Book of Common Prayer invited *1709–11*
from the General Assembly a condemnation of 'set forms.'
In 1709 its ruling was challenged by James Greenshields, an
Episcopal minister lately come from Ireland to Edinburgh,

where, after taking the Abjuration Oath, he set up a meeting
house and claimed the liberty conferred by the Act of 1695
to conduct public worship freely. As his congregation was
chiefly drawn from English residents settled in Edinburgh
since the Union, he used the Book of Common Prayer. The
Edinburgh Presbytery at once inhibited him from con-
ducting a form of public worship 'contrary to the purity and
uniformity of the Church established by law.' Greenshields,
denying its jurisdiction over him, eventually was put into
prison, where he lay for seven months. Appeals to the Court
of Session proving ineffectual, in 1710 he laid his case before
the House of Lords and brought home to English Episcopalians vividly, and for the first time, the plight of their
communion in Scotland. A Tory Parliament dealt sympa-
thetically with him: in 1711 the House of Lords reversed
the decision of the Courts below, and awarded him costs
and damages.

The effect of Greenshields' case was seen in a Toleration
Act (March 1712) which declared it free and
Toleration Act, 1712 lawful for the Episcopal communion in Scotland
to meet for divine worship performed after its
own manner by pastors ordained by a Protestant bishop,
and to use the liturgy of the Church of England, with liberty
to conduct marriages and baptisms denied to the nonconforming Episcopal clergy by the Act of 1695. An additional clause gave the measure a political bearing which
wounded Presbyterians, while it effectually barred Jacobite
Episcopalians. It required Episcopal and Presbyterian clergy
alike to take the Abjuration Oath, to pray during divine
service for the Queen and the Heiress Apparent, and bound
the subscriber to maintain the succession 'as the same is
and stands settled by' the Act of 1701, which required the
sovereign to be in communion with the Church of England.
Already outraged by the favour shown to Episcopacy, Presbyterianism resented an obligation to uphold the exclusive
claim of the English Establishment upon the sovereign's

attachment, and was released from it in 1719. Meanwhile, popular opinion held the Toleration Act a violation of the Union. It did not stand alone. On the top of it a Bill was passed restoring patrons to their ancient rights, provided they had taken the oaths and were purged of suspicion of Popery. Thus patronage, abolished *Patronage Act, 1712* in 1649 and 1690, was again restored by an Act fated to cause bitter controversy and division. It passed, in spite of the Assembly's protest, and was accompanied by a measure, wholly vexatious, an 'Act discharging the Yule Vacance,' directing the Scottish law courts to observe the Christmas vacation, a deliberate slight upon Scottish religious feeling repealed in 1715. A proposal (1713) to subject Scottish malt to a duty of sixpence the bushel, uniform with the English rate, was resisted on *Malt Tax, 1713* the ground that it was expressly exempt under the Treaty of Union 'during this present war.' A campaign of protest culminated actually in a motion in the House of Lords for the dissolution of the Union, which was defeated by only four votes, and whose practical result was the suspension of the malt duty till 1724, when the proposal was revived with notable consequences.

The Union therefore, though unshaken, was in disfavour when, in May 1714, the death of the aged Electress Sophia left her less agreeable son *George I, 1714–27* George Louis heir to the British crowns and promised the imminent succession of a prince who, though he had been heir presumptive for thirteen years, remained incorrigibly German and ignorant of his future subjects' manners, customs, and language. Four months later (August 1714) Queen Anne expired, after a sharp tussle in which the Jacobite leaders, Lord Bolingbroke, the Duke of Ormonde, and the Scottish Earl of Mar, vainly endeavoured to win the dying queen's assent to the proclamation of her half-brother, the Old Pretender. Seven weeks later the new sovereign landed in England and pointedly excluded the Tories from his favour. Bolingbroke, in March 1715, crossed the Channel to become 'James VIII's' Secretary of State. Ormonde followed him later. Mar— 'Bobbing John'—remained meanwhile to sound his prospects at the Hanoverian Court.

James was now in his twenty-sixth year, 'slender, tall, and comely,' fixed in his devotion to his father's religion and ready even by armed force to extirpate heresy from his kingdoms. For the moment his prospects were not promising. Bolingbroke's flight left his party leaderless in England, Jacobite sympathy expressed itself only in noisy demonstrations in Scotland, and the European situation was discouraging. George I's succession was explicitly recognized by the Treaty of Utrecht (1713) to which France had put her hand, while the death of James' benefactor Louis XIV in September 1715 handed France to the Regent Orleans, who had nearer interests to advance at home than those of the Pretender. But James was eager to be in action, and though his friends warned him of the futility of a landing in Britain unless it was backed by Continental succours, appointed July 31, 1715, for a rising. Mar's action supported his injudicious resolve. Convinced that the new Court of St James' was not disposed to advance his prospects, Mar boarded a collier in the Thames on August 2, 1715, and sailed to test the situation in Scotland, among whose Highland clans at least loyalty to the Stewarts could be supposed to survive. A month later (September 6) he raised the standard of James VIII and III at Braemar. Its gilt ball fell as it was erected, an omen of disaster which failed sufficiently to impress the superstitious gathering.

The event long dreaded—Scotland's parting from her ancient dynasty—summoned all who were not irrevocably pledged to a German sovereign to strike for the old line. At Aberdeen, Dunkeld, Gordon Castle, Brechin, Montrose, Dundee, Inverness, the Pretender was proclaimed. An attempt to seize Edinburgh Castle was narrowly frustrated. Before the end of September Mar was in Perth, and soon controlled the entire coast from the Moray Firth to the Forth. Highland and Lowland contingents swelled his force to 6000 foot and 600 horse in the course of November, and in the west the clans were in arms to harass Argyll's country. Embarrassed by want of troops, the government took other steps to confound the Pretender's partisans, suspended the Habeas Corpus Act, put a heavy price on James' head, and sent down Argyll, whose military apprenticeship under Marlborough and his family traditions recommended him, to command the forces in Scotland. By the end of September he was settled at Stirling, in command of less than 2000 men, while reinforcements were ordered from Ireland, and the United Provinces were summoned, under their Treaty (1713) obligations, to provide eight regiments of foot and one of horse.

Had Mar at once challenged Argyll's inferior force at Stirling, Edinburgh and the south lay open to him. But he preferred to await James' arrival, partly in hope of French reinforcement, counting also on the Pretender's presence to excite the loyalty of his followers, and desiring leisure to watch the disposition of England. He devised, however, an enveloping movement whose effect, if successful, would render Argyll's position at Stirling precarious. The clans were instructed to seize Inveraray and advance on Stirling from that quarter, while a strong force passed the Forth under Brigadier Mackintosh of Borlum. Mar's design failed on both wings. The clans withdrew from before Inveraray after threatening attack. Mackintosh, instead of combining with the Border Jacobites against Argyll's rear, made a dash upon Edinburgh (October 14) which Argyll in person forestalled. Resuming his interrupted commission, Mackintosh joined a force of English and Scottish Jacobites at Kelso a week later (October 22).

The Border force included a body of Northumberland

Jacobites under Thomas Forster, Member for the county, the Earl of Derwentwater, and Lord Widdrington. Unable to agree on their course of action, its Scottish and English leaders concluded on a compromise and, less than 2000 strong, set out upon the track on which in 1648 and 1651 the cause of the Stewarts met disaster. Few partisans joined, though in Lancashire the Roman Catholics were more responsive. Encouraged by assurances of a friendly welcome in Manchester, the insurgents marched to Preston where, as in 1648, the adventure collapsed. On November 12 an English force, advancing from Wigan, delivered an attack upon the Jacobites, reinforced by some 200 Lancashire Catholics and their retainers. It was beaten off after a hard tussle. Next morning General Carpenter arrived by forced marches from the north. The insurgents were *Preston,* 1715 trapped; to break cover with nine regiments of horse in pursuit would be futile. Forster sensibly proposed surrender, and on November 14 his force, in number about 1500, laid down their arms.

Almost simultaneously the Stewart cause received.: death blow in Scotland. By the first week in November 1715 Mar's strength at Perth was about 8000. Argyll could not muster half that number. But the Dutch contingents were on their way, and Mar judged it important to strike before their arrival. Instead of waiting to be attacked, Argyll evacuated Stirling and, marching northward, posted himself on Sheriffmuir, an undulating upland of the Ochils near Dunblane, where his superiority in cavalry would tell. On *Sheriffmuir,* November 13 action was joined: the left of each 1715 army was driven from the field, and both commanders claimed a 'drawn stake.' But for Mar's prospects the engagement was decisive: the Dutch troops arrived in the Thames the day after the battle, and his single opportunity to pass the Forth vanished. Simultaneously, Simon Fraser, intent to secure the Lovat title, wrested the North from Jacobite control, while Ormonde's descents upon

the southern English coasts (October—December) called out
no response. Everywhere the critical year ended gloomily
for the Jacobite cause.

Such a moment James, with characteristic fortune, chose
for his belated arrival. He landed at Peter-
head on December 22, 1715, and at Fetteresso   *James in*
issued his proclamation. It announced intention   *Scotland*
to relieve his subjects from 'the hardships they groan under
on account of the late unhappy Union,' promised to restore
Scotland's Parliament to its accustomed home, and offered
security to the Churches of England and Scotland. Enthusiasm marked his progress towards Perth, where a secret
resolution already had been formed to retreat to the north:
since Sheriffmuir, the Highlanders, chafing at inaction, had
deserted in considerable numbers. Meanwhile, Argyll, at
Stirling, reinforced by the Dutch troops, was at the head
of 9000 horse and foot and a powerful train, and James'
arrival coincided with stringent orders to him to advance.
On January 24, 1716, he reconnoitred towards Auchterarder
in a season more severe than a generation could recall. At
Perth confusion reigned. A futile effort was made to
impede Argyll by burning the villages between Perth and
Stirling and on January 31 the retreat began. Argyll
hotly pressed the pursuit. A rumour of his advance from
Arbroath hurried the Chevalier on board ship in Montrose
harbour. He never saw Scotland again, and left behind him
no happy or inspiring memory. Mar accompanied him,
leaving General Gordon to conduct the despondent troops
to Aberdeen and thence to Badenoch, where they dispersed.
The royal army indefatigably hunted down the fugitives,
while the Dutch troops left 'nothing earthly' undestroyed
along their route. By May tranquillity was restored.

That the Union survived an effort to overthrow it, whose
chances of success at the outset were probably as considerable as its prospects of failure, was due entirely to the
conviction that independence under a Catholic prince was

less preferable than partnership with England. The government recognized that excessive severity would overstrain the allegiance of a population most of whom admired, if they did not repeat, Mar's protest against the 'cursed Union.' Less than one hundred of the prisoners taken in Scotland were sent for trial to Carlisle. None of them was executed. Of those captured in England over 700 were transported and fifty-seven, including Kenmure and Derwentwater, were put to death. Lord Nithsdale was saved by his heroic wife, in whose clothing he broke prison. A number of leaders were attainted, and a Commission was set up (June 26, 1716) to ascertain the extent and value of their forfeited estates, sell them for public uses, and provide capital for the erection of schools in the Highlands. Thirty-four Scottish properties were disposed of, chiefly to the York Buildings Company, but without any benefit to the public uses proposed.

For a generation the Union was not seriously assailed. In February 1717 the Pretender crossed the Alps to his long exile in Rome, accepting Papal hospitality which seriously damaged his cause. Twice, however, the European situation offered him prospect of action. In 1717 Charles XII of Sweden, eager to recover the duchies of Bremen and Verden from Hanover, set on foot a conspiracy for a Stewart restoration in England. The English Jacobites subscribed money, but the government winded the plot. Charles XII's death in November 1718 having removed the Pretender's only apparent friend, Spain opportunely afforded him his last active employment. Under Cardinal Alberoni's vigorous rule she aimed at recovering the Italian provinces wrested from her in 1713, but was frustrated by Great Britain's determination to uphold the Utrecht settlement. Ormonde was summoned from Paris to lead an Armada against England. The Earl Marischal, exiled in France since the '15, was proposed to conduct a smaller expedition to Scotland. In February

The Swedish Plot, 1717

1719 James hastened to Spain from Italy. By March he was in Madrid, in time to receive early tidings of the destruction of his hopes: a Protestant *The '19* wind shattered Ormonde's Armada fifty leagues west of Cape Finisterre. After vainly begging another effort in his behalf, James returned to Italy and uneasy marriage (September 1719) with Maria Clementina Sobieska, granddaughter of Poland's warrior-king.

Once more Scotland was invited unaided to uphold the Stewart cause. In March 1719 the Earl Marischal sailed from Spain with a couple of frigates and a handful of Spanish infantry. A few days later Tullibardine and other Jacobite exiles in France followed from Havre. The two parties united at Stornoway and quarrelled over their course of action, till Tullibardine, producing a commission from James, decided to await the news of Ormonde's fortune. Early in April the three vessels sailed to Gareloch and anchored off Eilean Donan. In May Ormonde's collapse was known, British men-of-war entered Loch Alsh, and the insurgent force, 1100 strong, headed northward for safer country. But Major-General Wightman was advancing from Inverness. On June 10 he found his quarry in the Pass of Glenshiel and, after stubborn re- *Glenshiel, 1719* sistance, dispersed them. The Spaniards, declaring 'they could neither live without bread nor make any hard marches through the country,' surrendered next day.

For a quarter of a century Jacobitism found no friends abroad, while the Pretender, isolated and remote in Italy, scandalized his adherents by his domestic squabbles and the incompetence of those who managed his affairs. Without opposition a second Hanoverian sovereign reached the throne in 1727, though James hurried from Italy to be ready at an emergency. The Jacobite Lockhart of Carnwath, laying down his pen in 1728, bemoaned a hopeless situation: 'no projects formed, nothing done to keep up the spirits of the people, the old race drops off by degrees and a new one sprouts up, who, having no particular byass to the King [James], as knowing litle more of him than what the public newspapers bear, enter on the stage with a perfect indifference, at least coolness, towards him and his cause, which consequently must daylie languish and in process of time be tottally forgot.' None could discern in the youthful Prince Charles Edward (born December 31, 1720) the most vigorous champion of a waning interest.

Alberoni's defeat removed the Union's only active foreign enemy, while the general election of 1722 confirmed the Whigs, its natural protectors, in their ascendancy. Till 1742 Robert Walpole remained in power. His policy aimed at consolidating the Hanoverian monarchy by denying the Jacobites opportunity to oppose it behind enemy Powers. But his government was not free from aggravations which excited in Scotland renewed protests against the Union. The Peerage Bill (1719), which proposed to substitute twenty-five hereditary for her sixteen elected peers, was opposed as depriving her peerage of any direct influence upon the representatives of their order. Wider opposition was excited by a proposal (1724) to levy an additional sixpence a barrel on Scottish beer and ale. Unreasonably enough, the tax was declared to violate the Union's compact of fiscal equality. Walpole, yielding, imposed instead a threepenny duty on Scottish malt. A chorus of opposition rose against a proposal which threatened to raise the price of Scottish 'Twopenny,' a beverage of general consumption. The Edinburgh brewers refused to brew. Glasgow offered violent resistance to the Excise officers in June 1725, when, on the Act coming into force, they attempted to value the malsters' stocks. The mob gutted the house of the local Member of Parliament, whose advice was suspected to support the tax, and behaved in so disorderly a manner that peace was restored only after the arrival of a consider-

Peerage Bill, 1719

Malt Tax, 1724

able military force. The Malt Tax was imposed, not without
effect upon the relative consumption of ale and whisky.

Eleven years later Edinburgh was the scene of a riot
whose circumstances, commonplace in their
origin, have been immortalized by Sir Walter   **George II,**
Scott in *The Heart of Midlothian*. Andrew Wil-   **1727–60**
son, a notorious Fifeshire smuggler, was hanged at Edinburgh
on April 14, 1736, in circumstances which excited particular
sympathy. His offence was an attempt to recoup his losses,
through frequent seizure of contraband, by robbing a Customs officer at Pittenweem. Along with an accomplice he
was captured, tried, and sentenced to death. Precautions
were taken to prevent his rescue on the scaffold, which was
guarded by a detachment under Captain John Porteous.
Wilson, indeed, was hanged without interruption: but
thereafter the mob stoned the guards and cut
down his body. Whether at the orders of Por-   *The Porteous*
teous or not, his men opened fire: six persons   *Riot,* 1736
were killed and about twenty were wounded. Porteous was
found guilty of murder and sentenced to be executed on
September 8. Influence was exerted in his behalf, and on
the queen's authority respite was granted. Assuming the
postponement to be the prelude to pardon, a mob tore
Porteous from prison on September 7 and hanged him on
the Grassmarket from a dyer's pole. In spite of Scottish
opposition, a vindictive measure passed the Lords, which
proposed to imprison and incapacitate the Lord Provost of
Edinburgh, and could be represented as infringing the
liberties of the Royal Burghs guaranteed by the Act of
Union. Mitigated punishment eventually was imposed, but
popular indignation was not abated.

The House of Hanover was fortified by a full generation's
prescriptive right when its last rival faced it and
succumbed in 1745. Peace, which had persisted   *The '45*
in Western Europe almost continuously since its accession,
was broken by Walpole's declaration of war upon Spain

(Jenkins' Ear War) in October 1739; while the Emperor Charles VI's death exactly a year later threatened a wider conflict. In the War of the Austrian Succession it burst upon Europe and engaged France and Great Britain as enemies. Jacobite activity, long dormant in England and Scotland, revived as the prospect of war increased, and after the battle of Dettingen (June 1743) dissipated the fiction of peace between Great Britain and France, Louis XV gratified the Pretender at Rome by an undertaking to support his cause. James being no longer possessed of the physical vigour to repeat his exploits of 1708 and 1716, early in 1744 his elder son Prince Charles Edward left Rome for France. He was entering his twenty-fifth year, eager for action, a young man above the middle height and very thin. 'I go Sire,' he addressed his father, 'in search of three Crowns.' But, notwithstanding his daring adventure, Charles had neither head nor heart for great things, and reached France in time to witness the disappointment of his hopes: in March 1744 a French force assembled at Dunkirk to enter the Thames was shattered by storm. The enterprise was abandoned and Charles vainly petitioned Louis to repeat his preparations. Scottish partisans visited him in Paris and reported his determination to come to Scotland if he brought 'only a single footman' with him. Early in 1745 a message of caution was sent to him from his Scottish partisans. It never reached him, and the battle of Fontenoy (May 11, 1745) conveyed absurdly erroneous impressions of his Hanoverian rival's instability. A hasty message announced his coming: he followed to Scotland in July, and before the end of the month landed in Arisaig. On August 19 he raised the standard at Glenfinnan at the head of Loch Shiel and was soon at the head of 2000 clansmen, the half of them Macdonalds.

Charles' driving power, the glamour of his personality, and the military ability of Lord George Murray, his most valuable recruit in Scotland, claim their share in a remarkable achievement. But circumstances were Charles' best friend. Though the Union was no longer a rallying cry, as in 1708 and 1715, the government was unduly contemptuous of the Jacobite danger. The bulk of the British army was on the Continent. In Scotland the establishment consisted of three and a half battalions of infantry and two regiments of horse, in all about 3000 troops, all of them, except one foot regiment, raw and inexperienced. Sir John Cope, commanding in chief, showed little ability and no adaptability to strange and unexpected conditions.

Deciding to deal with the situation before it got out of hand, Cope, with the infantry under his command set out from Stirling on August 20 for Fort Augustus. Arrived at Dalwhinnie, he found his passage blocked by the clans in Corriyarrick Pass, a wild defile to Fort Augustus. Cope's prudent course was to fall back on Stirling: he chose to push on to Inverness, assuming that the North would be the scene of Charles' first activities. But the prince followed a bolder plan: a march on Perth would bring in recruits from the Atholl country, and Cope's cavalry at Stirling and Leith were inadequate to defend the Forth and Edinburgh. On September 4 Charles entered Perth and proclaimed his father. His most valuable recruit there was Lord George Murray, Tullibardine's brother, who had been 'out' in '15 and '19, a man of marked military ability to whom Charles entrusted the army's direction. After a week's stay in Perth the prince resumed the advance (September 11). On September 13 Gardiner's dragoons gave him the passage of the Forth at the Fords of Frew and fell back to join Hamilton's at Falkirk. Their combined 'canter o' Colt-Brig' cleared his path towards Edinburgh (September 16), whose walls were in no condition to offer resistance. But Cope's arrival by sea from Aberdeen was imminent and the authorities sought to manoeuvre for delay. The Camerons defeated the intention. In the small hours of September 17 they rushed the Nether Bow Port and seized the guardhouse and the gates.

At noon Charles entered the city. James VIII was proclaimed forthwith, and Holyrood, after more than sixty years, housed a prince of the ancient lineage. Four days later (September 21), advancing on Edinburgh from Dunbar, where he disembarked, Cope at length met his enemy near Prestonpans. Within fifteen minutes his force was scattered to the winds. 'The Army,' Charles wrote to his father, 'had a fine plunder.'

Prestonpans, 1745

Striking as his success was, the weakness of Charles' position could not be concealed. The Lowlands, which furnished his father with squadrons in 1715, now provided a single troop less than fifty strong. In Edinburgh few recruits were enrolled. On the side of his enemy vigour replaced apathy. Immediately after Cope's defeat 6000 Dutch troops reached the Thames from Holland, and before the end of October reinforcements from Flanders were available, with the Duke of Cumberland, who arrived on October 19. These succours were inadequately balanced by money, arms, and artillery (six four-pounders) from France, and on October 24 the Treaty of Fontainebleau bound Louis to render Charles assistance. Encouraged by these marks of interest, the prince was urgent to rouse his English adherents. Incredulous of the effect he anticipated from his appearance in England, Lord George and others objected that, if his adherents there were in earnest, they did not need the encouragement of his presence; while, if a French landing in England was imminent, it was sounder strategy to draw English troops to Scotland than to advance to meet them in a probably hostile country. But Charles was immovably resolved to go to England. With apprehensions of disaster Lord George concurred. As in 1715 the western track was chosen: it offered ground more suited to Highland tactics, and Lancashire's welcome was remembered.

England invaded

Charles bade farewell to Edinburgh on November 1. His army numbered 5000 foot, 500 horse, and 13 guns. A fort-

night later (November 15) Carlisle capitulated. Marshal
Wade was gathering forces at Newcastle. Another army was
concentrating about Lichfield, of which Cumberland took
command. But for the moment Charles advanced unchallenged. Preston gave enthusiastic welcome. Manchester
surpassed Preston in its acclamation: about 200 'common
fellows' were formed into the Manchester Regiment, under
Francis Towneley, the only material reinforcement the
march yielded. Charles was elated. His Council did not share
his confidence: retreat was already discussed among them:
the French had not landed, and no 'person of distinction'
had encouraged them. They agreed to proceed as far as
Derby, in order that the English might not say they had
not been encouraged to rise or the French to land. Already
the army was in touch with Cumberland's outposts, and a
third army was forming on Finchley Common, when, on
December 4, Charles entered Derby. Next morning his officers
waited on him with a positive refusal to proceed on an errand
clearly futile. Charles yielded with a bad grace, vowed he
would not again consult his Council, and kept his word till
the eve of Culloden. The retreat began forthwith, Cumberland's cavalry following in close pursuit. After fighting a
rearguard action at Clifton, near Penrith, on
December 18, Charles crossed the Esk and be-   *Clifton, 1745*
fore the end of the month was in Glasgow. The Manchester
Regiment, left behind to garrison Carlisle, surrendered to
Cumberland: the winter campaign ended.

During Charles' absence in England the situation in Scotland moved to his advantage. Since the end of September
Aberdeen was a Jacobite city, and in November Lord John
Drummond arrived from France with field-guns and 700
Scots and Irish in French service. Lord Lovat, courting
reward in both camps, stood by the government but let his
son lead out the Frasers. Having at his disposal a total force
of 8000 men and nineteen guns, Charles on January 3, 1746,
opened his last campaign. Stirling was in his hands four

days later and an assault on the castle was prepared. General Hawley, superseding Cope, approached to bring *Falkirk*, 1746 relief. As he lay at Falkirk on January 17 the clans fell decisively upon his camp. His defeat called for Cumberland, who took over Hawley's demoralized command. But dissension already weakened his enemy. Charles' reliance on his Irish companions from France was obnoxious to Lord George and the chiefs. They pointed to the army's alarming depletion from desertion, advising retreat to the Highlands and renewed activity in the spring. The counsel was sound but dashed Charles' prospects. In disorder that resembled flight the Forth was crossed on February 1. The goal was Inverness, conveniently accessible from the sea, in which to await the spring campaign. It fell on February 20; Fort Augustus to the French contingent a fortnight later. Only Fort William stood for the government; otherwise Charles' grip on the Highlands was close and firm. But Cumberland, heavily reinforced, slowly followed his retreat. The swollen Spey delayed his advance on Inverness till April 8, when he left Aberdeen with the last division of *Culloden, 1746* his army. On April 16 Jacobitism fought its last fight at Culloden. The clans charged heroically but without avail. No rendezvous had been named in case of defeat, and Prince and clansman thought only of escape. After five months of romantic adventure up and down the Highlands Charles was borne by a French frigate on September 20, 1746, to France, whence the Treaty of Aix-la-Chapelle (1748) expelled him. As an active Cause Stewartism did not survive his disreputable later career and his brother's acceptance (1747) of a Cardinal's hat.

A Scotsman described the Highlands in 1747 as the 'bar *Settlement of the Highlands* barous part of the island, hitherto a noxious load upon the whole.' Their population had been the mainstay of the fourth and last attempt since the Revolution to restore the House of Stewart and invited drastic action. The Disarming Act of 1725, having expired, was replaced (1746) by one of severer character. Not only was the possession of arms made punishable by heavy fines, and even transportation, but the wearing of Highland dress was forbidden. The bagpipe, defined as an 'instrument of war,' was put under legal anathema. But the foundation of the rebellion lay in the power possessed by the chiefs to demand the military service of their vassals as a condition of their tenure, a prerogative which persisted in spite of the Disarming Act (1716) passed after the earlier rising, which proposed to commute it for money. It was now (1747) enacted that from March 25, 1748, military tenure should be superseded by a money rental. At the same time the heritable jurisdictions throughout the Lowlands were withdrawn and vested in the Crown, with compensation to those persons whose rights were sacrificed. Along with these measures, the economic development of the Highlands, already begun by Marshal Wade, who in a period of eleven years (1726–37) constructed nearly 300 miles of military roads, contributed within half a century after the '45 to a change of manners and interests which completely revolutionized Highland society and enlarged the processes of Anglicization to which the Lowlands had been subjected at an earlier period in Scotland's history.

The Episcopal clergy, their numbers now dwindled to less than 150, had refrained in 1745 from the vigorous partizanship of 1715. But, in English *Episcopacy* eyes, they were deemed anti-Hanoverian, and Cumberland had not scrupled to destroy their meeting houses. After Culloden their chapels were closed in Edinburgh, and in August 1746 an Act empowered local authorities to shut Episcopal meeting-houses, attended by five or more persons, whose ministers had not taken the oaths by September 1, 1746. It also disfranchized and disqualified for a seat in Parliament peers and commoners convicted of more than one attendance at unlicensed meeting-houses within the year preceding the election, and condemned unlicensed ministers to imprisonment for the first and transportation for a subsequent offence. The Scottish episcopate being suspect, only ordinations by an English or Irish bishop were recognized, a restriction which practically proscribed the Scottish Episcopal Church as a distinct communion. A later Act (1748) even disqualified the few ministers ordained by a Scottish bishop who had qualified before September 1, 1746.

The deaths of James in 1766 and of Charles in 1788 purged Episcopacy of suspicion of Jacobitism: though the penal laws, adding another to the dark pages of Scotland's ecclesiastical history, were not even partially removed until 1792. But as an active force Jacobitism expired at Culloden. It had failed as a national protest against the Union. It had failed as a weapon in the hands of foreign Powers ready to use it for their own ends. Freed from the incubus of civil commotion Scotland at length realized that for which she had bartered independence, the material prosperity whose tardy coming had provided the enemies of the Union with their most plausible argument.

CHAPTER XV

REVIVAL AND REFORM

THE generation that followed the last Jacobite rebellion was, in certain aspects, the most remarkable in Scotland's experience. The destruction of the patriarchal power of the Highland chiefs, the abolition of the heritable jurisdictions of the Lowland nobility, the total eradication of the Jacobite party, among whom especially ancient Scottish manners and customs tended to survive, the gradual influx of wealth and extension of commerce—all of these causes united to render the people of Scotland of Sir Walter Scott's day a class of beings as distinct from their grandfathers as his contemporary Englishmen were distinct from those of Queen Elizabeth's day. A sudden surge of material prosperity encouraged a Renaissance of letters so vigorous and remarkable that, within two generations of Culloden, Scotland numbered among her sons men of international renown in many fields of intellectual activity—philosophers (David Hume and Thomas Reid): historians (David Hume and William Robertson): economists (Adam Smith): poets (Robert Burns and Sir Walter Scott). At the same time Scotsmen made themselves prominent in England as lawyers, churchmen, painters, architects, doctors, gave a Lord Chief Justice to the United Kingdom in 1756, an archbishop of York in 1761, a Prime Minister in 1762, and a Governor General to India in 1785. So prolific was the succession of Scottish men of genius flourishing on English soil that Englishmen complained of a 'plague of locusts' and humourists pictured John Bull 'choked by inadvertently swallowing a thistle.'

Generally indifferent to current politics, Scotland's in-

terest in the third quarter of the eighteenth century was
fixed absorbingly upon the development of her
economic resources. Her population at the time
of the Union was about 1,000,000. It grew to
1,265,000 by 1775 and to 1,608,000 in 1801. Imports increased from £465,000 in 1755 to £1,267,000 in
1775 and £1,493,000 in 1797: exports from
£284,000 in 1755 to £348,000 in 1775 and
£1,037,000 in 1797. The shipping of the Clyde, the principal
port, was reckoned at 5600 tons in 1735: it had increased
about twelve-fold by 1771. At the beginning of the century
Glasgow was a small town of about 12,000 inhabitants,
rural in its amenities: in 1801 it numbered over 70,000. In
1772 half the tobacco imported to Great Britain was consigned to its merchants. Similar, though not equal, progress
attended other towns. Paisley at the time of the Union was
a village of thatched houses sheltering a population of less
than 3000, selling coarse linen goods. The Union opened a
market in the colonies: the white sewing-thread industry
was introduced in 1725, and by the end of the century the
town's population was approaching 25,000. Dundee developed from a similar beginning to a population of over
23,000 in the same period. Aberdeen, a city of mean dwellings surrounded by a bleak moor, increased to a population
of 24,000 by the end of the century and made the Dee
navigable for vessels of large draft. Its principal industry
was stocking knitting. Inverness, in 1746, was a village of
hovels: it possessed few houses of stone and lime, and only
one which contained a room not occupied by a bed. Edinburgh, as the result of the Union, for many years remained
impoverished and listless, 'a penniless lass wi' a lang pedigree,' wrote a Scotsman of a later generation. But the
growing prosperity of the distinctively industrial centres
reacted upon its fortunes, enlarged it as the legal and banking
centre, and restored to it its former dignity. By the end of
the eighteenth century its population was about 66,000,

George III,
1760–1820

Commercial
and Industrial
Progress

with valuable industries of its own, particularly printing works and paper-mills.

By 1730 the country was stirring with new activity. Linen manufacture, the staple industry, increased by prodigious leaps: 3,000,000 yards in 1728 grew to 14,000,000 in 1771, over 36,000,000 in 1822. In the early part of the century woollens were the chief produce. English competition after the Union tended to swamp the native industry, and an expanding linen market in America depressed it further. But the War of Independence, by diminishing the call for linen, re-established Hawick and other Border towns in their staple trade. Prosperity created a demand for carpets, which were manufactured at Hawick and Kilmarnock. Cotton-mills were set up at Lanark in the eighties, and a wide expansion of cotton-thread manufacture ousted linen from Paisley and rapidly employed the activities of the west country. Meanwhile, the country's iron and coal resources were adequately explored for the first time. Dr John Roebuck, a Birmingham experimental chemist, founded the Carron Iron Works in 1760, the largest of their kind in Europe, the Elswick and Essen of their day, where not only every variety of ironwork was produced, but ordnance of the largest calibre, as well as light guns known as carronades, were cast.

Agriculture was revolutionized. At the beginning of the century its conditions were primitive: the almost universal type was the collective farm, whose *Agriculture* home land was cultivated on the 'run-rig' principle, according to which each tenant developed his own rig or strip, the grazing outfields being pasture common to all. Community of culture wasted the soil, through constant repetition of crops, discouraged enterprise, and forbade improvement. But after 1760 agriculture showed marked progress. The huge antique plough was replaced by the modern implement: thrashing mills and scythes superseded flail and sickle: afforestation was carried out in the teeth of ignorant opposition: potato and turnip cultivation became general: stock was improved: and the Montgomery Act of 1770, permitting the landlord to grant long leases and burden his estate with the cost of permanent improvements, was not least among the causes which promoted the remarkable development of Scottish agriculture in the last quarter of the eighteenth century.

Accompanying these evidences of industrial enlightenment were works of public utility which the country's advancing prosperity permitted and required. In 1722 a survey *Canals* was made, and statutory powers were taken forty years later, for the construction of a canal from Grangemouth to Bowling on the Clyde below Glasgow: the Canal was opened through its entire length in 1790. The Crinan Canal was completed in 1801, and the Caledonian Canal was begun (1803–23): the Union Canal was finished in 1822. Simultaneously Glasgow, cut off from the sea twenty miles distant at the beginning of the century, triumphantly achieved a stupendous work which deepened the Clyde and permitted the town's recognition as an independent port in 1780. Thomas Telford (1757–1834), at work *Roads* upon the roads, constructed nearly 1000 miles of them and 120 new bridges, advancing the country by a century and exposing wide tracts hitherto remote.

But to the world at large the most surprising and admired *Literature* evidence of Scotland's Renaissance was her literary activity and her weighty contribution to the processes of human thought. The Union closed a bleak period of literary sterility, freed Scotland's mind to explore outside the area of religious controversy, and afforded the material prosperity essential to the craft of letters. The result was a vigorous and patriotic outpouring *Alan Ramsay* of vernacular song, of which Allan Ramsay (1686–1758) is the earliest and most characteristic example. Of gentle descent, apprenticed in Edinburgh to a wig-maker, and incorrigibly addicted to verse making, his *Tea-Table Miscellany* (1724–32) and *The Evergreen* (1724–27) offered collections of old Scots songs and ballads, and stimulated a taste which his own *Gentle Shepherd* (1725) gratified. Eagerly purchased, it released its author from his wig-blocks, and settled him in the Luckenbooths to open the first circulating library in the kingdom. Happy among his books and in the society of the wits, the little kindly man lived for a generation, making Old Edinburgh vivid in his pieces. His mantle descended on Robert Fergusson (1750–74) Burns' admired prede- *Robert Fergusson* cessor. The son of an Edinburgh haberdasher's clerk, educated at St Andrews on a bursary, and dead in a madhouse before he was twenty-five, his vernacular poems are vivid pictures of Auld Reekie, bohemian Edinburgh, its taverns, scenes and people, and powerfully influenced his greater successor.

Robert Burns (1759–96) appeared opportunely at a moment when Scottish vernacular literature no longer *Robert Burns* boasted its early vogue. His settled aim, he announced in the Preface to his Kilmarnock volume (1786), was to sing the sentiments of himself and rustic compeers 'in his and their native language,' taking Ramsay and Fergusson as his examples, though the classics of English litera- ture were known to him. Urged later in life to express him- self in English, he had the judgment and the will not to forsake an idiom most congruous to the thoughts in him seeking utterance. He remains irrevocably Scotland's national poet. Burns was born at Alloway, near Ayr, on January 25, 1759, eldest of seven children of his father, tenant of a few acres of bare soil. Burns followed his father's sinking fortunes from farm to farm at a ploughman's wage, with a brief intermission at Irvine (1781) to learn flax-dressing, till the older man died in 1784. In the same year he read Fergusson's poems and awoke his own faculty. Settled at Mossgiel, a farm of 118 acres in Mauchline parish, Ayrshire, his Muse found utterance. The familiar *To a Mouse, To a Mountain Daisy, The Cotter's Saturday Night, The Vision*, and other masterpieces were the work of this season of hot inspiration. Jean Armour, a Mauchline mason's daughter, fired his inflammable heart and laid the cares of paternity upon an exchequer already light enough. Burns, desperate, packed his chest, set his face to the Indies, and, to furnish funds for the voyage, issued at Kilmarnock his *Poems chiefly in the Scottish Dialect* (1786). Success was instant. Before the year's end he was in Edinburgh eagerly welcomed by the literati. Two editions of the Kilmarnock volume were called for in 1787 and its author was acclaimed as the 'Caledonian Bard.' Marriage to Jean Armour (1788) and a failing effort to resume the old farm life at Ellisland near Dumfries followed. Here Burns wrote *Tam o' Shanter*, and tilled the ground till the end of 1791 when, already appointed an Excise gauger at £50 a year, he removed to Dumfries, where he wrote *Auld Lang-syne, Scots wha hae, A man's a man for a' that, Ye Banks and Braes o' bonnie Doon*, and others. He died on July 21, 1796.

Sir Walter Scott's (1771–1832) many-sided genius epitomizes the national revival which is a topic of this chapter. Whether in his lyrics, romantic poems, or novels, a spirit of passionate patriotism inspired them all. No other country boasts a writer whose pen with equal prodigality unfolded its history. None could furnish an equipment of such intimate learning to its reconstruction. His romantic disposition, Jacobite partiality, the locality of his upbringing, which from early youth made familiar to him the drama of Border history, the accident of physical frailty which drew him to books for recreation, the inspiration he inhaled from Edinburgh, all moved him to recreate the past. So intimately did he wrap the histories of every wynd and gable in Auld Reekie round him, that, after his death, his son-in-law could never revisit them without feeling as if he were treading on Scott's gravestone.

Sir Walter Scott

Scott's earliest considerable work, *Minstrelsy of the Scottish Border* (1802), laid the spell of the past upon him. Its success encouraged him to employ his pen on a long poem, a romance of Border chivalry in 'a light-horseman sort of stanza' agreeable to the romantic story he had to unfold. *The Lay of the Last Minstrel* (1805) made him the most popular author of the day. *Marmion* followed in 1808, a series of vivid scenes culminating in Flodden Field, strongly appealing to national sentiment. In 1810 the *Lady of the Lake* appeared and drew visitors from all over the island to visit Loch Katrine, whose beauties it revealed. In *Rokeby* (1813), with less success, Scott explored the scenery of an English county in the days of Cromwell and Prince Rupert. Bannockburn and Bruce inspired the *Lord of the Isles* (1815). It was Scott's last romantic poem. Either he felt his vein exhausted, or withdrew from a field in which Byron, he admitted, 'hit the mark where he [Scott] did not even pretend to fledge his arrow.' In his forty-third year he abandoned poetry for prose and entered a domain in which he reigned unchallenged.

Waverley, first of the novels, was published in July 1814. It was an attempt, Scott explained, 'to embody some traits of those characters and manners peculiar to Scotland, the last remnants of which vanished during my youth.' The whole series, with infrequent excursions into foreign climates, attempted for Scotland something of what Maria Edgeworth achieved for Ireland. As a Clerk of Session Scott doubted whether it was decorous to write novels, and declared that if he owned his authorship 'it would prevent me the pleasure of writing again.' Until his bankruptcy, though the secret had long been penetrated, his novels continued to appear as 'By the Author of Waverley.' In 1819 he broke new ground with *Ivanhoe*, fearing that by confining himself to Scottish subjects he might exhaust the interest of his readers. In 1822, having been created a baronet two years before, he played a prominent part in welcoming George IV to

REVIVAL AND REFORM

Holyrood. Four years later (1826) the crash of financial misfortune bent but failed to break his spirit. From that moment till the end every ounce of his energy was expended in clearing the load of debt. His novels did so, but not in his lifetime. In September 1832 he died. His extraordinary fertility, gallery of character, graphic power of delineation, range of antiquarian knowledge, and general accuracy, are qualities of the novels which may yield to those emphasized here—their stimulation of patriotism through the medium of history, their interpretation of Scotland to her English partner hitherto ignorant and indifferent.

It was, however, chiefly in the domain of metaphysics that Scotland influenced the thought of her neighbours. From first to last the Scottish Philosophy, so called, had its citadel in the Universities which, by the middle of the century, boasted a highly active and expert academic society. First of the more notable philosophers to hold a University Chair was Francis Hutcheson (1694–1746), whose unconventional lectures at Glasgow did much to diffuse a taste for analytical discussion and a spirit of liberal enquiry. Seven years before his death David Hume (1711–76), a Berwickshire laird's son, published at Edinburgh *A Treatise of Human Knowledge* and followed it in the next twelve years with a series of works which excited lively controversy. His sceptical opinions defeated his candidature for the Glasgow Chair of Logic in 1752. But in that year he obtained the Keepership of the Advocates' Library, Edinburgh, a post which afforded both materials and leisure to write his classic *History of England* from the Conquest to the Revolution. His fame now was international: as secretary to the British Ambassador in Paris he was welcomed with effusion at the Court of Louis XV. In 1767 he was appointed Under-Secretary of State for the Home Department, settled in Edinburgh two years later, and there died in 1776.

Hume is the parent of modern philosophy. His standpoint was sceptical. The mind's perceptive apparatus, he supposed, consists of *impressions* and *ideas*, the difference between the two residing in the degrees of force and liveliness with which they declare themselves. The external world and its objects, space and time, free will, existence, knowledge, all of these experiences are merely ideas based on mental impressions and are not demonstrably of material or actual reality. Religion, Providence, final causes, are consequently riddles, an inexplicable mystery. Though his purpose was constructive, Hume's logic led to complete scepticism and exposed him to the indignant criticism of orthodoxy.

The only competent reply to Hume in Great Britain came from Thomas Reid (1710–96), born at Strachan, *Thomas Reid* Kincardineshire, and from 1752 to 1763 Professor of Moral Philosophy in King's College, Aberdeen. In 1764 he proceeded to Glasgow to fill the Chair in that subject vacated by Adam Smith, and published his *Inquiry into the Human Mind on the Principles of Common Sense.* Admitting the validity of Hume's reasoning from Hume's own premises, Reid, however, insisted that there are certain primary and universal truths which *Common Sense, i.e.* common understanding involving general consent, compels the human intelligence to accept, *e.g.* the existence of an external world, free will, causation, matters consequently withdrawn from the suspicion of non-existence in which Hume's logic involved them. The analysis answered Hume's pessimism with a message of consolation, and till the middle of the nineteenth century continued to influence the philosophic thought of Europe.

While the Universities were reconstructing a system of philosophy, a Glasgow Professor of Moral Philo- *Adam Smith* sophy was propounding a new science. Adam Smith (1723–90), born at Kirkcaldy in 1723, was called to the Chair of Logic at Glasgow in 1751. In the following year he exchanged it for that of Moral Philosophy, a subject whose treatment, by tradition at Glasgow, included some exposition of social theory. As early as 1753 Smith was instructing his class in those principles of free trade and economy which he enforced and illustrated in his classic treatise. A tempting financial offer drew him from an ill-paid Chair in 1764 to accompany the young Duke of Buccleuch upon a tour abroad. He visited France with his pupil, and at Toulouse, 'in order to pass away the time,' began to write the book which made him famous, his labours being stimulated by contact with the French economists, his exact indebtedness to whom is a point of controversy. Upon the conclusion of his tutorship he returned to Kirkcaldy, where he completed his classic work, *An Inquiry into the Nature and Causes of the Wealth of Nations* (1776). Two years later he proceeded to Edinburgh on his appointment as Commissioner of Customs, and died there in 1790. He is frequently styled the founder of political economy, though he was anticipated in some respects by other writers. He was, however, the first to isolate economic facts and give them scientific treatment, while he expounded the doctrine of free trade and other modern principles.

Until the French Revolution kindled her sudden interest *Scotland's* and excited a demand for Parliamentary and *political* municipal reform, Scotland's political sense but *backwardness* little developed: she played a subordinate and undistinguished part in the United Kingdom's politics, though in John Stewart, third Earl of Bute (d. 1792), and Henry Dundas, first Viscount Melville (d. 1811) she produced prominent statesmen. Her population was too small, her middle class too impotent, to mould Parliament to the likeness of its English counterpart. To the end of its existence it was a feudal, not a national body. Its three Estates sat in a single Chamber on a platform of equality as the King's vassals. It lacked the democratic constitution of the General Assembly, and on the eve of the Reform Bill, in the whole of Scotland, counties and burghs, there were few more than 4000 whose possession of a vote invited active interest in political questions. Nor did the apparatus of local government encourage a political sense. Until 1469 the officials of each burgh, including its Commissioners to Parliament, were elected by its 'whole community.' An Act of 1469 ordered the retiring Councils to choose their successors annually, a method which set up in each burgh a narrow oligarchy of 'honest and substantial burgesses' in whose hands the choice of representatives at Westminster was confined till the Reform Bill. In 1832 municipal voters numbered only about 1400, and county voters were few more than 3000, of whom about half were 'nominal' and fictitious, being persons collusively granted the territorial qualification for a vote for the period of an election. Subtracting them, the Parliamentary voters for the whole of Scotland on the eve of the Reform Bill were about 3000 out of a population approaching 2,500,000. Though the Scottish Estates were merged into the British Parliament in 1707 their antiquated method of electing county and burgh members survived until 1832: so little was it representative of the nation that the municipal franchise was restricted to sixty-six Royal Burghs.

Upon a country pulsing with new vitality, with swelling populations already grouped in thriving centres of industry, impatient of the 'taciturn regularity' of the old order, first the War of American Independence and then the French Revolution burst with startling announcement. The spirit of liberty, it was remarked, took 'a northern turn' and Parliamentary reform came prominently before a public hitherto indifferent. In December 1792 a Convention of Friends of the People assembled at Edinburgh, repre- *Friends of* senting eighty societies from thirty-five towns *the People* and villages lying, for the most part, within the industrial area. Insignificant in numbers—about 140—it voiced the new aspirations of democracy. There was a short

period, chiefly in 1793 and 1794, when the Scottish Jacobins
aped French forms and phraseology, and gravely alarmed
Scottish Toryism. In January 1793 a series of political trials
exhibited it in highly nervous mood. The most prominent
Thomas Muir of them was that of Thomas Muir, indicted
for seditious speeches and circulating seditious
publications—especially Paine's *Rights of Man*. Lord Braxfield, who tried him, conducted the political trials of 1793–
94 with an 'indelible iniquity' that makes him the Jeffreys
of Scotland. 'Come awa, come awa,' he addressed a dila-
tory juryman at Muir's trial, 'and help us to hang ane o' thae
daamned scoondrels.' Muir was sentenced to transportation
to Botany Bay for fourteen years.

So far from intimidating the reformers, Braxfield's ferocity
spurred them to new vigour. In October 1793 the Scottish
and English Friends of the People held an international Convention at Edinburgh, where annual Parliaments and manhood suffrage were demanded. Vindictive sentences were
imposed upon the ringleaders, the Habeas Corpus Act was
suspended (1794), the law of treason was extended, and
persons suspected of Jacobinical principles were subjected
to intolerant persecution. But the menace of Napoleon's
ambition intervened to divert public attention from the
reformers, and after the Treaty of Amiens (1802) Whig
opinion began to rally against Tory domination. In the
The 'Edin- autumn of 1802 the first number of the *Edin-*
burghReview,' *burgh Review* appeared, and provided the younger
1802 Scottish Whigs—Sydney Smith, Lord Brougham,
Francis Jeffrey, and Francis Horner—with an organ for
their opinions. The *Review* astonished by its moderation,
and, appearing in the very citadel of Dundas' Tory influence,
placed the Whigs in a new relation to the public interests
of the day. Still greater commotion was caused by Dundas'
impeachment for peculation in 1805. Though he was ac-
aquitted, the fall of a minister who for thirty years had
been undisputed master of Scotland staggered Scottish

Toryism and broke its spell. Pitt's death within a twelvemonth (January 1806) dissolved his government: the essentially Whig ministry of 'All the Talents' took its place and chose its Scottish officials from the party of reform.

The conclusion of peace with France in 1814 produced a rebound. A new generation came into action, whose mind, stimulated by the Revolution, was too young to be rendered cautious by its atrocities, and therefore found Tory caution irksome. Moreover, the first effects of peace were cruelly disappointing. Foreign trade contracted, wages fluctuated violently, rents expanded, wheat rose steadily in value. Societies similar to those of 1794 sprang up in the towns. A democratic society known as the Hampden Club, whose objects the House of Commons declared to be 'nothing short of a revolution,' was active, *Hampden Club*, 1817 and the government got wind of secret preparations among the Glasgow operatives, pledged 'either by moral or physical strength' to obtain manhood suffrage and annual Parliaments. The ringleaders were arrested and tried for sedition (1817).

In 1819 the sufferings of the poor impelled them once more to agitate for Parliamentary reform. At Manchester a series of meetings culminated in the so-called *Peterloo*, 1819 Peterloo Massacre (August 16). A similar 'sedition of the stomach' spread disorder in the west of Scotland. Riots were general, and a proclamation placarded in Glasgow and Paisley in name of a Committee for forming a Provisional Government seemed to confirm the government's worst forebodings. It called a general strike for April 1, 1820, to secure the rights which 'distinguish the freeman from the slave.' A series of encounters known as the 'Radical War' embroiled the troops and the *The Radical War*, 1820 strikers. Nearly fifty persons were apprehended, of whom three out of twenty-four convicted of treason suffered death.

For ten years the cause of reform drifted hopelessly. But
the year 1830 gave the death blow to Tory rule
William IV, in Great Britain. George IV passed away at a
1830–37 ripe age in June and a month later Paris blazed
a second time in revolution. In November Grey's Whig
ministry replaced Wellington's and took office avowedly on
the principle and for the conclusion of Parliamentary reform. In June 1832 the first English Reform
Reform Act, Bill passed into law and its Scottish counterpart
1832 was approved a month later. Since the representative system in Scotland was more remote from modern
conditions even than that of England, the Scottish Bill was
the more revolutionary measure. The electorate of self-
elected Councils in the burghs was superseded by the en-
franchisement of householders paying a uniform £10 rate.
In the counties the Parchment Barons', or 'nominal' voters,
were abolished: the franchise was conferred on freeholders
of real (landed) property valued at £10 a year, and also on
tenants paying a rent of £50 and over on a nineteen years'
lease. Eight new burghs were distributed among the existing
groups returning Members, and the total of burgh Members
was advanced from fifteen to twenty-three by giving Edinburgh and Glasgow—the latter hitherto submerged in a
group—two each, and by allotting one each to Aberdeen,
Dundee, Greenock, Paisley, Perth. The national strength in
Parliament was therefore increased from forty-five to fifty-
three. A claim on behalf of the Universities was defeated.
Scottish representation in the House of Lords was not
altered, but the disability of eldest sons of peers to sit for
Scottish constituencies was removed.

By unexpected transposition Parliamentary preceded
burgh reform. The latter had been brought for-
Burgh Re- ward prominently in 1784 and a fainthearted
form, 1833 effort at reform was made in 1822. In a Parliament returned by the new electorate the complementary
measure could not be delayed, and before the end of 1832

the Lord Advocate was in a position to announce the government's decision to carry it. In March 1833 he introduced two Bills, one affecting the newly enfranchised burghs, the other applicable to the sixty-six Royal Burghs. In the former councils were instituted, elected by holders of the £10 Parliamentary franchise. In the majority of the Royal Burghs the councils were made similarly elective, though a few, in which the £10 householders were less numerous than the old councillors, retained their constitutions. The Bills became law in August 1833.

The passing of the Reform Act diverted Scotland's interests after a long interval to ecclesiastical matters and logically revived the old problem *Dr Thomas* of Patronage. A people who, after long struggle, *Chalmers* had won the privilege to choose their Parliamentary representatives were armed to assert similar liberty in the selection of their spiritual pastors. Their right to do so had never ceased to be asserted in principle by the Evangelicals, the most powerful body within the Establishment, under the leadership of Dr Thomas Chalmers (1780–1847), while the Act of 1712 had produced an alarming growth of Dissent, whose chief cause was the imposition of unwelcome ministers by patrons on unwilling congregations. As a matter of statesmanship, therefore, circumstances called for reconsideration of that measure.

The Non-Intrusion controversy or Ten Years' Conflict round the subject of patronage had its immediate origin in the General Assembly of 1833, *Patronage* to whose members Chalmers introduced the measure henceforth known as the Veto Act. Upon a review of the early traditions of the Church it claimed for every congregation an absolute veto on the intrusion of a pastor imposed upon it contrary to the wishes of a *Veto Act,* majority of its membership, while leaving to *1834* the patron the right of presentation. The proposal was lost by twelve votes: it was easy to alarm waverers by emphasizing the fallibility of an unintelligent electorate and a probable levelling down of ministerial standards. But outside the Assembly feeling was strong in its favour. Legal advice had been invoked and was declared to be favourable: the Whig government's sanction and co-operation was alleged. The motion was approved in most of the Presbyteries and was carried in the Assembly of 1834 by a considerable majority.

The Veto Act definitely challenged the Patronage Act, *The Auchterarder Case*, 1834 and made collision inevitable between ecclesiastical and civil authority standing respectively behind them. In August 1834 the parish of Auchterarder provided an arena of battle. The patron, Lord Kinnoull, having presented a young licentiate named Robert Young, nearly five-sixths of the parishioners intimated their dissent, but without alleging specific reasons. The Auchterarder Presbytery accordingly refused to admit Young who, along with his patron, appealed to the Court of Session (1835). After a considerable interval, the Court by a majority decided (1838) that in rejecting Young without first making trial of his abilities the Presbytery had acted illegally and in violation of their duty. An appeal by the

Victoria, 1837–1901 General Assembly to the House of Lords evoked (1839) a judgment even more unequivocal and disconcerting to the champions of ecclesiastical independence. Not merely was the decision

The Marnoch Case, 1838 of the Court of Session confirmed, but the inability of a Presbytery to reject the patron's presentee on any ground but his incompetence to fulfil his duties was expressly stated. Similar cases arose elsewhere, notably at Marnoch in the Presbytery of Strathbogie, the majority of whose members were actually suspended and deposed by the Assembly for daring to admit the patron's nominee and complying with the directions of the Court of Session.

Clearly the single hope of agreement between civil autho-

rity and the Church's resolution to assert its spiritual
independence resided in some legislative proposal which could reconcile them. Champions   *The Claim of
of compromise having appeared in Parliament   Right, 1842*
in 1840 and 1841, whose proposals failed to satisfy the bel-
ligerents, a crisis was reached. 'The war of argument is now
over,' said Dr Chalmers in 1841: 'the strife of words must
give place to the strife of opposing creeds and opposing
purposes.' To this point the Non-Intrusionists had not ventured openly to advocate the abolition of patronage. But
the government's attitude was unequivocal: patronage was
established by Act of Parliament, and so long as it rested
on that foundation must be upheld. Events, on the other
hand, had shown that while patronage survived, friction
between Church and State was apparently inevitable. Therefore, though his action invited a charge of inconsistency
against the party that passed the Veto Act, Dr Chalmers,
early in 1842, supported a proposal to abolish patronage
and by the act remove the grounds of strife persisting now
for nearly ten years. By a large majority the Assembly of
1842 condemned patronage as the main cause of the difficulties in which the Church was involved, and approved a
statement of its position entitled a 'Claim, Declaration, and
Protest,' commonly cited as the Claim of Right: it asserted
that the rights and liberties of the Church had of late been
assailed to an extent that threatened their complete sub-
version, concluded that its government could not be carried
on subject to the coercion exercised by the Court of
Session, and protested that Acts passed without the Church's
consent and prejudicial to its government as settled at
the Union were, other than in their civil consequences, null
and void.

To a case so argued there could be only one answer. In
March 1843 a private member invited the House of Commons
to appoint a Committee of enquiry to examine the Claim of
Right and the grievances of which it complained. Both sides

of the House, Whigs and Tories, were emphatic in condemnation of its contentions. Sir Robert Peel's standpoint was unyielding: no government could admit claims which in their essence were incompatible with the supremacy of civil order or transfer the right of patronage to 'a variable and irresponsible multitude.' By a great majority the motion for an enquiry was negatived.

Two months after Parliament's decision the last scene was enacted. Already in the preceding autumn a 'General Convocation of all the right-minded clergy' assembled at Edinburgh and by an overwhelming vote resolved to secede from the Established Church unless concessions were made to its convictions. On May 18, 1843, the momentous decision was carried into effect. On that date the General Assembly met for the last time as the undivided Court of the Scottish Church. After the opening prayer in the Assembly Hall, the retiring Moderator, instead of constituting the Assembly, read a document in name of more than two hundred ministers protesting against the invasion of the Church's rights and summoning those who supported him to proceed elsewhere to find the liberty denied them under the Establishment. Followed by more than four hundred ministers, over one-third of the parish and unendowed clergy of the whole Church, he passed from the Hall to another already prepared for their reception. By acclamation Dr Chalmers was called to the Moderatorship of the new Free Church of Scotland. On May 23, 1843, 396 ministers and professors—a number subsequently expanded to 474—put their signatures to an Act of Separation which renounced the benefices they held under the Establishment.

The abolition of Scotland's archaic representative system in 1832 as significantly as the Union itself indicated her absorption into the United Kingdom and brought her distinctive political existence to an end. The Disruption of 1843, the last bout in a conflict between Church and State whose acrid controversies had fired three centuries, as

The Disruption, 1843

clearly marked a terminus. The half-century that followed these events was one of confirmation and correction. The political reform of 1832 was carried further by the Acts of 1867–68, which gave burghs the *Reform Acts,* 1867–1918 household and lodger franchise, reduced the owner and tenant qualifications to £5 and £14 respectively in the counties, and increased Scotland's representation from forty-five to sixty seats. The Acts of 1884–85 further extended the franchise and increased the sixty Members to seventy-two. Under the recent (1918) Redistribution Act Scotland is represented by seventy-four in the Commons: her representative peers, as in 1707, are sixteen in number.

Of the other event the sequel is a story of correction. Though irreconcilable congregations of the early dissenting Secessions continue to stand aloof, the Scottish Presbyterian body has steadily moved in a *Church Union* direction of comprehension. In 1847 the United Presbyterian Church was formed out of dissenting congregations hitherto apart. In 1900 that body united with the Free Church of 1843 to form the United Free Church of Scotland. Its reunion with the Establishment from which its component elements at different times seceded is now (1921) imminent.

INDEX OF PERSONS AND PLACES

For EU product safety concerns, contact us at Calle de José Abascal, 56–1°,
28003 Madrid, Spain or eugpsr@cambridge.org.

www.ingramcontent.com/pod-product-compliance
Ingram Content Group UK Ltd.
Pitfield, Milton Keynes, MK11 3LW, UK
UKHW020320140625
459647UK00018B/1943